Crystal Naylor

VICTORIOUS!
GLORIOUS!
CHURCH!

Crystal Naylor

VICTORIOUS! GLORIOUS! CHURCH!

Our Soon Coming King, Inc.

The opinions expressed in this manuscript are solely the opinions of the author. The author has represented and warranted full ownership and/or legal right to publish all the materials in this book.

VICTORIOUS! GLORIOUS! CHURCH!
All Rights Reserved.
Copyright © 2012 Crystal Moore Naylor
v7.0

Cover Photo © 2012 Crystal Moore Naylor. All rights reserved.

This book may not be reproduced, transmitted, or stored in whole or in part by any means, including graphic, electronic, or mechanical without the express written consent of the publisher.

Scripture quotations are from The King James Version of the Bible.

PUBLISHER: OUR SOON COMING KING, INC.
WEBSITE: www.osck.org

VICTORIOUS! GLORIOUS! CHURCH! - © 1996 By Rev. Crystal Naylor
Additionally Copyrighted In 2009, 2010, And 2011
By Apostle Crystal Moore Naylor

Copyright Registration: TXu 767-929

ISBN: 978-0-9707429-0-2

PRINTED IN THE UNITED STATES OF AMERICA

AUTHOR'S EMPHASIS: APOSTLE CRYSTAL MOORE NAYLOR HAS TAKEN AUTHOR'S PREROGATIVE IN EMPHASIZING CERTAIN WORDS IN SCRIPTURES AND THROUGHOUT HER BOOK, BY USING BOLD PRINT. APOSTLE NAYLOR HAS ALSO CAPITALIZED CERTAIN WORDS THAT WOULD NOT NORMALLY APPEAR CAPITALIZED. THIS HAS BEEN DONE BY THE AUTHOR FOR VISUAL ENHANCEMENT FOR THE READER.

Blessed Are The **Pure In Heart**: For They Shall See **God**.

Matthew 5:8

TO GOD BE THE GLORY!

BECAUSE

JESUS CHRIST IS LORD!

BEHOLD, I HAVE GRAVEN THEE UPON THE PALMS OF MY HANDS; THY WALLS ARE CONTINUALLY BEFORE ME.

ISAIAH 49:16

Table of Contents

Dedication i
Foreword... iii
Commendations v
About the Author xi
Acknowledgements xiii
The Rapture.. xv-xix
Preface xxi

1: Introduction - Israel 1
    Israel 4

2: Introduction - Spiritual Israel 11
    Spiritual Israel 16

3: Are You Married To The Lord?............................... 23

4: The Second Advent – The Return Of Jesus Christ 37

5: The Holy Spirit – Who Is He And How Does He Help Us? 45

6: God Is Love And He Dwells In You – The Believer 57

7: No Greater Love Than This (Jesus) 61

    Visual: Increased Harvest – Seeds 67

    Visual: Keys To Receive Your Harvest – Your Inheritance 68

8: Healing Of Spiritual Emotional, Physical, Social and Financial Hurts Through Obedience - Walking in (Love) and Doing God's Whole Word.. 69

    Scriptures - The Word Of God-Spiritual, Healing, Wealth, Protection, For Our Children 76-78

9: Breaking Generational Curses Through Love (Jesus) Galatians 3:12-14.. 79

    Visual: FAITH Is – Hebrews 11:1 85

    Visual: Tree Of Life Or Tree Of Death? 86

    Visual: Choose Life Or Choose Death..................................... 87

    Breaking Generational Curses Through Love (Jesus) – Part II.. 88

    Breaking Generational Curses Through Love (Jesus) – Part III 92

    Breaking Generational Curses Through Love (Jesus) Part IV ... 96

    Visual: Faith Speaks – To Reap You Must Sow 100

    Breaking Generational Curses Through Love (Jesus) Part V ... 101

    Visual: Jesus Christ – The Strongest Man 104

    Visual: Some Strong Holds 105

    Visual: Some Strong Holds 105

10: The Greatest Of All Is Love... 107

    Visual: The Fruit Of The Spirit 112

    Visual: Intimacy With God.. 113

11: See My Glory – See Me 115

12: Total Salvation – Jesus – God's Will Fulfilled....................... 121

    Includes Glorified Bodies Given At The Rapture................... 121

13: Come And Dine 125
    Come And Dine – Part II 135

14: Total Salvation And God's Glory (Don't Rob God) 145
    Total Salvation And God's Glory (Keep Your Vows) 148
        Visual: Seed To The Sower 164
        Visual: Seed Time And Harvest Time 165

15: Total Salvation and God's Glory Do You Want My Glory? 167

16: Victorious! Glorious! Church! 185
    Visual: I AM That I AM - ALMIGHTY GOD 195
    What Is Total Salvation? 196
        Visual: God's Plan For Man..................................... 199
        Visual: We Believe.. 200
    Prayer of Salvation 202
        Visual: God's Holy Temple - Born Again Man 203
        Song: My Soon Coming King - By Crystal Moore Naylor....... 204
        The Heart: The Visions Explained -
        By Apostle Crystal Moore Naylor 205
        Visual: The Rapture Vision II -
        By Apostle Crystal Moore Naylor..206

Dedication

I dedicate this book to **my Lord and Savior Jesus Christ**, who is **my Friend, my Everything and my King**, who will shortly take His body home. It is my prayer that every member of the body of Christ will be awake and ready for Jesus' return like the five wise virgins as we await the Lord's return. I also pray that every member of the body of Christ will each have pure hearts and clean hands (Godly motives). I also pray that we will seek to glorify the Lord in every area of our lives and be busy about the Father's business in Jesus' name amen.

BLESSED ARE THE PURE IN HEART: FOR THEY SHALL SEE GOD.
Matthew 5:8

TO GOD BE THE GLORY BECAUSE JESUS CHRIST IS LORD!
PRAISE GOD! AMEN!

Love in Jesus Christ,
Crystal

Foreword

It is my pleasure to write about Apostle Crystal and this book. Apostle is a loving wife that is worthy of all the blessings of God. She has been able to walk as a strong wife to me as well as a mother of our three sons. Apostle has walked in love over forty-five years that I have known her and has been able to fulfill her calling from God. She has more than enough love for the family and for those outside of our family.

Apostle Crystal Naylor is a powerful anointed woman of God and walks in sonship. She has spent a great deal of time ministering to the needs of others. As you read this book, you will be able to see her dedication to saving souls. Apostle was quick to answer the call of God to operate within the five-fold ministries.

Apostle has worked long hours in the ministry and is determined to finish the race that God has set before her. She has dedicated her life to reaching souls for the kingdom of God. She has been able to overcome obstacles that have been placed before her in this race and is very quick to give God the honor and glory.

We thank God for Apostle Crystal's desire to serve the body of Christ, her desire to see that none should perish, and her desire that the kingdom of God would grow mightily in this world. She has a tremendous desire to see the devil defeated in the lives of everyone.

This book was written to glorify God. It is Apostle Crystal's prayer that those who read this book will be strengthened in their faith and that their desire would become a desire to serve Almighty God. It is also Apostle's desire that laborers for God will be encouraged to reach out to those who are lost or are falling away from God.

Reading this book will definitely cause a change within you that will become evident on the outside. To God Be The Glory!

Pastor Louis Naylor, Sr.
Her Loving Husband

Commendations

My Mother,

For over 40 years Crystal Moore Naylor has been there for me, from childhood to adulthood, whenever I have needed anything, even just an ear to bend. She has always been there.

My Mother has devoted her entire life to helping others from sacrificing for family to being there for the sick and elderly, as well as for others. She has always put others first. She is the most generous, unselfish, and loving person I have ever known. I thank God that he has given me my mother and I love her with all my heart. All who read this book will find it an inspiration and a blessing.

Louis Jr.

Apostle Crystal,

Is a strong, loving, and caring person. She gives to anyone in need, without expecting anything in return. Her love for the Lord shines brightly in every aspect of her life, and she has been a blessing to numerous people in countless ways.

Apostle Crystal has dedicated her life to the Lord and leading souls to His Victorious Glorious Church. It would be easy to write a long list in reference to Apostle Crystal's accomplishments, as well as the people she has blessed, but the ink in the pen would run dry. Thank God for her leadership at Total Salvation Church, but most of all thank you mother for being Mother. I believe that what my mother has written will help each person spiritually.

Love,
Christopher

My Mother,

She is a focal point in my life. She has instilled the values of temperance and forgiveness in me. She is always eager to listen and always willing to help. She will call to express love or concern or just to let you know that you are in her prayers.

She always makes time for both physical and church families. She never lacks in charisma and always encourages me to persevere. Wisdom and kindness are ever-present in her demeanor and I am thankful that I was placed into her life and I love her dearly. I pray that her words from this book touch your life as they have mine,

Matthew

It is with great joy that I give reference to Apostle Crystal Naylor and Total Salvation Church, Inc. I have known Apostle Crystal for quite a few years and have had the honor and privilege to be with her, her husband, and her church family many times.

She has a heart for people that supersedes prestige, power, or platforms of influence. All that she does is with a heart of giving and love as she invests so much for the good of others. I have seen her sacrifice at the expense of her own personal needs in order to demonstrate to another their intrinsic value. She is a woman who walks in such maturity as she accepts responsibility for her life and future as well as continually is motivated to see the goals and objectives of her life and the church fulfilled.

She also demonstrates amazing interpersonal skills as she can truly relate and connect to what another thinks, feels, and how they perceive any given situation. She has demonstrated repeatedly the ability to build trust with others because she is a person who possesses the competencies needed to succeed, but most importantly, the character and pure motives of one who is trustworthy. Her influence has not just had local or national impact but a compelling global effect.

It is with great confidence that I give reference but also commendation to this precious woman of God and friend!

Sincerely,

Dr. Melodye Hilton
Christian International Apostolic Network Mid-Atlantic Regional Leadership

Apostle Crystal Naylor is the Presiding Apostle of The Total Salvation Church in Maryland, USA. I have known her for about eight years. She has ministered with me in Africa and the UK. She functions effectively as an Evangelist, Pastor and Prophet. She has preached the gospel in various parts of the world including Africa, China, UK and the United States. Apostle Naylor is used of God in leading people to the saving grace of Jesus and in the healing ministry.

Apostle Naylor is a woman of integrity, commitment to the word of God and love for people. Her love and commitment propels her to take the gospel sometimes at great cost to distant lands. She models what she preaches.

I strongly recommend her for any opportunity to preach the word of God.

Apostle Sunday A. Popoola PhD
Int. Director, Apostolic Mentoring Networks.

Apostle Crystal Naylor loves the Word of God. As a woman of God, she has demonstrated her love for Him in so many different ways over the thirty-five years that we have known her, and writing this book is no exception. Her book, Victorious! Glorious! Church! was an inspiration from God and written with passion, love, and a special anointing that has governed Crystal's life for many years.

It covers a multitude of biblical principles from which new and mature believers alike will reap the benefits of God's manifested power in remarkable ways. My wife Cynthia and I look forward to a life-transforming experience move of God in all who take pleasure in reading this remarkable book.

Joseph Trammel, Sr.
Pastor, Church of Christ
Boyds, MD

Apostle Crystal Naylor is an inspiration to us and all who know her. My husband Joseph and I have known her for over thirty-five years and she has always been an example of a believer and a faithful servant to Jesus Christ. Over the years we have witnessed her devotion to the Lord and have been the recipient of many of her anointed faith filled prayers.

We believe that this book inspired by the Word of God, will inspire others to great faith, to servant hood and to fall deeper in love with our Lord and Savior Jesus Christ. In the process of transformation readers who believe will also be inspired to become more like Christ while walking as He walked.

>Cynthia Trammel
>First Lady, Church of Christ
>Boyds, MD

Apostle Crystal Naylor is an anointed Woman of God who preaches, and teaches the word of God without compromise. I have witnessed as she has ministered the Word of God and people were saved, delivered, healed, and received their victories. I was present on one occasion as Apostle Naylor ministered to a lady that was deaf in her ear and was instantly healed. Apostle Naylor also ministers in the prophetic ministry.

Apostle Naylor has been a very special friend of mine for over twenty years. She lifts up the name of Jesus Christ not only in talk, but, she practices what she preaches. She has ministered locally, nationally, and internationally, and impacted may lives for the Kingdom of God.

Apostle Naylor is on fire for the Lord. She walks in love, she is concerned about souls, and she is a woman of integrity. Apostle Naylor ministers Total Salvation to the whole man, spirit, soul, and body.

This book is a blessing and I highly recommend this book to every believer to read, it will bless you tremendously!

>In His Service,
>Evangelist Martha Charles

This book is a must have for the believers in the Body of Christ. It will equip the believers in understanding the times that we are in and how important it is to spread the Word of God. Christ is coming back for a Victorious Glorious Church! As Apostle Naylor set at the feet of the Lord, as she meditated in His Presence, He began to write His Words on her heart. This book was designed by God, it was written by God through the Power of His Holy Spirit, and Apostle Naylor was the instrument that He used to bring it forth.

Psalms 45:1 says "My heart is overflowing with a good theme; I recite my composition concerning the King; My tongue is the pen of a ready writer." Apostle Naylor's obedience is a Blessing to the Body and as you read this book, you will "Hear the Father's Heart."

Prophetess Monya B. Smith

About the Author

The author of this book, Apostle Crystal Moore Naylor, is truly a gift to the body of Christ from God. She is a dedicated wife, mother and a tremendous blessing to many.

Apostle is married to Pastor Louis Naylor, Sr. and is the mother of three sons, Louis, Jr., Christopher, and Matthew. She has four grandchildren, Louis III, Yasmin, Sierra, and Justice.

Apostle Crystal is an author of two other books. She is an anointed poet and artist as well as a powerful minister of the gospel of Jesus Christ

Apostle has been in the ministry of God for over twenty-five years. She ministers as an Apostle, Prophet, Pastor, Evangelist, and Teacher and hears constantly from God for guidance. She is constantly preaching and teaching God's word to anyone that will listen. Apostle Crystal is an ordained Apostle under the Christian International Apostolic Network.

Apostle not only ministers locally, but has ministered internationally in Nigeria, Africa several times. She has also ministered in China, London, England and in Egypt, and she is looking forward to continued traveling abroad to carry God's gospel. Apostle has a very special place in her heart for ministering to all people.

Apostle Crystal's greatest desire is to walk in the perfect will of

God. She has a desire to see that none should perish but all should come to know God.

> Love Always
> Pastor Louis Naylor, Sr.

Acknowledgements

I would first like to thank and praise the Lord who told me to write this book, and then gave me two visions of the rapture which I drew. Truly God is worthy of **all** the praise, honor, and glory, for without Him this book would not have come to pass. What you will read is a result of the teachings and revelations that the Lord has given to me because he is my number one mentor, Amen! **THANK YOU JESUS! TO GOD BE THE GLORY, BECAUSE JESUS CHRIST IS LORD! AMEN!**

I also thank and praise Almighty God for my husband Louis, who throughout our over forty years of marriage, has always been there for me. I thank and praise God for you Lou, and for the loyalty, and continued support of me and my endeavors.

I also thank the Lord for both my parents, Mr. and Mrs. Moore, who are now in heaven with the Lord Jesus Christ, for their training me, and for my mother mentoring me and teaching me as a child to walk in love, forgiveness, and to grow in Godliness. Special thanks to our three sons Louis Jr., Christopher, and Matthew for their support of whatever I have undertaken for God's glory. Special thanks to our youngest son Matthew who did the original typing of my poem, titled **"The Rapture"**, while the Lord was speaking the poem to my spirit.

Special thanks to those who helped me with the typing of this book: to my husband and friend Lou, also a special thanks to Deaconess Joyce, Minister Beverly, and most of all to the Lord Jesus Christ who helped me with the typing of His book.

I also give thanks to every person that prayed for this book to come forth by the Spirit of the Lord and helped in any way. Special thanks goes to Apostle Dr. Sunday Popoola.

I pray that the Lord will richly bless each of you in Jesus' name. Amen!

Special thanks to you **ROSE**, for your many prayers

Psalms 45:1 – My heart is inditing a good matter; I speak of the things which I have made touching the king: my tongue is a pen of a ready writer. Amen! To God Be The Glory! Praise God, Amen!

The Rapture

For the rapture my soul awaits,
For I know in my spirit the time is late

Jesus Christ is my Soon Coming King, and
It's for Him my heart leaps, and for Him I sing

The date and the table is set,
For we who will be raptured are blessed.

Jesus Christ is the Captain of my soul,
For I know He is the one who is in control.

Oh how I love Him, and long for His return,
Oh yes, it is for Him that my spirit yearns.

For years many have mocked, and they have scorned,
They say He'll never rapture us, He'll not come for His own.

I know He's coming, and He told me it won't be long
Before He takes us back to Heaven, our home!

I know He is coming, and He is coming quite soon!
I will be His bride and He'll be my groom.

To this my spirit does bear the witness,
That is why I'm so busy, about my Father's business.

So don't be discouraged, and don't give up,
Let's do what He tells us so we'll be all caught up.

Oh how I love my Father, and Jesus the Son,
And the Holy Spirit they are all One.

For Heaven's my true home that I long for,
And Jesus Christ is the door.

To behold Jesus Christ, the one I so adore,
To bow before Him, and to be in His presence forever more.

                                              Copyrighted 1996 By Rev Crystal M. Naylor

The Rapture

Are you ready? Don't wait! Today, accept Jesus as your SAVIOR.
Tomorrow? Well, that might be too late

Don't wait! Accept Him, it's not yet too late
So you too will be ready for His appointed date.

I love Him and long for His return,
Oh yes, for Him my spirit yearns!

But I know my Father, God the Creator of all things has
Had much patience, that's why He waited for the early,
And the latter rain.

But now the time has come, that Jesus Christ
The Son must come.

That is why we must yield to Him, and do His will,
As we yield we'll be like Him in more ways than one,
The Father, The Holy Ghost, and The Son.

He's coming, yes He's coming real soon! It may be morning,
Night or noon, I know He is coming so I have no gloom. Why?
Because I know He's coming soon.

By the signs that we see, we know that He's even at the door.
By these signs and by His word, we know we'll be mortal no more.

It may be spring, summer, winter or fall,
But we know now is the season we're sure to hear His call.

The last trumpet will sound and the dead in Christ shall arise
From the ground. Then we who are alive, and yet remain, will
Arise in Christ forever changed.

Without a spot, without a wrinkle, or any such thing,
Because Jesus is our soon to come KING.

Because of His blood we're holy without a blemish,
Because Jesus made sure that the work was finished.

For in a moment and in a twinkle of an eye
We'll arise to Jesus Christ, Himself in the sky.

Copyrighted 1996 By Rev Crystal M. Naylor

The Rapture

Yes, we will be like Him because of His VICTORY.
When we see Him, we'll be like Him Eternally.

Immortal, Victorious, and Glorious,
His Bride forever we'll be....... ....

His Victorious, Glorious Church to Him we do yield.
Victorious, Glorious, Church,
His Will Is <u>FULFILLED</u>! AMEN!

        To God Be the Glory
        Praise God! Amen!
        Love in Jesus Christ,

        Rev. Crystal M. Naylor
        April 15, 1996

        Copyright 1996 by Rev. Crystal M. Naylor

Preface

I believe with all my spirit, soul and body that we are the generation that will be alive when Jesus comes for His **Victorious! Glorious! Church!** Many years ago, God told me that when I entered the ministry to which he had called me, that it would be just before the return of Jesus Christ. At that time, God told me I was not to share what he had told me with anyone, not even with my husband. Several years later while I was in prayer early one Sunday morning, God directed me to tell the Pastor of the Church, which I was a member of at that time, "that God had told me that when I entered the ministry that he had called me to, that it would be just before the return of Jesus Christ and to tell him before the morning church service."

I was reluctant to do this, thinking, who am I to tell the Pastor of the Church something like that, but I knew God had told me to share what he had told me. I feared God more than man and went to knock on the pastor's office door. However, as I was about to enter the Pastor's office, a dear sister in the Lord asked if she could go into the office with me to see the Pastor because she also had something that she wanted to share with him. Although I did not want to tell him what God had said in front of her, I said yes, not wanting to be rude. She shared a dream that the Lord had given to her about heaven and the saints that had been raptured that were entering into heaven's gates. I also shared what God told me to tell the Pastor while she was present.

Later that same day the Women's Choir of the church was celebrating their anniversary. An evangelist that had never been to our church was the guest speaker. The title of his message was "Prepare For The Soon Return Of Jesus Christ." This was a great confirmation to me, although I truly needed no confirmation because I knew what God had told me. Since that time, the Lord has spoken to my spirit, "the time is at hand", and it won't be long before Jesus comes to take his people home to heaven. May your heart be encouraged and blessed as you read this book that the Lord instructed me to write several years ago.

The cover of this book is an enhancement of vision one of the Rapture which was given to me by the Lord a number of years ago. Almighty God told me to write this book before 1995. I give God all the Glory, Honor, and the Praise, for he alone is worthy. In 1995, the Lord gave me a double vision of the Rapture. The first vision was in the morning praise and worship service. The second vision was in the evening praise and worship service on the same day Sunday, at the church that I was a member. Prior to that time years before the Lord had given me a pencil sketch, and a cut and paste of the Rapture, that was to be the cover for my book, that the Lord wanted me to do. After the double vision of the Rapture, I did a quick color sketch of the vision that I had seen during praise and worship. I also did a poem titled The Rapture on April 15, 1996. I gave copies of my color sketch of the Rapture to my husband and family, the pastor of the church, and several friends. Shortly after this I asked a lady of the church who was on the praise and worship team and a graphic artist if she would do my drawing of the Rapture for the cover of my book **VICTORIOUS! GLORIOUS! CHURCH!** After giving her a copy of my color sketch she said yes, however, the Lord dealt with me to do the picture myself, and I obeyed him. What you see is a result of my obedience to God.

The lady that was a graphic artist of our church later showed me a pencil sketch of the rapture that was very similar to mine. One of the youth leaders and his wife had done a similar drawing to mine unknowingly and they wanted the graphic artist to do theirs for a bulletin for a Wednesday night youth service. Their's would show youth in a cartoon style being raptured from the earth to Jesus, while mine showed born again people being raptured from the earth to Jesus in a realistic style.

I was asked what to do, I told all I did not want to get in the way of what God was doing, and to pray. The youth leader and his wife decided to do something different for the youth service. I shared all this with the Pastor of the church. She asked me why I thought the Lord would give them the same sketch, even though the youth leaders sketch was not in color or detailed like mine with all ages of people being raptured? I told her I did not know why but I had heard that when God is surely going to do something in the earth, he confirms it in twos. (Read Genesis 41:32)

Later, after my husband and I were called by the Lord to pastor a church, I realized that by the Lord having one of the youth leaders sketch a very similar sketch without either of us knowing what the other was doing, he was probably letting the Pastor know that indeed this was of God and not of me.

I shared all of this to encourage you, for indeed our Lord Jesus Christ is so very, very, very, very soon to come for his own. I believe we have no time to waste. Therefore, let us yield ourselves as Jesus did. Let each of us say, nevertheless not my will Father God, but thy will be done in me, in Jesus' name! Amen! Praise the Lord! To God Be The Glory! AMEN!

My prayer is that, if you are saved, but not living for God, that you will repent, and be converted (changed), and never backslide again. If you are not saved, accept Jesus Christ as your Savior today, and live everyday as if you knew that it would be the day that Jesus would rapture (catch away) his church. Remember it might be today!

For we who are saved and living for Jesus, I pray that we would have our fire for the Lord and the things of God rekindled for some, and increased to the highest level possible for us all. It is my prayer that we as the body of Christ would live and serve the Lord with all our spirit, soul, and body in all that we think, say, and do. I pray that we all in Jesus Christ's body would have pure hearts and clean hands (right motives - Godly motives) in all we think, say, and do. I also pray that the body of Jesus Christ brings much glory to the name of our Lord and Savior, and very, very, very, very <u>Soon Coming King Jesus Christ</u>, Amen.

Psalm 24:3-5
v/3 - Who shall ascend unto the hill of the Lord? Or who shall stand in his holy place? v/4 He that hath clean hands, and a pure heart; who hath not lifted up his soul unto vanity, nor sworn deceitfully. v/5 He shall receive the blessing from the Lord, and righteousness from the God of his salvation.

To God Be The Glory! Praise God! Amen!

Crystal M. Naylor

1

Introduction - Israel

<u>Jeremiah 32:40</u> - And I will make an everlasting covenant with them, that I will not turn away from them, to do them good; but I will put my fear in their hearts, that they shall not depart from me.

ISAIAH 59:16-21. - *And he saw that there was no man, and wondered that there was no intercessor: therefore, his arm brought salvation unto him; and his righteousness, it sustained him. V17 - For he put on righteousness as a breastplate, and an helmet of salvation upon his head; and he put on the garments of vengeance for clothing, and was clad with zeal as a cloke. V18 - According to their deeds, accordingly he will repay, fury to his adversaries, recompence to his enemies; to the islands he will repay recompence. V19 - So shall they fear the name of the Lord from the west, and his glory from the rising of the sun. When the enemy shall come in like a flood, the Spirit of the Lord shall lift up a standard against him. V20 - And the Redeemer shall come to Zion, and unto them that turn from transgression in Jacob, saith the Lord. V21 - As for me, this is my covenant with them, saith the LORD; My Spirit that is upon thee, and my words which I have put in thy mouth, shall not depart out of thy mouth, nor out of the mouth of thy seed, nor out of the mouth of thy seed's seed, saith the LORD, from henceforth and for ever.*

In Zechariah 2:8, Israel is referred to as the apple of God's eye. Israel was chosen as God's chosen people because of God's covenant to Abram as stated in Genesis 12:1-3. The Israelites were fewest in numbers of all people. God's power can often be shown greater with fewer numbers. Thereby, God is magnified, rather than man and God gets the glory when his purposes are fulfilled. Deuteronomy 7:7 states, "The Lord did not set his love upon you, nor choose you, because ye were more in number than any people; for ye were the fewest of all people."

As we look at Israel and Spiritual Israel, we must always keep in mind that the Church or Spiritual Israel has <u>not replaced</u> Israel, and never will replace them. It is also important to remember that **Jesus Christ came through the lineage of Abraham, and that Jesus Christ was an Israelite.**

God chose Abram and later named him Abraham. God knew that Abraham was a man that would serve him, and teach his household to serve Jehovah God as well. God had made a covenant with Abraham in Genesis 22:17-18. He reminded Abraham of this covenant which stated, "That in blessing I will bless thee, and in multiplying I will multiply thy seed as the stars of the heaven, and as the sand which is upon the seashore; and thy seed shall possess the gate of his enemies; And in thy seed shall all the nations of the earth be blessed; because thou hath obeyed my voice."

From Abraham and his wife Sarah, Isaac the son of the promise, was born. From Isaac and his wife Rebekah, two sons were birthed, Esau and Jacob. Through Jacob's lineage, one day, Jesus would come. God later changed Jacob's name to Israel, and he had twelve sons. These twelve sons represented the twelve tribes of Israel. From these few people and their wives, multitudes of Hebrews were birthed, who were named Jews or Israelites. So we can see how God can use little when the person's heart is willing to bring forth abundance in any and all areas that God desires them to.

Eventually, <u>Jacob</u>, whose name God <u>had changed to Israel,</u> moved with his small family of seventy which included his eleven sons to Egypt at the request of Joseph, who was then ruling in Egypt, second to the Pharaoh. Through God's divine providence, Joseph was exalted and many lives were spared because of him. Joseph, who had suffered at the hands of his older brothers years earlier, had been sold into slavery and taken to Egypt. God imparted great wisdom to Joseph which he shared with Pharaoh and because of Joseph's pure heart, his family and many others were spared from certain death, due to the many years of severe drought, Genesis 47:11-28. After Joseph's death, there arose a different Pharaoh that did not know Joseph. This wicked Pharaoh made God's people slaves for over four hundred years. God raised up a deliverer by the name of Moses who delivered Almighty God's people by mighty signs and wonders. It is believed that the Hebrew people, also called the Israelites who were named after Israel, had grown into the millions. So we can see how God was able to use a few to bring forth multitudes as he had prophesied to Abraham. In Genesis 15:5-6, we read God's covenant to Abraham where God says, "And he brought him forth abroad, and said, Look now toward heaven, and tell the stars, if thou be able to number them: and he said unto him, So shall thy seed be. And he believed in the Lord; and he counted it to him for righteousness."

Although the sins of God's people separated them from him, God clearly declares that he alone is their Victory; he is their Salvation. He is Jehovah-Nissi, The Lord Our Conquerer, Banner and Victory.

In Isaiah the word of God lets us know that the sins of God's people, had caused a spiritual separation between them and their living God. In Isaiah 59:1-2, Isaiah lets the people know that, *"Behold the Lord's hand is not shortened that it cannot save; neither is his ear heavy, that it cannot hear: But your iniquities have separated between you and your God, and your sins have hid his face from you, that he will not hear."*

God's people, the Jews, sinned in three areas: (1) **In Not Keeping the Sabbath,** Numbers 15:32-36, Nehemiah 13:17-18, Isaiah 58:13-14, Ezekiel 20:13, and Ezekiel 22:26, (2) **In intermarriage with the heathen,** Deuteronomy 7:3-4, I Kings 11:1-2, and Nehemiah 13:23-29, and (3) **In idolatry, they also sinned against their True and Living God,** I Kings 21:26, II Kings 17:12, Ezekiel 6:1-5 and Zechariah 13:2.

These sins had to be faced and dealt with by the appropriate disciplinary measures if the nation was to carry on its witness. However as we read God's word we also see God's love for Israel then, as well as today. How great is God's love for mankind.

Israel

Of the three areas of sins among the Israelites, the **breaking of the Sabbath** was frequently done. The keeping of the Sabbath was a sign that God truly ruled Israel. To break his Sabbath law was to rebel against God, an act meriting death. Therefore, all work, except acts of mercy or necessity, was forbidden on the Sabbath. (Isaiah 58:13-14; Matthew 12:1-13; Exodus 3l:14). In the book of Nehemiah, chapter 13, verses 15-22, it states that Nehemiah stopped men from various countries from bringing in their goods on the Sabbath to do business with the Jews in Jerusalem. He also commanded the Levites to cleanse themselves, and to keep the gates closed on the Sabbath so that it would be sanctified. One of the reasons that Israel was taken into Babylonian captivity was because of their breaking of the law and their not keeping the Sabbath.

The word Sabbath means cessation or rest. As God is our example, he shows us through his word that six days he worked, and the seventh day he rested. The formal institution of the Sabbath is a basic part of the mosaic law. Each division of the law contains specific sections relating to the practice of the Sabbath, the moral law, the ten Commandments, the civil law, and the ceremonial law. In Exodus 31:12-18, the Lord told Moses to tell the children of Israel that their keeping the Sabbath was a sign between God and his people throughout their generations, that they may know that I am the Lord that doth sanctify you. The Sabbath day itself was holy to God and he expected it to be holy to his people.

As the Lord revealed his name to his people as Jehovah-Mekad-dishkem, he let them know that he would purify them and make them holy as they set aside the Sabbath as a day of rest, a day to worship him. Then the Lord would set them aside, and separate them for his purposes. Exodus 31:15 says, "Six days may work be done: but the seventh is the Sabbath of rest, holy to the Lord: whosoever doeth any work in the Sabbath day, he shall surely be put to death."

The Sabbath was to be a period of refreshing. God used himself as the example of how he worked six days and rested on the seventh. This was to be a perpetual covenant, a sign between Israel and God. God wanted their living pattern to imitate his. He wanted man to rest and to think about and enjoy the blessings of their God. He desired that man give him praise and worship for their blessings. In Leviticus 23:3 the Lord said, "Six days shall work be done: but the seventh day is the Sabbath of rest, a holy convocation; ye shall do no work therein: it is the Sabbath of the Lord in all your dwellings."

In Numbers 15:32-36, we see a rebellious man caught gathering sticks on the Sabbath day and he was brought to Moses and Aaron and to all the congregation. The Lord told Moses the man was to be put to death by stoning outside of the camp. Afterwards, the Lord told Moses to tell the children of Israel to make fringes in the border of their garments, a ribbon of blue, a fringe for them to look at and remember all the commandments of the Lord and to do them, and they were not to seek after their own heart or own eyes which caused them to go a whoring, but they were to remember and do all of God's commandments and be holy unto their God. (Numbers 15:37-40).

God said, "I am the Lord your God, which brought you out of the land of Egypt, to be your God: I am the Lord your God." (Numbers 15:41) We can easily see how important the Sabbath is to God and although his people continually disobeyed him, he continued to remind them that he was their Source, their Righteousness, their Victory, their Salvation. He and he only was worthy of their obedience, their love, and worship. Although they continually were warned, they chose to disobey, thereby bringing judgment upon themselves.

God had also commanded his people to maintain the Sabbatical year, (Leviticus 25: 1-5). During the seventh year, they were to let the land rest. During the Sabbatical year, the Israelites were to cancel all debts owed them by fellow Israelites, and they were to free Hebrew slaves remembering that they were once slaves in Egypt. (Deuteronomy 15:1-18). The fiftieth year, the year of Jubilee, was celebrated by the Jews (Leviticus 25:10-13). This year was also holy unto the Lord and was expected to be observed by the people of God.

The anger of God fell on Israel because the Sabbatical year was not observed. Jeremiah reminded them of the covenant God had made with their forefathers, who had come out of Egypt from slavery themselves, and that in the seventh year they were to let their Hebrew brothers go free. However, they chose to disobey the word of the Lord. They chose to do it their way. Because they did not listen to God speaking through the prophet Jeremiah, the Lord allowed them as well as King Zedekiah, king of Judah, to be given into the hand of their enemy, which was the king of Babylon and his army. As prophesied, Judah was burned with fire and became desolate. (Jeremiah 34:1-22).

Throughout God's word, we see God's people choosing to be disobedient and breaking the covenant they had with God. They did not keep the Sabbath day nor the Sabbatical year.

The **second sin** that the Israelites committed was **intermarriage with heathens**. In Deuteronomy 7:3-6, the Lord commanded His people not to have anything to do with the Hittites, Girgashites, the Amorites, the Canaanites, the Perizzites, the Hivites, and the Jebusites. The Lord told his people not to give their sons or daughters in marriage to them. The Lord also told them that in doing so, their sons would stop following Him, the true and living God, and they would begin to serve other gods, and the Lord's anger would be kindled against them and destroy them suddenly.

The word of God even tells us in I Kings 11:1-2, that King Solomon loved many strange women including Pharaoh's daughter. These women were Moabites, Ammonites, Edomites, Zidonians, and Hittites. King Solomon had been told by God not to go unto them nor were they to come in unto him because if he did, they would surely turn away his heart from his living God to their idol gods. I Kings 11:3 tells us that he, king Solomon, had seven hundred wives, princesses, and three hundred concubines, and that they turned King Solomon's heart to their gods. His heart was not perfect with the Lord his God, as was the heart of David, his father. The Lord continued to raise up prophets to tell his people not to intermarry with the heathens. If they married them, it would cause them to sin against God. But God's people disobeyed the Lord and intermarried, and they began to do the same things their heathen spouses were doing, which was worshiping idol gods, which had been prophesied. God's people lost their first love for their living God. Even though God in his love and mercy warned his people, they continually refused to listen to his words.

The **third sin** the Israelites committed was **idol worship**. Throughout the word of God, it tells that many of his people worshipped idols rather than their living God. Genesis 31:34 states that Rachel had stolen some of her father's idols. Aaron, who was Moses brother, helped the Israelites make the golden calf at the foot of Mount Sinai when the Israelites lost their patience waiting for Moses to return. Throughout the word, we see idolatry, the worship of pagan gods practiced by many of God's people. A primary reason for this idolatry was their sin of intermarrying with the heathens who worshipped idols. The Israelites forsook their living God to the extent that they even offered their sons and daughters to the heathen god molech and caused their children to go through the fire as sacrifices to the idol god molech. God had already warned and commanded his people that they were not to do this as stated in Leviticus 18:21, II Kings 16:2-4 and Jeremiah 32:35. It was a custom of many of the heathen nations to cast their children into the fire to please their idol gods.

In Ezekiel 16:13-22, the prophet tells the people how God had blessed them abundantly, with gold, silver, with fine linen, silk and embroidered cloth. He had even given them the best food to eat, fine flour, honey and oil. Their fame had even gone forth to the nations. In v/14, he reminds them that it was because the Lord had bestowed his splendor upon them, that they were renown among the heathens. Instead of the Israelites trusting, thanking, and obeying their living God, they played the harlot and sinned in every way possible with that which God had blessed them. With the garments God gave to his people, they decked the high places, and they even took the gold and silver he gave them and made images of men and committed whoredom. They offered their meat, fine flour, oil and honey, that God had given them to feed his people, to the idols. They also took their daughters and their sons which the Lord had given them and sacrificed them to idols to be destroyed. They slaughtered God's children and offered them up to idols by causing them to pass through the fires. All these abominations the Israelites did and they did not remember the days of their youth or where God had brought them from. The Lord declared in verse 23, Woe, woe unto thee! saith the Lord God.

Today in our nation America, we see the same results of idolatry, the sacrifice of our children. Abortion is legal in this country as well as many other countries. Sadly, even some who call themselves Christians are defending this so called right to choose abortion and even practicing the killing of the unborn child. Yes, God is a merciful God, but he is also the righteous judge and surely our nation shall be judged severely because of this and many other abominable sins. Even now we can see the beginning of God's judgments upon this wicked nation. So many times today idols are in the lives of believers, whether consciously or unconsciously. An idol is that which one values more than God our Creator, that which is placed before him, be it food, family, job, cars, recreation, money, friends, children, whatever or whoever takes the place of God in their lives.

The word says in I Samuel 15:23, "For rebellion is as the sin of witchcraft, and stubbornness is as iniquity and idolatry." God's people received judgment from God and punishment for their sins from the hands of their many lovers, those that they went a whoring after, those they wanted to be like, which were the heathen nations, (Ezekiel 16:37-39). The Lord declared that Sodom, their sister, and her daughters had <u>not</u> done as they had done, that the Jews were more corrupt then they were, (Ezekiel 16:48). Indeed God's judgment did come, and many of the Jews were destroyed because of their rebellion, and disobedience to God and his word and his prophets. Praise God, even as prophesied through the word of God, a remnant would be saved.

Under the anointing of God, Ezekiel prophesied in Ezekiel 6:1-14 that God's people would be destroyed because of all the evil abominations that the house of Israel had done. He prophesied that the Israelites would be destroyed by the sword, famine and plague; but that a remnant would escape as stated in Ezekiel 6:8, "Yet will I leave a remnant, that ye may have some that escape the sword among the nations, when ye shall be scattered through the countries." The remnant would remember the Lord among the nations that they would be carried to as captives. These Israelites would recognize and realize how they had hurt the Lord by their adulterous hearts which had turned from him, and they would acknowledge how they had allowed their eyes to play the harlot after idols. Then they would loathe themselves and the evil that they had committed. They would recognize all their abominations and know that what God said was not in vain. They would realize that God would do just what he said through his prophet. Unfortunately, they would only recognize this after the judgment of God had come upon them for their sins. They would know that the Lord is God! Although judgment had to come because of the three areas of sin of the Israelites - **(1) breaking of the Sabbath, (2) intermarriage with the heathen, and (3) idolatry**,- God first warned them and called his people to repent, so that the judgment would not have to come. However, because of their continued rebellious hearts, they brought judgment upon themselves. Even though judgment came, the Lord promised through his word, there would be a remnant saved. God gave the promise of a day of restoration, and the promise of the Redeemer, his son Jesus Christ, who would come to redeem mankind through the shedding of his precious holy blood. To God Be The Glory. Praise God! Amen! (Genesis 3:15, Isaiah 52:3, 10, and Jeremiah 32:37-40)

We must always remember that God loves his people the Israelites, and that he will never forget his people. They are the apple of his eye and that God's son, Jesus Christ, was born of Jewish lineage, of the tribe of Judah. (Luke 3:23-38 and Matthew1:1-17) God chose the Jewish nation not because they were the largest, but because they were the smallest, to show forth his power, as well as because of his covenant to Abraham and his seed. As Christians, we are to love and to pray for the Israelites, Psalms 122:6.

As we see prophecy after prophecy being fulfilled before our very eyes today such as the Israelites returning to their homeland, we should rejoice. Jeremiah 23:7-8 states, "Behold the days come, saith the Lord that they shall no more say, the Lord liveth which brought up the children of Israel out of the land of Egypt; But the Lord liveth, which brought up and which led the seed of the house of Israel out of the north country, and from all countries whither I had driven them: and they shall dwell in their own land." We should rejoice that the scales of spiritual blindness are being removed from many Jewish people's eyes as they are realizing that Jesus Christ was born of a virgin, as prophesied in Isaiah 7:14 and that this prophecy was fulfilled as recorded in the gospel of Luke 1: 30-38, and other gospels. Some have realized that Father God is the Father of Jesus Christ, Luke 2:30-38. Many scriptures in the bible tell us that Jesus Christ is the Messiah, and Praise God, many have and are accepting Jesus Christ as their Savior, including Israelites. We should also rejoice that as we see so many of God's prophecies being fulfilled, we can be assured that Jesus Christ will indeed shortly return to rapture his Victorious! Glorious! Church! It states in I Thessalonians 4:17, "Then we which are alive and remain shall be caught up together with them in the cloud to meet the Lord in the air and so shall we ever be with the Lord." Amen! Even So, Come Lord Jesus, Revelation 22:20. **AMEN!**

2

Introduction - Spiritual Israel

Acts 3:19-21 - Repent ye therefore, and be converted, that your sins may be blotted out, when the times of refreshing shall come from the presence of the Lord; v/20 And he shall send Jesus Christ, which before was preached unto you; v/21 Whom the heaven must receive until the times of restitution of all things, which God hath spoken by the mouth of all his holy prophets since the world began.

THE CHURCH IS presently in the time period of restitution. Restitution may be defined as bringing back to a former condition, to restore, a recovery. To find the former state, we need only look to God's Word. The former state is seen in the Garden of Eden before Adam and Eve sinned. They were in perfect harmony and union with their Creator, God. They were able to commune and fellowship with God. Nothing separated them from their Elohim, their Creator. They had dominion over everything; even the animals were subject to them. It was not until they sinned through disobedience to God's one command to not eat from the tree of knowledge of good and evil that the separation of the perfect oneness they had with God began. Sin, death, sickness, disease, and all that the curse of the broken law brought, came into effect in the earth and the lives of mankind. Praise God, we are presently at the end of this age which is referred to as the Gentile age, church age, or age of grace. We are now seeing prophecies rapidly being fulfilled before our very eyes. Acts 3:19 speaks of the day in which we are presently living. The word says, "**Repent** ye therefore, and be **converted**, that your sins may be blotted out, when the times of refreshing shall come from the presence of the Lord." Repent means to turn away from sin, disobedience or rebellion, and to turn back to God. It also signals a change of mind, a feeling of remorse or regret for past conduct. The word converted or conversion means to turn away from evil deeds or false worship and to turn toward serving and worshiping the Lord. Conversion is more than one repenting of a sin; it is a <u>wholehearted</u> turning to God.

Conversion is also the inward experience, which is sometimes referred to as the new birth. This conversion was explained by Jesus in John 3:3-8. Jesus explained conversion to Nicodemus as a new spiritual beginning in a person's relationship with God. Jesus explained that the new birth or being born again, is not of flesh and blood but with water (the word) and of the Spirit of God.

We, who are Christians, who have experienced this conversion or new birth that Jesus spoke of to Nicodemus, must today be totally yielded to Almighty God. If we sin, we must be quick to repent so that our hearts remain pure before God. So that during the mighty move of God, we will be able to flow with God's Spirit and be used by him as he does a short work of righteousness in the earth (Romans 9:28).

In Acts, chapter three, Peter boldly spoke God's words and told how faith in the name of Jesus, had caused the lame man at the gate of the temple called Beautiful to walk and had given him perfect soundness in the midst of the people. Indeed, this man's time of refreshing from the presence of the Lord had come for him and he was restored. A time of restoration in his body had taken place. His body was restored to how God had originally ordained it before the fall of man minus the glory that originally covered Adam and Eve. He had been lame from his mother's womb, a result of the curse that had come upon mankind in the Garden of Eden. Peter and John demonstrated Holy Ghost boldness as they declared what was rightly this man's inheritance because of the Holy One, the Prince of Life, Jesus, who Peter declared that the rulers had rejected.

Today, at the close of this end time age in which we are now living, satan is using drastic means both overtly and covertly to try to entrap members of the body of Christ. He is using drugs, all types of television programs, movies, plays, to entice and entrap both the saved and the unsaved. Today, some music has subliminal messages, as well as overt messages that glorify suicide, hell, premarital sex and many other things that are wicked and perverse. When possible, satan tries to use believers against believers; whatever the reason, be it prejudices because of different Christian denominations, race, or gender. He really does not care what the entrapment is as long as it works to separate believers. He causes strife, dissent and confusion to entice a person to sin, and to draw them from God.

Much like God's people of the Old Testament, there is a choice that must be made whether to be totally yielded to God and his purposes for the born again believers' lives, or to not yield. Revelation 3:16 clearly tells us that those who are lukewarm, and not hot, that the Lord will spue them out of his mouth. If every born again Christian is a part of Jesus Christ's body, and if he has promised to spue those who are lukewarm out, then when this occurs they are no longer a part of the body of Jesus Christ. Once he does, they are no longer attached to the True Vine, Jesus, who is the life giver! Jesus desires that the body of Christ, which is the Church, his bride, be **victorious**, victorious in every area, spiritually, physically, emotionally, socially and financially. He desires that we walk in his finished works at Calvary's cross in which he gave **Total Salvation** to his body. It's the reason Jesus shed his precious blood, for our inheritance. The word salvation, both in the Hebrew as well as the Greek, means so much. Both words are very similar in meaning. Salvation means to be saved, health, prosperity, healing, victory, deliverance, and more. This is all in Jesus Christ. Jesus paid the price so that whosoever would believe on his name could receive the most important part of **Total Salvation** which is to be saved. This is the greatest miracle and greatest part of a believer's inheritance, Amen! It does not have to stop there because every believer has an inheritance while we are in this earth, as well as when we get to heaven. While here on the earth, much like an inheritance from a will, it must be claimed, the same is true with our inheritance paid for by Jesus Christ; we must accept it. As we accept what is rightfully ours and press into receiving it by faith through believing and acting on the word of God, which are our promises, this indeed, pleases Father God. That's why he sent his son Jesus Christ to die on the cross; to pay the price for the redemption of the world. Jesus became the Testator of the New Testament Covenant, which is the believer's will, which is <u>God's holy word</u>, <u>our promises</u>. When we as believers enter into the kingdom to receive our inheritance, we do so by faith, the same way that we were birthed into God's kingdom when we were born again.

As we continue to enter into the kingdom of God, it is then that we receive more and more of our inheritance, our **Total Salvation** gift which is **Jesus Christ**. This is the reason that Jesus shed his precious blood on Calvary's cross for us, that we could be saved and then receive our covenant blessings. We must always keep in mind that it is not a name it, claim it game. It's having a spiritual and personal relationship that as believers we grow into with the Lord Jesus Christ as we seek him first. As Jesus Christ becomes first in our lives, we will become more and more intimate with him. As we do, we will come to know him as not only as our **Savior**, but also as our **Friend**, the **Lover** of our souls, our **Lord** and **Master**, our **Healer** and **Deliverer**, our **Sanctifier**, our **Victory**, our **Righteousness**, our **Provider**, our **Husband**, as well as our very, very, very, very, **Soon Coming King** and much more. The ways that we come to know Jesus are endless, and we will continue to grow in him and know him better even after we leave this world and continue our relationship with Jesus in heaven. This relationship will continue even when we return to rule and reign with Jesus Christ during his millennial reign on this earth, and beyond throughout eternity. Indeed, **Jesus Christ** is our **Great I AM**, our **All and All**, our **Alpha** and **Omega**, our **Everything!** Much like we who have spouses that we love and respect and continue to grow more in love with, we also continue to learn new and exciting things about one another. The same is true concerning our relationship with Jesus Christ, but on a much higher level. As we seek him, we come to "seek first the kingdom of God and his righteousness, and all other things shall be added unto us" (Matthew 6:33).

Faith pleases God. As we seek him, we must seek him in faith.

Hebrews 11:6 tells us, "But without faith it is impossible to please him, for he that cometh to God must believe that he is, and that he is a rewarder of them that diligently seek him."

When we first sought Jesus in faith, it was then, we became a born again child of Almighty God, and Jesus became our Savior. Being saved is the greatest gift of our inheritance. There is no greater gift than to be born again, blood washed sons and daughters of God. Moreover, Jesus shed his precious blood for our **Total Salvation** and he desires that as believers, after becoming born again, that we continue to enter the kingdom of God and receive all that he has for us because of his precious shed blood on Calvary's cross.

The Church of Jesus Christ is made up of Jews who are the natural branches and non-Jews who are not the natural branches. Both have accepted Jesus Christ as their Savior and are born again believers. Praise God for the Jews and the non-Jews of all races who have been born again and who make up the Church of Jesus Christ, which is his body. We must always remember that, the Jews or Israelites, are the natural branches of the good Olive Tree, who is Jesus Christ. The branches who have been grafted into the good Olive Tree, and are not natural Jews, may be referred to as Spiritual Israel and we will never take the place of Natural Israel. As Spiritual Israel, we are the branches that have been grafted into the good Olive Tree, who is Jesus Christ, and we must always recognize Jesus as our life giving source and draw whatever we need from him for he is our great **I AM**. Amen!

The Church of Jesus Christ must not boast itself against the Jews who are not yet born again. We must love them and pray for them and believe that God is able to graft them in again as scales are removed from their eyes and they realize that Jesus Christ is the Savior. Amen! In Romans 11:21-24, it states "For if God spared not the natural branches take heed lest he also spared not thee. V/22, Behold therefore the goodness and severity of God: on them which fell, severity; but towards thee, goodness, if thou continue in his goodness: otherwise thou also shall be cut off. V/23, And they also, if they abide not still in unbelief, shall be grafted in: for God is able to graft them in again. V/24, For if thou wert cut out of the olive tree which is wild by nature, and wert grafted contrary to nature into a good Olive Tree:

how much more shall these which be the natural branches, be grafted into their own Olive tree?"

Spiritual Israel

Jesus says to His church, "I AM whoever, whatever you need that agrees with my word and my will for your life." Your time of refreshing from the presence of the Lord is now; your time of restoration is now. It is not when we get to heaven, and yes, as believers that truly love Almighty God, we look forward to going to heaven. God wants the members of his body to demonstrate who he is in the earth now. God desires that we reflect on what he looks like and how he acts. We cannot do this apart from a very intimate relationship with him. Jesus loves his body. He laid down his life for his body to redeem us, to purchase us back from the devil. Amen! He waits for his church as a whole to seek him to come to know him in an intimate and personal way. Psalms 9:10 says, "And they that know thy name will put their trust in thee: for thou, Lord, hast not forsaken them that seek thee." The words "to know" in the Hebrew is yada, which is the same word that was used in Genesis 4:1, where the word says that Adam knew (yada) Eve, Adam was physically intimate with his wife Eve, and she conceived, and gave birth. God desires that every member of his body come to <u>know</u> (<u>yada</u>) him, as a husband does his wife and a wife her husband on an intimate level. The more we know God, the more we become like him. The more that God's people come to know him the more they are able to conceive and birth God's plans and destinies for their lives into the earth.

When we daily spend quality time with the Lord in the word, which is alive, which is Jesus, who is the Word, we come to know Jesus in a more personal way. For example, if an acquaintance, someone you had recently met, called you, more than likely you would not recognize his voice; he would have to identify himself. However, if a close friend or a close family member that you had contact with on a regular basis called, you would instantly recognize his voice. So also with the Lover of our souls, Jesus Christ, he desires that we know him (yada him), know him as a kinsfolk, kinsman, for he is our Kinsman

Redeemer. Yada means to understand, be sure of, to ascertain by seeing. These are only a few Hebrew definitions of yada. God desires that we know his son Jesus Christ in a personal and intimate way because as we come to know, ascertain by seeing Jesus more, we also come to know the Father. Jesus said in John 14:9, "he that hath seen me hath seen the Father." Indeed Jesus will manifest who he is to those who will believe and receive the gift of **Total Salvation.**

As we seek God daily with our **whole heart**, it is then that we come to know him. When we pray from a pure heart and our motives are right, and when we love God with our whole being, it is then that we come to know him. When our desire is to please God, even above ourselves, it is then that we come to know him. When we spend time in the presence of God daily in praise and worship, it is then that we come to know him. When the greatest Lover and Love of our life is **JESUS CHRIST**, then we come to know HIM and we become like HIM. Why? Because above everything and everyone, we are seeking to know JESUS in a more personal and intimate way. Therefore, as we do this, we begin to see and recognize Jesus as he manifests himself to us. As we daily spend quality time in fellowship, communicating with our Lord and Savior, Jesus Christ, we become more and more in love with Jesus, the Lover of our souls. It is then that we will look forward to and cherish the intimate time we spend with our LOVER, and as we are quiet and allow him to speak to us. Jesus said in John 10:27-28, "My sheep hear my voice, and I know them, and they follow me: And I give unto them eternal life; and they shall never perish, neither shall any man pluck them out of my hand." God is always speaking to us, but many times we don't take the time to be still and listen to what he wants to say, how rude! As we listen to God, we come to know him better. As we put God's Word first place in our lives, we grow spiritually, our minds are renewed, we are cleansed and we become more like Jesus. We come to know him as we daily eat the Lamb, the Living Word, Jesus.

Instead of being conformed to the world, we become transformed as our minds are renewed. We become more and more transformed into the image of Jesus Christ, who is our very, very, very, very Soon Coming King, Amen!

As we who are born again Israelites or Spiritual Israelites yield to God to do his will, to please him, to make him happy by doing the Word after hearing it, we will come forth as the **Victorious! Glorious! Church!** and Father God will release Jesus from heaven to take his bride home. Jesus said in Matthew 24:14, "And this gospel of the kingdom shall be preached in all the world for a witness unto all nations; and then the end shall come." Praise God even after the church has been raptured, (caught up) the gospel will continue to be preached. During the tribulation period as recorded in Revelation 7:3-8, for a period of time there will be twelve thousand Jews that will be sealed by God's angels from each of the twelve tribes of Israel on the earth. There will also be the two witnesses on the earth for a period of time (Revelation 11: 3 - 14). Also Revelation 14:6 – 7 states that an angel of God will fly in the midst of heaven that will preach the everlasting gospel to every nation and people on the earth. Even when the wrath of God is poured out, we still see God's great love being demonstrated.

I believe that we are the generation that will see Jesus' return to take his body home, but as his body, we have a work to do. We must wear the whole armor of God (Ephesians 6:10-18) and we must pray for the body of Christ. Jesus is our example. In John 17:1-3, Jesus prayed for his body long before we were ever born. Today, we are the hands, feet, and mouths of Jesus in the earth. We are his royal priesthood and its time that we act like it.

It is time that we see others as God does. Jesus paid the price to save mankind. Each of us must accept for ourselves the free gift of salvation that Jesus provided by shedding his blood on Calvary's cross. God sees the end result because he knows the beginning from the end and everything that is in between. Praise God! The Lord sees the body of Christ as being mature, each joint fitly joined together, each member in its place doing its job. God sees his **<u>Victorious!</u>, <u>Glorious!</u>, <u>Church!</u>,** Amen!

God is the ALPHA, the Beginning, the OMEGA, the End (Rev 1:8), and the AMEN, The So Be It (Rev 3:14). He dwells mightily in his body, which is his temple, the body of Christ. The Lord desires to work through us, his body of Christian believers. He desires to use us, but we must be willing to yield to God's will for ourselves.

God is holy and He commands that we his people be holy. I Peter 1:15-16 says, "But as he which hath called you is holy, so be ye holy in all manner of conversation; Because it is written, Be ye holy; for I am holy." The word of God in I Peter 2:9-10 states that, "But ye are a chosen generation, a royal priesthood, a holy nation, a peculiar people; that ye should show forth the praises of him who hath called you out of darkness into his marvelous light: Which in time past were not a people, but are now the people of God; which had not obtained mercy, but now have obtained mercy."

It's time that we act and demonstrate whose we are and what God says we are. As a royal priesthood, we must be prayer warriors, not only for ourselves, but for others. I Peter 2:12 says, "Having our conversations honest among the Gentiles that whereas they speak against you as evildoers, they may by your good works, which they shall behold, glorify God in the day of visitation." Yes, the Gentiles, or unsaved, will be drawn to Jesus by the works of the body of Christ, by the very lives that we live, as living epistles that glorify God by our lifestyles. How else will the unsaved know what Jesus looks like unless they see Him manifested in us, in the way we talk, act, even in the ways God prospers us as we put God and his agenda first place in our lives. As God manifests himself to us as our provider, we must always give him the glory and credit for what he has done for us. Amen!

As members of Jesus Christ's body, God's word says in Romans 15:1, "We then that are strong ought to bear the infirmities of the weak, and not to please ourselves." Yes, we are to pray for our families, ourselves, and others' special needs, but how many Christians are consistently praying for the body of Jesus Christ? We are members of Jesus and members of one another, and certainly we should regularly pray for one another. Why? So that the carnality among the body will stop, so that God's character will increase in every member, and so that we all will be mature members in the body of Jesus Christ. I encourage you to yield to God and allow him to <u>increase</u> in you. Ask the Lord to give you a deeper love and fear (holy reverence) for him first of all, as well as a deeper love for the things of God. Also, ask God to give you a deeper love and burden for the saints of God, every member of the body of Jesus Christ, as well as a deeper love and burden for unsaved souls. We must pray that the unsaved will accept Jesus as their Savior. Regularly pray Ephesians 4:13-16, remembering that we who are saved are all members of one another.

Prayer

Heavenly, Loving Father, I come to you in the precious name of Jesus Christ, my Brother, Savior, Friend, Master and Lover of my soul and my very, very, very, very, Soon Coming King.

I thank you Father God that I am your blessed, blood washed, born again child of God. I love you. I adore you. I worship only you, my true and living God. I give you thanksgiving and all the honor, glory, and the praise for who you are to me, and for all you have done and will do in my life.

Father God, in the blessed name of Jesus, help me to examine my heart for any sin, and I now confess it aloud to you and ask for your forgiveness of any sin, known or unknown in my life. I repent of every sin and I forgive all. Lord, you said in Isaiah 1:18, "Come now and let us reason together, saith the Lord: though your sins be as scarlet, they shall be as white as snow; though they be red like crimson, they shall be as wool," and I thank you. I thank you for the precious blood of Jesus Christ that was shed for my sins and I ask that you apply the precious blood of Jesus Christ to my sins and to me in Jesus' name! Amen!

I thank you that I am now in right standing before you because of the precious shed blood of Jesus Christ.

In Isaiah 43:26, You said, "Put me in remembrance: let us plead together: declare thou, that thou mayest be justified." So now, I put you in remembrance of your word.

In Psalms 37:4-5, you said "Delight thyself also in the Lord; and he shall give thee the desires of thine heart; Commit thy way unto the Lord, trust also in him, and he shall bring it to pass."

Father God in Jesus' name I pray for the body of Christ. Your word says in Isaiah 53:12 that Jesus made intercession for the transgressors. I especially pray for the backsliders, as well as the body of Christ as a whole. You told your disciples in John 20:23, "Whosoever sins ye remit, they are remitted unto them, and whosoever sins ye retain, they are retained." I am your disciple today and I remit the sins of the body of Christ as well as those members who are backslidden, and I ask that you would forgive them and apply the blood of Jesus Christ to each one's sins and I thank you Father God in Jesus' name, Amen!

I pray that you, Father God, in Jesus' name, would create in each member of Jesus Christ's body, including those who will become members, "a clean heart, O God; and renew a right spirit within us." I also pray that each member will be quick to repent, in Jesus' name of anything that is unpleasing to you, Father God. I pray that you will give each of us clean hands and that we will not lift up our souls unto vanity, nor swear deceitfully in Jesus' name, Amen!

I also pray Ephesians 4:13-16, that we will <u>all</u> come in the unity of the faith, and of the knowledge of the Son of God, unto a perfect man, unto the measure of the stature of the fullness of Christ; That we henceforth be no more children, tossed to and fro, and carried about with every wind of doctrine, by the sleight of men, and cunning craftiness, whereby they lie in wait to deceive; But speaking the truth in love, may grow up into him in all things which is the head, even Christ. From whom the whole body fitly joined together and compacted by that which every joint supplieth, according to the effectual working in the measure of every part, maketh increase of the body unto the edifying of itself in love. In Jesus' name, Amen!

In Ephesians 5:25-27, God's word says, "that Christ loved the church and gave himself for it; that he might sanctify and cleanse it with the washing of water by the word, that he might present it to himself a glorious church not having spot, or wrinkle, or any such thing; but that it should be holy and without blemish."

So I intercede on the behalf of the church, that each member will be like the five wise virgins that took oil in their vessels with their lamps, and that we will be ready to go in with the Lord Jesus Christ to the marriage (Matthew 25:1-12). Amen!

I confess by faith I Thessalonians 5:4-6,9: That the church, which is the body of Jesus Christ is not in darkness, that that day should overtake us as a thief.

I thank you Father God in Jesus' name that we are the children of light and the children of the day: we are not of the night, nor of darkness.

"Therefore let us not sleep, as do others, but let us watch and be sober, for God has not appointed us to wrath, but to obtain salvation by our Lord Jesus Christ."

I thank you that your glorious church shall be a victorious church that is watching and ready, for your word says in I Thessalonians 4:16-17, "when the Lord himself shall descend from heaven with a shout, with the voice of the archangel, and with the trump of God and the dead in Christ shall rise first, then we which are alive and remain shall be caught up together with them in the cloud to meet the Lord in the air: and so shall we ever be with the Lord", Amen! In Jesus' name, Amen!

Father God, in Jesus' name, we thank you for your **VICTORIOUS! GLORIOUS! CHURCH!** which shall shortly be caught up to meet the Lord in the air in Jesus' name! We stand on your word in Matthew 19:26, "With men this is impossible, but with God **all** things are possible." Amen and Amen! Praise God! To God Be The Glory!

Let us always remember that God has not given up on His church and we can do no less, for we are members of Jesus and members of one another. I Corinthians 12:12-13 says, "For as the body is one, and hath many members, and all the members of that one body, being many, are one body: so also is Christ," "For by one Spirit are we all baptized into one body, whether we be Jews or Gentiles whether we be bond or free, and have been all made to drink into one Spirit."

Therefore, let us pray for one another in the body of Christ consistently, remembering Romans 15:1 which says, "We then that are strong ought to bear the infirmities of the weak, and not to please ourselves." Amen.

3

Are You Married To The Lord?

Isaiah 54:5 - For thy maker is thine husband; the Lord of host is his name; and thy Redeemer the Holy One of Israel; The God of the whole earth shall he be called.

THE QUESTION AND the title of this chapter, "Are You **Married** To The Lord?" is for every person, male or female, young or old. To be **married** to the Lord, requires certain things. We will look at what God's word says is required. We will look at the prophet Hosea, who God used to demonstrate his love toward his backslidden people. Hosea was a prophet to the Northern Kingdom during the reign of Jeroboam II. His ministry overlapped that of Amos, Isaiah and Micah. During the time of Hosea, there was a great religious apostasy. God's people were deserting their faith in the true and living God. Hosea is sometimes referred to as a minor prophet, not because he was any less important than the major prophets, but because of the length of his message. The book of Hosea is one of the shorter books of the prophets. Hosea, I believe, is a type of Jesus Christ. Throughout God's holy word, we see many types or examples of the heart of the Lord. Hosea received the word from the Lord to take a wife, who was a harlot. Can you imagine how Hosea must have felt knowing that this woman that he **married** had slept with who knows how many men and was not the chaste and pure virgin that most men took for wives. In Hosea, we see that he indeed was already **married** to the Lord himself because he loved the Lord first and foremost above anything, even above his own desires or wishes. He desired more to be obedient and to please the Lord to whom he was **married**.

Before looking at Hosea, I just want us to look at a few of God's covenant names in the Old Testament. In Genesis 17:1, we find that God renewed his covenant with Abram when Abram was ninety-nine years old. At this time, God appeared to him and told him, "I am the **<u>Almighty God</u>** or **<u>El Shaddai,</u>** the All Sufficient God, the God who is more than enough." Praise God! **El Shaddai** commanded Abram to walk perfect before him, to <u>mature in faith</u>. God said, I will make my covenant between me and thee and multiply thee exceedingly. God told Abram that his name would no longer be Abram, but Abraham and God called the things that were not as though they were by changing his name to mean Father of a Multitude. In Genesis 17:5, God told Abraham he had already made him a father of many nations! Praise God, it had not been manifested yet in the physical, but in God's mind it was already done and he was bringing Abraham to a place to see things as he saw things as being already done. God was helping him to walk in faith even by changing his name.

Abraham, like many of God's people had missed it with God. God had made him a promise to give him a child and when that child was not manifested, Abraham and Sarah decided to help God out. Abraham had a child named Ishmael by Hagar the handmaiden of Sarah. Ishmael was the son of the flesh. Today, because of the act of Abraham's and Sarah's self wills to have a child by Hagar, there is the Arab nation. In Genesis 17:1-25, the Word of God tells us that the son of the promise, Isaac, from which the nation of Israel would come, was born even later in their old age. In verse 1, when God appeared to Abraham and revealed his covenant name as **Almighty God** or **El Shaddai**, it tells us that Abraham was ninety-nine years old. In verse 25 it tells us that Ishmael, the son of the flesh, was 13 years old. God promised in verse 21 that Sarah would bear to Abraham, the son of the promise Isaac, the set time in the next year.

After Isaac's birth, Sarah cast out Hagar and her son, Ishmael. God consoled Abraham and told him that from both sons, nations would come forth, but from Isaac, his seed would be called and all nations would be blessed. Jesus Christ later came through the lineage of Abraham's and Isaac's ancestry. The Jewish or Israelite nation descended from the lineage of Abraham, as well as his son of the promise Isaac, that he conceived with his wife Sarah. From Ishmael, the son of the flesh that Abraham conceived with Hagar, Sarah's handmaiden, the nation of the Arabs was birthed. Both the Jews and the Arabs are still at odds today. Keep in mind that God had told Abraham that he was **<u>Almighty</u> <u>God</u>**, or **<u>El</u> <u>Shaddai</u>**, but still Abraham and Sarah tried to work things out by trying to help God. The result of not trusting God was the son of the flesh. Praise God, for indeed he was merciful and patient with Abraham and Sarah even after they missed him, just as he is with you and I today. However, God does not expect us to keep missing the mark, but to be perfect, as God told Abraham, and as Jesus said in Matthew 5:48, "Be ye therefore perfect, even as your Father which is in heaven is perfect (mature), full of faith, obedient to do God's will instead of our own will."

Later, God gave Abraham a command to take his only son whom he loved, Isaac, to the land of Moriah and offer him for a burnt offering. Abraham did not argue and I believe he was full of faith, because early the next morning he took Isaac to the land of Moriah as God had instructed. He even took the wood for the burnt offering. In faith, he set out to look for the place where God wanted him to offer up Isaac for a burnt offering. Indeed this took faith. In Genesis 22:5, Abraham told the men that were with him to stay there with the ass, that he and the lad would leave them to <u>worship</u> and that they would come again to them. Faith speaks through action!

In Genesis 22:6, we are told that Abraham took the wood for the burnt offering and laid it upon Isaac his son to carry. I believe that Abraham is a type or a picture of God the Father and Abraham's son Isaac is a type of Jesus Christ who became the ultimate sacrificial lamb. Isaac was made to carry the wood that he was to be sacrificed on, just as Jesus was made to carry the wooden cross of Calvary that he was placed upon. When God the Father gave his only begotten Son, he showed his love for all of mankind. Praise God, Jesus paid the price for all to be saved through his precious shed blood. II Corinthians 5:21 says, "<u>For he hath made him to be sin for us, who knew no</u>

sin; that we might be the righteousness of God in him." Not only did Jesus take our sins, but he also took our sicknesses, diseases, death, and more including every curse of the broken law. Galatians 3:13 tells us, Jesus was made a curse for us, but all men have not accepted the free gift of becoming saved which is the first part of God's **Total Salvation package. Once a person is born again, this allows them to enter into various other parts of Total Salvation.**

Abraham showed that he loved God more than his son of the promise, Isaac, because he, like God, was willing to offer his son to be sacrificed. When Isaac asked Abraham where was the lamb for the burnt offering Abraham said, "my son, God will provide himself a lamb for a burnt offering." In obedience, they went to the place that God had shown Abraham and built the altar. Abraham bound his son and placed him on the altar. Here, we see Abraham speaking words of faith and doing the will of God. Also, Isaac was obedient to his father's will because he was allowing himself to become the sacrifice, just as Jesus was obedient to his Father's will to be offered as the perfect Lamb of God on Calvary's cross. In Genesis 22:11-14, as Abraham took the knife to slay his son, the angel of the Lord called to him out of heaven and Abraham said "Here am I." The angel said, "Lay not thine hand upon the lad, neither do thou anything unto him; for I know that thou fearest God, seeing thou has not withheld thy son, thine only son from me." Praise God! God indeed provided Abraham a ram caught in the thicket and revealed his covenant name **Jehovah-Jireh**, as stated in verse 14, "And Abraham called the name of that place **(Jehovah-Jireh)** - The Lord will provide - his provision shall be seen. Truly Abraham was **married** to his God."

Throughout the word of God, God manifested himself through his names to his people. These names refer or point to who God is to his people, and that Jesus would pay the price for **Total Salvation**. Praise God! **Hosea's** name means **salvation**. Through Hosea's obedience to God's will for Hosea to take a wife who was not a pure virgin, but a harlot who did not respect her husband, in that she slept with other men; God was able to use Hosea as a sign to show Israel themselves. Even though Gomer, Hosea's wife, was unfaithful to him, Hosea still was devoted to her. He still showed his love for her in providing a home, clothing, food and giving her his name. Although Gomer continued to have other lovers, Hosea remained faithful to her even though she was continually unfaithful to him.

Much like Hosea's harlot wife, Israel had forsaken their first love, their living God, with whom they were in covenant. They were to be God's people, his examples to the heathen nations. They were to worship God and him alone. As the Israelites were obedient to God, he would manifest his covenant names physically in their lives, i.e. "**Jehovah-Nissi**" (the Lord their banner, their victory), **"Jehovah-Tsidkenu"** (the Lord our Righteousness) as well as many other covenant names. They were once **married** to the Lord but they turned their backs on him and were worshiping idols. They were seeking to hear from gods of stone and wood. Even the priests were sinning against God. Instead of Israel being faithful, she was living the life of a harlot, or adulteress, much like Gomer, who continued to be unfaithful to her husband, Hosea the prophet. Hosea was a type or a picture of Jesus Christ. Gomer was sinning as a harlot against Hosea, just as Israel was sinning against their living God. Gomer would sleep with whomever she pleased and did not even acknowledge the one who truly loved her, her husband Hosea. Israel was doing the same thing; they were sinning against God. They turned their backs on the one who really loved them, the one who provided for their every need.

The question for each of us is, "Are we **married** to the Lord?" We are now living in the closing moments of this age of grace and indeed Jesus Christ is very, very, very, very soon to return to take his bride home to heaven with him. The question, Are you **married** to the Lord?, is very, very serious! Some may say, "Well, I'm a man; I'm supposed to be the groom!" Yes, Praise God, in the natural realm, but not in the spiritual realm. The word of God tells us that in Christ Jesus, there is neither male nor female (Galatians 3:28). Jesus Christ's bride will not only be females but it also will be made up of males. Praise God! He will be the only **Bridegroom**. What happens in this earthly realm when a male and female marry? When they marry, a covenant is made and both vow to keep it by saying I do or I will; many times it is in writing. A covenant is simply an agreement and it is not to be taken lightly, which is why it is so important to seek the Lord and be led by the Lord when considering marriage.

Today many do not place much emphasis on morals or Christian values, but we as children of God should be doers of God's word and not hearers only. Yes, both males and females should be virgins when they enter into marriage. Both should be chaste and pure. Whether they are young or old, one must not be swayed by what their peers or friends say or do. You must do what the word of God says to do. Remember that your body is the temple of God. I Corinthians 3:16-17 states, "Know ye not that ye are the temple of God, and that the Spirit of God dwelleth in you? If any man defile the temple of God, him shall God destroy; for the temple of God is holy, which temple ye are." Yes, God does live in every truly born again child of God. When we do not obey the word of God and allow sin to rule, it brings death (i.e. aids, accidents, alcoholism, etc.). James 1:15 says, "Then when lust hath conceived, it bringeth forth sin: and sin, when it is finished, bringeth forth death."

God's word declares that he commands us to be like him, to walk in holiness, in faith, and in love before him and our fellow man. In Hosea 2:19-20, God tells his people he has "betrothed them to himself in righteousness, in judgment, loving kindness and in mercies, and in faithfulness that they may know the Lord." In II Corinthians 11:2, Paul says that the church is to be **married** to <u>our husband, Jesus Christ</u> and that we are to be a chaste virgin. When Jesus walked this earth, he spoke of himself as the Bridegroom in Mark 2:18-20. The disciples of John and the Pharisees asked why Jesus' disciples did not fast. Jesus told them as long as the bridegroom was with them, they did not need to fast but, when the bridegroom would be taken away from them, they would fast in those days.

In Matthew 25:1-13, Jesus told the parable of the five wise virgins and the five foolish virgins. Through this parable, Jesus warned his disciples then, and we today, what would happen to those who are not prepared, not totally committed or **married** to him. Jesus warned those who are lukewarm, whose hearts are divided like Gomer, Hosea's wife, and like the Israelites during Hosea's time. God continued to plead with his people to <u>love only him</u>, so that his judgment would not come upon them. Almighty God also desired that they would have continued fellowship with him and that he could manifest his covenant names in their lives. God wanted to bless his people and to manifest himself to them through his names even as he had manifested himself to Abraham as **Jehovah-Jireh** and **El Shaddai**, and even as he had manifested other covenant names to their fore parents in the past. God is a covenant God, he is a loving God, giving, and forgiving, however, he is also a jealous God and a God of judgment.

We each must decide if we truly desire to be **married** to the Lord. No one can make the decision for us, just as no one can choose where we will spend eternity. We each must accept Jesus into our hearts for ourselves. Jesus stated in Matthew 25:1-13 that all ten were virgins. He said that five of these virgins were wise and five were foolish. The five wise virgins took oil in their vessels with their lamps. Oil often symbolizes or refers to the Holy Spirit. At midnight, when the cry was made, "behold the bridegroom cometh, go ye out to meet him", they arose and trimmed their lamps and the five foolish asked the five wise to give them some of their oil, for their lamps had gone out. The wise virgins said, "no, unless there not be enough for us and you, but go to those that sell and buy for yourselves." And while they went to buy the Bridegroom came; and they that were "ready", *prepared, totally sold out to the Lord, truly* **married** *to the Lord in their hearts*, went in with him to the marriage: and the door was shut. Afterwards came the other virgins saying "Lord, Lord, open to us." He answered and said, "Verily I say unto you, I know you not. Watch therefore, for you know neither the day, nor the hour wherein the Son of man cometh." To paraphrase, the five wise virgins were those who had made themselves ready, males, females, young and old, who were on fire for God, not lukewarm, those who not only studied his word but also were doers of God's word. They were living godly lives, holy unto the Lord. They loved the Lord whom they were **married** to in their hearts, and they placed no one or anything above him or his word. The wise virgins received all that Jesus had as they entered into heaven with the Lord.

The five foolish virgins were not living consistent lives. They were not totally **married** to the Lord in their hearts, because their hearts were divided. Perhaps they did not want to stop going to clubs, or parties with the world. Perhaps they would not stop sexual sins such as adultery or fornication, whether, heterosexual, bisexual or homosexual. Perhaps they loved to cause strife among the brethren or tell lies. Whatever the reasons, the five foolish virgins were not totally committed to the Lord and were not allowed to enter with Jesus, the Bridegroom, into heaven. Why not take time now to examine yourself to determine where you are in your relationship with the Lord. Are you among the five wise virgins whose vessels were filled? Are you a vessel of God's whose light is shining as a bright light before men, so that your life will glorify Father God? Or do you find yourself among the five foolish virgins, rebellious, wanting to do things your way? Do you still want to be like the world in some areas of your life? James 4:4 states: "Ye adulterers and adulteresses know ye not that the friendship of the world is enmity with God? Whosoever therefore will be a friend of the world is the enemy of God."

If you desire to have a close relationship with Jesus, the **Bridegroom,** then make him first in your life. One way to give him first place in your life is by placing his word first as you consistently read and study the Bible. After reading the word, it must be applied to one's daily life, so that your mind may be renewed. When a person decides to continue to read, study and apply the word of God to their life continually, he or she will become a disciple of Jesus. In John 8:31-32, Jesus said, "If you continue in my word, then are ye my disciples indeed; and ye shall know the truth, and the truth shall make you free." As you read, study, and apply the word of God to your life, you will not be conformed to the world but be transformed by the renewing of your mind. As this is done consistently you will become conformed to the image of Jesus Christ. Amen!

God desires that every member of the body of Jesus Christ be totally committed to him in all areas of our lives. In Ephesians 5: 21-33, it tells us that Jesus Christ is the head of the church, which is his body, and that the husband is the head of his wife. God's word admonishes the wife to reverence her husband, and the husband to love his wife even as Christ loves the Church and gave himself for it. God is showing us through his word his divine order. Through the word, God shows us what is expected of a man and woman who are **married** to one another, as well as his body that is **married** to Jesus Christ, the Bridegroom. The Lord expects that we remain faithful to our spouses, as well as to him throughout our entire lives. Amen! When a marriage covenant is made, God sees that, and two become one. Galatians 5:19-21 says God forbids adultery and fornication, as well as other sins. I Corinthians 6:15-20 says, "Know ye not that your bodies are the members of Christ? shall I then take the members of Christ, and make them the members of a harlot? God forbid. What? Know ye not that he which is joined to a harlot is one body? For two, saith he, shall be one flesh. But he that is joined unto the Lord is one spirit. Flee fornication. Every sin, that a man doeth, is without the body; but he that committeth fornication sinneth against his own body. What? Know ye not that your body is the temple of the Holy Ghost which is in you, which ye have of God, and ye are not your own? For ye are bought with a price: therefore glorify God in your body, and in your spirit, which are God's."

It is important that husbands and wives remain faithful to one another and faithful to the Lord. If you are not **married**, the Lord still wants you to be faithful to him and if you are born again, recognize that he is your spouse, your marriage partner, your Bridegroom, and he wants you ready when he comes to take us to the supper of the Lamb. Revelation 19:7-9 states, "Let us be glad and rejoice, and give honor to him: for the marriage of the Lamb is come, and his wife hath made herself ready. And to her was granted that she should be arrayed in fine linen, clean and white: for the fine linen is the righteousness of saints. And he saith unto me, Write, Blessed are they which are called unto the **marriage supper of the Lamb.** And he saith unto me, these are the true sayings of God."

It is time for husbands and wives to come together as one to pray at night, during the day and before going to work or school. It's time to teach the children God's word, the Bible. It is a necessity that the family attend church regularly and join a Bible believing and teaching church of God's word. The mothers and dads, both parents, should be godly examples to their children. If a husband is truly head of his wife, he will not abuse his wife, verbally or physically, or the children. He will be like Christ in every way. The wives will submit to their husbands as unto the Lord. Mothers and fathers, what has the Lord told you to do that you have not yet begun or completed? Some of you may be saying well I can't do anything, or God only wants to use the pastor or those who sing in the choir. Not so, he wants every believer to become yielded vessels to him that he can work through. One way God desires to use his people is in intercessory prayer. An intercessor is someone who is willing to stand in the gap who prays for others who have special needs. God then is able to move us to new levels in him, in his glory. We must become like the five wise virgins who were obedient to have their vessels filled with oil and like Hosea the prophet who was married to the Lord and continuously demonstrated his love to God through his obedience. Oil also refers to the joy of the Lord, which is our strength. (Nehemiah 8:10). As we yield to be totally **married** to the Lord with our whole heart, we will strive to become like Jesus in every way and every area of our lives. Then we will say, "Not my will Lord, but your will be done in my life" in every situation.

If we are truly **married** to the Lord with our whole heart, we will be like Abraham who laid who he loved, his son Isaac, on the altar to be sacrificed. We too will find that most times God will give what we consider the most precious back to us with added blessings. Nothing must be more important than our living God, whether it is our own lives, children, jobs, money or ministry, absolutely nothing is to be before Almighty God!

If we are truly **married** to our living God, it will show forth in our lives in various ways. We will want to please God by our faith. Hebrews 11:6 says, "But without faith it is impossible to please him: for he that cometh to God must believe that he is, and that he is a rewarder of them that diligently seek him." We will please him by our obedience because it demonstrates submission and our love for him. John 14:23 says, "If a man loves me, he will keep my words: and my Father will love him, and we will come unto him, and make our abode with him." I Samuel 15:22 says, "Behold to obey is better than sacrifice, and to hearken than the fat of rams." We will please God by demonstrating love. Ephesians 5:2 says, "And walk in love, as Christ also hath loved us, and hath given himself for us an offering and a sacrifice to God for a sweet smelling savour." Galatians 5:6 tells us, "faith worketh by love", if healing or other blessings are to be manifested, we need to walk in love and yes God is sovereign. Praise God, when we walk in love we also will be quick to forgive as well as to repent when me miss it. Amen!

In Abraham's life, we have seen that he was **married** to the Lord. God blessed Abraham abundantly and made an everlasting covenant with him and his seed after him. In Genesis 22:18, the Lord says, "And in thy seed shall all the nations of the earth be blessed; because thou has obeyed my voice." Praise God, in the fullness of time Father God sent Jesus to be born of a virgin. Jesus, the Son of God, who was clothed in flesh, came through the lineage of Abraham; therefore all nations of the earth indeed are blessed. Praise the Lord!

If God's men, women, boys and girls, are truly **married** to the Lord; they must be holy. Why? Because God is Holy, and he has commanded his people to be holy as stated in (Leviticus 20:7 and in I Peter 1:15-16). God has always commanded his people to be holy. Yes, in the book of Hosea, the Lord says he is **married** to the backslider, but he wanted them then, as well as his people through the generations to be truly married to him. God desires that those who are backslidden, who are lukewarm, those who are straddling the fence with one foot in the world and one in church, to come out from among the unclean things and be separate. God wants his people to stop sinning and be pure and holy virgins. He desires that each would say even as Jesus said not my will, but thy will be done.

Hosea did the will of the Father. In so doing, I believe that he pleased him in his obedience. Jesus himself said in John 8:29, "I do always those things that please him." If we truly love the Lord, are truly **married** to him, we will be like Hosea, and be a living epistle to all people. We will be like Abraham who spoke words of faith that God would provide a sacrifice. He then demonstrated his faith in laying on the altar what God had asked for, his son Isaac.

If we are truly **married** to the Lord, we will be the **bride** that is preparing herself to be ready to meet her **Bridegroom, JESUS CHRIST**. We will be like the five wise virgins in Matthew 25:1-13 with their lamps and oil in their vessels. Oil is a symbol of the anointing of God as well as the Holy Spirit. We will be ready to receive all that Jesus paid for mankind when he offered Himself as the Sacrificial Lamb to give to man **Total Salvation,** which includes the baptism of the Holy Ghost with the evidence of speaking in tongues. This free gift is available to all who desire it after they have accepted Jesus Christ as their Savior.

You may ask why this gift is needed. Acts 1:8 states, "But ye shall receive power, after that the Holy Ghost is come **upon you**: and ye shall be witnesses unto me both in Jerusalem, and in all Judea, and in Samaria, and unto the uttermost part of the earth." So the word of God clearly tells us that Jesus wanted his disciples to wait for the promise of the Holy Ghost to come **upon them**. Jesus said they would receive power. The Greek word for power is dunamis, a miracle working power from the same root word that gives us our modern day word dynamite. This Holy Ghost power would empower them to be effective witnesses of Jesus so that they would be able to fulfill the Great Commission that Jesus gave to all his disciples, both then and Christians throughout the ages (read Mark 16:15-18). The disciples of Jesus Christ are to be lights so that others will desire to receive the free gift of **Total Salvation**, which included the **greatest gift of all, becoming saved.** Being saved means that a person has accepted Jesus Christ as their Savior. Without first becoming saved or born again, one cannot receive the baptism of the Holy Spirit. Upon becoming saved, immediately the person is delivered from the power of darkness and is translated into the kingdom of Father God's dear Son, Jesus Christ (Colossians 1:13). It is then up to every born again Christian to decide how much they desire to receive of Father God's free gift of **Total Salvation**, who is **Jesus Christ;** because of his precious shed blood on Calvary's cross, we have received so much including healing, deliverance, prosperity, victory, and more. **Jesus** is our **Total Salvation**.

Proverbs 11:30 says, "The fruit of righteousness is a tree of life and he that winneth souls is wise." If we are truly **married** to the Lord, we will plant the seed of God's word into the hearts of those who are unsaved. Those who are truly **married** to the Lord, whether male or female, young or old, will become spiritual fathers and mothers whom our Bridegroom Jesus Christ can and will use to nurture and encourage the spiritual babies that have been birthed into God's kingdom. We must be yielded vessels fit for the master's use and allow God in us to be manifested through us.

In God's word, we have seen Hosea's love for his wife, Gomer as well as God's love for his people. We must remember what Romans 5:8 says, "But God commendeth his love toward us, in that while we were yet sinners, Christ died for us." Why, because he loved mankind so very much. Father God loved mankind so much that he sent Jesus Christ, his only begotten Son, to redeem man back to himself (John 3:16).

We must allow agape love, which is the God kind of love, the sacrificial love, to be manifested in our lives daily! When love is manifested, God is manifested. Jesus tells us in John 14:23, "If a man loves me, he will keep my words and my Father will love him, and we will come unto him, and make our abode with him." If we obey God, we will do his word, which is to keep the commandments of love. We will first of all "love the Lord our God with all our heart, and with all our soul, and with all our mind" (Matthew 22:37-39), and we will also do the second commandment, which is like the first, "we will love our neighbor as ourselves." We will not allow anyone or anything to take the place of God being number one in our lives. Jesus said also in John 14:21, "He that hath my commandments, and keepeth them, he it is that loveth me; and <u>he that loveth</u> me shall be loved of my Father, and I will love him, and will manifest myself to him." Jesus will show us healing, deliverance, and various parts of our **total salvation** gift as we yield completely to him and believe and receive all that Jesus purchased for us on Calvary's cross, **total salvation**. If we are truly **married** to the Lord, we will desire to please the Lord and love others, as he does, with agape love, which is the God kind of love. As we do, we will begin to see others with our spiritual eyes as well as our physical eyes. Yes, God hates sin, but he loves the sinner; that is why he sent Jesus to redeem man. We must have agape love for homosexuals, lesbians, prostitutes, drug addicts, alcoholics, and for all men. "For all have sinned and come short of the glory of God" (Romans 3:23). Praise God! Through the precious shed blood of

Jesus Christ, all have been redeemed; however, each must make the choice to choose life by accepting Jesus as his Savior, or choose death by refusing him and his gift of salvation.

Today is the day of salvation. Hosea's name means salvation. Whatever you need is in **Total Salvation,** who is **Jesus Christ.** He is for you today. Amen!

4

The Second Advent - The Return Of Jesus Christ

Matthew 10:38-39 - **And he that taketh not his cross, and followeth after me, is not worthy of me. v/39 He that findeth his life shall lose it: and he that loseth his life for my sake shall find it.**

PRAISE GOD, INDEED we are a blessed generation to be seeing almost daily prophecies fulfilled right before our very eyes. We have seen and are seeing the doors opened for the exodus of Jews from various countries to their nation of Israel. This prophecy was recorded by Jeremiah in chapter16:14-15; "Therefore, behold, the days come, saith the Lord, that it shall no more be said, the Lord liveth, that brought up the children of Israel out of the land of Egypt; But, the Lord liveth, that brought up the children of Israel from the land of the north and from all the lands whither he had driven them: and I will bring them again into their land that I gave unto their fathers." Praise the Lord that is exactly what the Lord God has done and is doing. For, if God says a thing, he indeed will do it. It was reported by the news media that multitudes of Jews have already made an exodus from Russia and thousands more are waiting and planning to leave. This great number does not even include the thousands who have already made their exodus from various other countries to their homeland and nation of Israel.

What Jeremiah, the prophet said under the anointing of God, the Holy Spirit, was referring to the great exodus of the Hebrew people when God delivered them from the hand of Pharaoh out of Egypt. Jeremiah prophesied that there would come a time when an even greater miracle would be performed. We have been blessed to see this prophecy being fulfilled as the Jews exodus from all parts of the world, even the land of the north, which refers to Russia. Praise God, the Lord wants us to recognize that it is indeed his hand that has delivered them and not man, and that they are returning to their homeland, Israel, just as God prophesied through the prophet Jeremiah. In the book of Matthew, chapter 24, the disciples asked Jesus what would be the sign of his coming or return and the time of the end. Jesus began to tell the signs in verses 32-34. He gave the parable of the fig tree. The fig tree was referring to Israel. Jesus said, "Now learn a parable of the fig tree; when his branch is yet tender, and putteth forth leaves, ye know that summer is nigh: So likewise ye, when ye shall see all these things, know that it is near even at the door. Verily I say unto you, this generation shall not pass, till all these things be fulfilled." The fig tree referred to is Israel, which has only been recognized as a nation since 1948. Indeed Israel is putting forth leaves, therefore we are to know that summer is nigh or near. Isaiah 35:1, I believe also speaks of the fig tree and Israel blossoming. It says in Isaiah 35:1, "The wilderness and the solitary place shall be glad for them; and the desert shall rejoice and blossom as the rose." Indeed Israel is blossoming as a rose. It is a major exporter of various fruits and other commodities, although it was once dry and barren. The Lord said when we see these things to know that summer, or our redemption, is near, that Jesus is even at the door. As stated in Matthew 24:34, "Verily I say unto you, this generation shall not pass, till all these things be fulfilled. Heaven and earth shall pass away, but my words shall not pass away." Matthew 24:32-35 lets us know that we are this generation that shall see the second advent of Jesus Christ. The **second coming** will be in **two parts**. First, the rapture will occur when Jesus comes in the air for his own, followed by his appearing at the end of the tribulation period, as recorded in Revelations 19:11-16, when he comes as the **Lion of Judah** to set up his millennial kingdom on earth.

About 2,000 years ago, many were looking for the prophecy in Micah 5:2 to be fulfilled concerning Jesus Christ's first coming. "But thou, Bethlehem Ephratah, though thou be little among the thousands of Judah, yet out of thee shall he come forth unto me that is to be ruler in Israel; whose goings forth have been from of old, from everlasting." This prophecy told where Jesus would be born hundreds of years before his birth was fulfilled. Isaiah 7:14 prophesied that he would be born of a virgin, also hundreds of years before this great event took place. For many years, people were looking for the advent or the coming of the Messiah, Jesus Christ. Christ's first coming was to pay the sin debt, to redeem mankind through his precious shed blood, so that souls could be saved. For even the Son of man, Jesus Christ, came not to be ministered unto, but to minister and to give his life a ransom for many! (Mark 10:45)

Christ's first coming was to bring salvation; he was Emmanuel (God with us). Jesus took on flesh like man. He came to become the last Adam, to buy mankind back, and although he was very God, he humbled himself and became man, so that when he walked this earth, he experienced the same things that you and I go through, Praise God! Yet he never sinned! To God Be The Glory! Amen.

When we think of the first coming of Jesus, God's word tells us that Jesus was born of the virgin, Mary who had been overshadowed by God, the Holy Spirit. After his birth, baby Jesus was laid in a manger in a stable. Think of how the angels did not appear to the king or to those in the palace, but they appeared to the (so called by men) common folks. An angel announced the birth of Jesus to shepherds in a field. Then a multitude of heavenly host sang praises about the birth of our Savior and the shepherds were told where they could find Jesus (Luke 2:7-15).

Many today sing about the wise men from the Orient. Indeed they were wise, for they recognized the times in which they were living. They no doubt studied the writings by men of God like Daniel, Micah, and others, as well as the stars. They were awake and not sleeping. They were looking for the prophesied King of the Jews, Jesus Christ, the Savior of the world.

The wise men had traveled a great distance following a star that led them to Jerusalem. Upon arriving, they went where one would assume the very Son of God would have been born, the palace, only to find he was not there. When Herod, the king, heard they were looking for the King of the Jews, he was quite upset. He called all the chief priests and scribes to demand where Christ would be born. They told Herod, it had been written by the prophet, the place would be in Bethlehem of Judaea (Matthew 2:1-5). Upon receiving this information, the wise men found the young child, Jesus, and they fell down and worshiped him. They also gave the Christ child gifts of gold, frankincense, and myrrh. Each of these gifts pointed to Jesus Christ. The <u>gold</u> speaks of Christ's deity, and is indeed, God manifested in the flesh (Philippians 2:6-7). The <u>frankincense</u> speaks of the sweet smelling fragrance of Jesus. Ephesians 5:2 states, "And walk in love, as Christ also hath loved us, and hath given himself for us an offering and a sacrifice to God for a sweet smelling savour." <u>Myrrh</u> was pointing to Jesus' crucifixion in the years that were to come. Myrrh was used in several ways. When Jesus hung on the cross, they gave him wine mixed with myrrh to drink which was used to anesthetize, but <u>he did not receive it</u> (Mark 15:23). Myrrh was also used for burial. In John 19:39, it is recorded that Nicodemus brought myrrh to prepare the body of Jesus Christ for burying.

At the first coming of Jesus to the earth, there were those who were much like the wise men that were also aware of the season of time in which they lived. Simeon, Anna, Mary and Joseph were looking for the first advent or first coming of Jesus Christ with great anticipation. God's word tells us that it was revealed to Simeon that he would not die before he had seen the Lord's Christ. When Mary and Joseph brought Jesus to the temple, Simeon recognized Jesus. He took Jesus in his arms and blessed him, for his eyes had seen God's Salvation, God the Son, who was Jesus Christ (Luke 2:25-35).

We, who are the blood washed born again Christians, today with great joy and anticipation, should be looking forward to Jesus Christ's first part of the <u>second advent</u>, or second coming when he comes in the air to **rapture His church**!

In studying Gods holy word, we find that there are four seasons, or time periods. Indeed, our living Father God is an orderly God. Just as God ordained and created four seasons of weather, spring, summer, fall and winter, the four spiritual seasons or time periods of God that he has ordained are times when he has, is and will deal with various groups of people in specific ways. The first season is the Age of the Gentiles which was before Abraham. The second is the Age of the Jews, from Abraham to Christ. The third season is the Gentile Age or the Church Age which is continuing today and will continue until the very close of this season when the rapture occurs. The fourth is the Age of the Jews, when the Tribulation Period begins. As we rapidly approach the close of the Church Age or the Gentile Age, we must yield ourselves totally to God to be sanctified.

And now, at this end time, it is especially important for us who have accepted Jesus Christ as our Lord and Savior to be totally committed and sold out to him in every single area of our lives. Christ must be first place in our lives. Daily, we must spend quality time with Jesus so that he can increase in us, and we can decrease. As the second advent of Jesus Christ is so rapidly approaching, the world needs to see Jesus Christ in those who profess to be Christians. We must truly realize that we are the only Bible, good news, gospel that many will see and hear. Christians must realize that by the very way we talk and act, it can cause an unsaved person to want Almighty God who is inside of us. However, the opposite is also true, the way some Christians live can cause an unsaved person to say, "No, I don't want God." Which is why, as Christians, we must live sanctified lives that glorify God. Sanctification brings about holiness or purification. Sanctification may be defined as separation from the world and being set apart for God's service. Holiness may be defined as moral, ethical, wholesomeness, freedom from moral evil. Holiness is one of the essential elements of God's very nature that is also required of his people. Hebrews 12:14 says, "Follow peace with all men, and holiness, without which no man shall see the Lord."

In I Thessalonians 4:4-7, the word of God is speaking to believers, informing the born again children of God what not to do, to keep our vessels unto sanctification and honour, a sense of what is right or proper. In I Corinthians 6:15, we are told to be sanctified and that a child of God should flee fornication. To fornicate, means having sexual relations outside of marriage, which would also include both hetero and homosexual sins, male and female. Adultery would include sexual relations with someone other than your wife or husband. Being separated from your spouse does not exempt you. It is still adultery, <u>all</u> of which falls under sin. Christians are commanded to not be a part of concupiscence (evil passions) even as the Gentiles (or unsaved) that know not God. Why, you may ask? After Jesus Christ's resurrection, he sent the Holy Spirit to indwell every person that becomes born again. God, the Holy Spirit is our paraclete, the one who has come along side to help us and to empower us. He comforts us, leads us, and teaches us. Praise God, he dwells inside of every born again child of God. Amen! We must become more sensitive and more aware that our bodies are not our own, that they have been bought with the precious price of the shed blood of Jesus Christ and that we are the temples of the Holy Ghost. (Read I Corinthians 6:19-20.) God has always commanded his people to be holy, to be separate, to be a peculiar people unto him, his living epistles in this earth. Although the word of God in I Thessalonians 4 commands us to be sanctified (set apart, separate) vessels of honor, we still must realize that Christ has called us to minister to the needs of others. Yes, we are to be separated, different from the world, but we must share the love of God inside of us with the world.

We must truly realize that God lives inside of us! We are a spirit that lives in a body and we have a soul that houses our will, emotions and our intellect. When we truly recognize that Christ is inside of us, we will not want to go any place that we would be embarrassed to have God find us. We will not want our eyes to see something that we would not want Jesus, sitting right beside us to see, be it porno pictures, x-rated movies, or magazines, or even some of the junk that's on television, computers or any electronic device. We would not even want to listen to something that we would not take Jesus with us to hear, be it gossip, lies, or even the truth if it's not edifying or building up a person. If it tears down, we should not listen or speak!

As I Peter 1:15 says, "But as he which hath called you is holy, so be ye holy in <u>all</u> manner of conversation." It is important to watch and control the unruly member, our tongue, and not allow idle talk or jesting, but instead, we should begin to control this part of the body to be used to spread love to build others up, to encourage, and to comfort. Our conversations should be ordered by what God's word says. It is time to recognize and realize that our vessels or bodies house the very God who created the universe. Wherever we go, he goes because he is in those who are born again. We should become more cognizant that whatever we do or say, God knows. He is omniscient (all- knowing) and omnipresent (everywhere at the same time). God dwells inside of every born again child of his, which is why we are commanded by God to keep our vessels in sanctification and honor. As Christians obey God's command concerning sanctification and honor, we will be ready when the Second Advent or Rapture occurs. Amen.

In Matthew 10:38-39, Jesus said, "And he that taketh not his cross, and followeth after me, is not worthy of me. He that findeth his life shall lose it: and he that loseth his life for my sake shall find it." I believe that this scripture is very important at this end time hour for every believer. I have already mentioned that there are four seasons of time and that we are at the very close of the third season of time referred to as the Age of the Gentile, or the Church Age, or the Age of Grace. During this season, Christ has been dealing primarily with the non-Jews. Praise the Lord! God is sovereign and there have also been many Jewish converts during this season of the Gentile or Church age. However, the next age will be the period of time referred to as the tribulation period, in which time, the Jews will become the focal point. During the tribulation period, God's judgment will be poured out upon this entire world. During this time, even more Jews will come to the Lord and be used by God to bring many souls into God's kingdom (Matthew 24:14-22).

There will also be one hundred and forty-four thousand Jews that will be sealed by Almighty God during the tribulation period **(Revelation 7: 2-8).** I believe that we are very near to this point of time, which is why it is so very important that true believers make the choice to be totally sold out and committed to God, not lukewarm. God said in Revelation 3:16, that he would rather people be hot or cold. Those who are lukewarm members of the body of Christ and they do not become hot, at some point they will be spued out of the mouth of Jesus Christ. Jesus is coming back and when he does, he is not taking the lukewarm or any sin with him. If we commit sin, the blood of Jesus Christ is available for Christians who truly repent. The blood of Jesus Christ cleanses each from all unrighteousness; but he does not expect his people to continue in that sin.

Jesus is coming back for a <u>glorious church</u>, a body of believers who are totally committed to him in all areas, a church without spot or wrinkle or any such thing, one that is holy and without blemish (Ephesians 5:27). I Thessalonians 4:16-18 says, "For the Lord himself shall descend from heaven with a shout, with the voice of an archangel and with the trump of God: and the dead in Christ shall arise first: Then we which are alive and remain **shall be caught up** together with them in the clouds, to meet the **Lord in the air**: and so shall we ever be with the Lord. Wherefore comfort one another with these words."

As Christians, we must take up our cross and continually follow Jesus by dying to self and yielding to Almighty God to do his will. As we lose our lives for Christ's sake, it is then that we find it. As we yield to God and his will for our lives, we fulfill God's destiny for our lives. It is then that we find the joy of the Lord in whatever we do that God has ordained for us. We also have peace in knowing that through our obedience, God is able to bless others through our yielded lives. Whether it be through intercession, singing in a choir, cleaning a neighbor's home, being a witness by the lives we live, by sharing God's word with others as he directs us, or in raising godly children. Whatever we do, when we lose our lives, we find them in yielding to the Lord. God is then truly glorified. Amen!

So as we see the day approaching of the **Second Advent**, or the **Second Coming of Jesus Christ**, let us continue to take up our cross and follow Christ. Let us lose our lives for his sake so that we may find ourselves with **him** in the **Rapture! Amen!**

5

The Holy Spirit - Who Is He And How Does He Help Us?

<u>John 16:13</u> - **Howbeit when he, the Spirit of truth, is come, he will guide you into all truth: for he shall not speak of himself; but whatsoever he shall hear, that shall he speak: and he will shew you things to come.**

I WOULD LIKE us to look at God, the Holy Spirit, who he is, and how he helps us. In the word of God, he is referred to as the Spirit of Truth, the Comforter, the Holy Spirit, and the Holy Ghost, but each of these names is referring to the third person in the Godhead or Trinity. God the Father, God the Son, and God the Holy Ghost make up the Trinity. They are each separate persons, yet they are one; and they are in total and complete agreement with one another.

The word tells us that God the Father is a Spirit, and God the Son is now the resurrected glorified Lamb of God, who is also God in flesh, and that God the Holy Ghost or Holy Spirit, is also a Spirit. Humans are also spirits. We are also a type of trinity because we live in a body, which is our covering or shell. Inside our body, lives our spirit and soul. The soul comprises the mind, the will, and our emotions. When God the Holy Spirit enters into a person's spirit, the person becomes born again. At that moment, the Holy Spirit becomes one with the born again person's spirit. The word says that we are being conformed into the very image of God's son, Jesus Christ (Romans 8:29). As we yield our minds to be renewed by the word of God, it is then that a believer begins to walk in the Spirit (Romans 12:1-2).

The word tells us that our bodies are the very temple of God. When a person becomes saved, God dwells in his temple, not made with hands. This is referring to the physical body of born again believers that houses or covers our spirits in which God comes to dwell. Some people believe that they can be saved and not have God, the Holy Spirit, dwelling inside of them, however, this is not true. When a person accepts Jesus as their Savior they are immediately born into God the Father's family and become a part of Christ's body. We are actually joined to Jesus Christ. As members of God's family, we are immediately entitled to all of God's promises and blessings, but it does not stop there. God gives his born again people the Holy Spirit to dwell inside of us. The Holy Spirit is our key to victorious living because he is our power source. This is one of the reasons it was necessary for Jesus to leave his disciples, so that the Holy Spirit could begin his work on the earth. When Jesus was with his disciples, he gave them the power to heal the sick, cast out demons and perform miracles. Before Jesus Christ ascended back to heaven Jesus told his disciples to wait for the **Holy Ghost** to come **upon them** in Jerusalem, Acts 1:4 and Acts 1:8. When they received the baptism of the Holy Ghost, they received additional power. Unfortunately, many saved people do not realize who they are or whose they are, and what belongs to them. As Hosea 4:6 says, "My people are destroyed for lack of knowledge" and this is exactly what the enemy is trying to do to the Christian family.

In John 20:21-22, we find that Jesus is talking to his disciples after his resurrection and he says, "Peace be unto you: as my Father has sent me, even so send I you. And when he had said this, he breathed on them and saith unto them, Receive ye the Holy Ghost." Here we find that they now have received the Holy Spirit to dwell on the inside of them. But Jesus lets the disciples know that they will receive even more power, and they are to wait to receive the baptism with the Holy Ghost and fire. In Acts 1:8, Jesus tells his disciples that they shall receive power after the Holy Ghost is come **upon them, not in them**, but upon them.

All "born again" believers have the Holy Spirit dwelling on the inside of them. In I Corinthians 6:19, we are reminded of this, "What? don't you realize that your body is the temple of the Holy Ghost, who is in you, whom God has given you, and that your body doesn't belong to you?" Throughout the book of Acts, we can find that many people were saved, and we know to become saved or born again means that God the Holy Spirit begins to dwell inside of the person's spirit. This occurs when an individual accepts Jesus Christ as their Savior. What is not automatic is the baptism with the Holy Ghost upon a person. Although this baptism is available to all who are born again each must choose to receive this special gift from God. The baptism with the Holy Ghost with the evidence of speaking in other tongues endues the person with God's supernatural power. Once a person is baptized with the Holy Ghost that person is then able to work to their fullest potential in the gifts of the Spirit as God intended, as he yields to God.

In Acts Chapter 8, we read that Philip had gone to the city of Samaria and preached Christ to some of the Samaritan people and they accepted Jesus as their Savior and even received water baptism. They had not received the baptism with the Holy Ghost. When the Apostles, Peter and John arrived, they prayed for these Samaritans to receive the Holy Ghost. After praying, they laid their hands on them; and they received the Holy Ghost upon them. Another way the word lets us know how to receive the Holy Ghost is to ask God the Father, as stated in Luke 11:13, "If you then, being evil, know how to give good gifts unto your children; how much more shall your heavenly Father give the Holy Spirit to them that ask him?" What I want to emphasize is that if you are born again, then the Holy Spirit lives inside of your body in your spirit. But God desires that his people also receive another gift, the baptism with the Holy Ghost and fire, which gives added and very much needed supernatural power. The word of God tells us about people who received the baptism of the Holy Ghost and power, which came upon them after being born again. (Acts 8:16-17 and 10:44-46)

It is time for the body of Christ, which is made up of every born again believer, to realize that God has given us the keys to victorious living. A major key to increased levels of victory is the baptism of the Holy Spirit and with power! Praise God! The Holy Spirit is the very power that is within us. God put his Spirit inside of every born again believer to help his people. We only need to read and study God's word to see the reasons Jesus knew that his disciples needed power. Jesus told his disciples that he was giving them the power to do the same miraculous works that he did while he was on earth. (Luke 10:19) The word continually reminds us that we can do **nothing!** in our own strength, but that "I can do all things through Christ which strengtheneth me." (Philippians 4:13)

The devil has blinded some in the body of Christ, but God wants everyone in his body to realize who we are in him. We are the children of the most High God and King, Jesus Christ. He is our Savior and Brother, who has already given us power! Praise God! We must realize that this power dwells within you and I, who are members of the body of Christ. God desires that each believer make up their mind to use the power of the Holy Ghost living inside of them and to also receive the supernatural gift of the Baptism of the Holy Ghost with the evidence of speaking in other tongues, just as the disciples in Acts 2:4 received this gift. This baptism of the Holy Ghost upon a Christian gives the additional power needed to believers as Jesus stated in Acts 1:8.

The Holy Spirit is called the Spirit of Truth and as John 16:13 says, "when the Spirit of truth is come, he will guide you into all truth: for he shall not speak of himself; but whatsoever he shall hear, that shall he speak and he will shew you things to come." So, from this scripture, we can see that Jesus is letting us know that the Holy Spirit is our Guide or Teacher and that one of his purposes is to teach us **all** truth and that when the Holy Spirit speaks to us he is not telling us what he thinks, but he is giving us what God the Father tells him to tell us. Praise the Lord!

The Holy Spirit leads and directs our paths in the things we say and do if we allow him to. If we are yielded to God and obedient, he can and will teach us the mysteries of God, because God wants us, his children, to know all truth. Some people say, "Well that's a mystery of God", but the word says that God wants us to grow up into the knowledge of Jesus and to be guided into all truth by the Holy Spirit inside of us. That is one of his jobs or purposes.

Jesus tells us that another purpose of the Holy Spirit is to show us things that are to come or things that will happen to us or others in the future. I am sure that many of us have had the Holy Spirit to do just that. Many times he warns us of danger that is near or he may tell us to go visit someone. If we are obedient to visit, we find that an individual had a very serious need that we already knew about because the Holy Spirit had told us, or even showed us through a dream or vision (I Corinthians 2:10-12).

The Holy Spirit strengthens us and gives us joy. The word says the joy of the Lord is our strength. If we lose our joy, then there goes our strength. When we keep our joy and do not allow problems and negative situations to take our joy, it is then that we become victorious over whatever the problem is that faces us.

The Holy Spirit is referred to as the Comforter. When there is a heavy burden, like the loss of a loved one, the Holy Spirit is right inside of us to give us comfort. Jesus said, "I will never leave thee, nor forsake thee", (Hebrews 13:5) and we know Jesus keeps his promises to us, Praise God! He is not like man who sometimes falls short. He is always with us, right inside of us in the person of God, the Holy Ghost. Jesus also said that when he would leave his disciples to go back to heaven, that he would pray to Father God and that he would send another Comforter, that being God the Holy Ghost. (John 14:16)

There are many, many ways that the Holy Ghost or Holy Spirit helps we who are born again if we allow him to work. He helps us through prayer. The Holy Spirit prays God, the Father's, perfect will as stated in (Romans 8:27-28). He can and will pray to God on our behalf or on the behalf of someone else. He will also sing praises to God as we begin to yield to the Holy Spirit inside of us. He will even give us songs. At times we find ourselves awakened from a sleep singing praises to God or praying to him. This is our spirit and the Holy Spirit as one. When a believer awakens from sleep praying in the Spirit, God the Holy Spirit may have been interceding for the person's physical body that was asleep, or for someone else. As we yield to the Holy Spirit, we can speak, pray and sing in tongues to God. Yes, there may be times that we may not always know what was said, but Praise God! He knows! Other times after singing, praying or speaking in tongues, God will give us a vision, or speak to us and let us know exactly what was prayed for, or tells us the words we praised him with in song.

It is good to be yielded to God, the Holy Spirit, because as the word tells us, he knows all things, which includes things to come. And many times in this life, the enemy, who is the devil, and his demons have set traps for God's people and our loved ones, as well as persons we don't know. Praise God, if we will pray in the Spirit, **(those who have been baptized with the Holy Ghost and speak with other tongues)** it will allow the Holy Spirit to speak through us to God, and many of the devil's traps can and will be defeated. Amen!

Brothers and sisters we are living in perilous times. The devil is busy walking to and fro **as** a roaring lion, seeking whom he may devour. We read the newspaper and watch the television, computer, or view other electronic devices only to see the sin and wickedness of many of the people in our generation. When we think that we have heard of something so wicked that there could be nothing worse, we find something more sinful and wicked has happened. The Bible speaks of just this. We are seeing prophecy taking place right before our very eyes. But it does not stop there. The enemy is attacking the Christian family in every way imaginable. Families are being torn apart, some of the youth are rebellious; husbands and some wives don't speak kind words to one another, if they are even speaking at all. Many times relatives won't help one another. Some even tell lies on each other. Even in the church, the devil tries to cause division and dissension.

It is time to realize that what is happening to our families and church families is a plot of the devil to destroy God's people if he could. The devil would have God's people to leave their husband or wife, the children to leave home, and even members of our church family to fight one another and others; and to leave the church that they were to planted in. In this age in which we are living, there are many, many more temptations now than there were during earlier generations. Everyday we hear of a new temptation. Today, various illegal drugs are easily available. Sex before marriage is often encouraged and made to look glamorous and promoted as the "in thing" to do, even in some schools. Some music and music videos teach that what is morally wrong based on the word of God is in; and to sin is glorified, encouraged and condoned. Even gambling has been legalized and glamorized, for we hear "play the lottery, play to win." Pornography is easily available on internet and in convenience stores where only a short time ago we would not have thought such things would be allowed in these and other places. If an individual chooses, he can have the pornography wired through cable television and more. Just a few short years ago, we would have never thought these things would happen. Now, not only has it happened, but it is accepted, and not just by the unsaved persons, but by some persons who say that they are saved and members of the body of Christ.

When a Christian's daughter becomes pregnant, or a son is responsible for a girl's pregnancy, many parents encourage abortion, killing the unborn child. Our society has legalized it and says abortion is not murder. What does God say? Does he say that murder of an unborn child is legal? Some husbands and wives even have extra marital affairs. Brothers and sisters, aunts and uncles, cousins and even parents and grandparents in some families tell lies on one another! You can <u>kill</u> with the tongue also! All of these things are an abomination to God. Abomination may be defined as an extreme disgust for, horrible, offensive, to hate very much, loathsome. All of these things I have mentioned are tricks and plots of the enemy. We must stop and think before we enter into these areas. To whom are we yielding our members? To whom are we yielding the parts of our body? - God or satan?

The things that have been mentioned are only a few of the tricks and plots of the enemy. Many times satan's schemes are not so obvious but very, very subtle. You almost don't realize that it is he and his demonic spirits at work in the Christian family, in the home, or in the church. The devil is on the job, but we must not be deceived. He does come against both the Christian family and the church family as well. Now that we have looked at some of his maneuvers, let's examine what God would have us to do about satan's schemes. We have already mentioned that every born again believer has been given a major key to victory in this life and that key is God the Holy Ghost living inside of us. Greater levels of his power are given to those who are Holy Ghost baptized Christians. But just like a key, unless we use it properly, the locked door will not open. So it is with the Holy Spirit; we must use the power, and allow him to flow through us to others.

Every born again believer must realize who the Holy Spirit is, that he is God who lives inside of them. He is always there. When we are asleep and when we are awake; wherever we are, he is with us. As Jesus said in Hebrews 13:5, "I will never leave thee, nor forsake thee," Praise God! Jesus keeps his promises because we are in him and he is in us, in the person of the Holy Ghost. Therefore, he is always with us. After we realize that we have been blessed to have God live on the inside of us, we must realize that he is inside of us to help us. He is our **Intercessor** to God the Father when we pray in Jesus' name, especially when we don't know how to pray for a person, situation, or even ourselves. The Holy Spirit always knows. When we pray in other tongues, Romans 8:26-27 states, "Likewise the **Spirit** also helpeth our infirmities: for we know not what we should pray for as we ought: but the **Spirit** himself <u>maketh intercession for us</u> with groanings which cannot be uttered. And he that searcheth the hearts knoweth what is the mind of the Spirit because he <u>maketh</u> <u>intercession for the saints</u> according to the <u>will of God."</u> Praise God! Thank You! The Holy Spirit leads , guides , and tells God's people what comes directly from God the Father. The word of God lets us know that the Holy Spirit will show us things to come. Why? Because our God is omniscient, which means he is all knowing. Praise God! He knows what traps the enemy has set for us and our loved ones each and every day; and he wants us to become aware of them also.

Those of us who are saved must realize that we are in a very real battle for our lives and the lives of our loved ones, as well as many that are unsaved. For those of you who may have had to go to war and fight the enemy, or if you have had loved ones who have gone to war, I am sure those persons can tell you how real the enemy was. Well, the spiritual enemies of God's people are even more real, and unless the gift of discerning of spirits is in operation, you will probably never see them. This enemy is around us, our houses, our jobs, and our churches in some instances. **But Praise God so are God's angels, and they are on the job also! They are at work helping God's people and carrying out God's plans. Amen!**

Unlike the Holy Ghost, demons will try to force themselves upon people, and even enter into them and possess them, if they are unsaved. When a person engages in sinful activity, many times they are entertaining demons. What happens when a person entertains their company? Most times they stay longer. The more one looks at pornography, the less his conscience bothers him until he is hooked. If a lying spirit is attacking a person, at first the person tells an occasional lie, however as he continues to lie, finally he doesn't even care who he hurts! We must not yield to temptation, which includes a variety of sins. Although a born again believer cannot be possessed, because the Holy Spirit is inside of his spirit, he can be oppressed by demonic spirits. However, possession and oppression are both bad. As born again believers, we must stand in the gap for our families, for those who are saved and those who are unsaved, through prayer.

The war that is raging is very real but because many can't actually see the demons around us, they are unaware of their presence. When we see our loved ones not acting Christ-like or our church family fighting, we must realize that satan is working to destroy Christians in any way that he can, if we allow him. We should praise God because we have the power of God the Holy Ghost inside of us, therefore, we should be making satan and his demons tremble with fear. Each day when we get up and each night when we go to bed, we should and must put on the whole armor of God. When a person goes to war, they put on special clothing, as well as take guns and ammunition, which are their weapons. We too must put on our special battle clothing and take our weapons and ammunition, and we must use them! God has given us our weapons and armor for protection, so please use it daily! Because we are fighting a spiritual war, we must put on spiritual clothing and use spiritual weapons. We must fasten truth to our loins; we must put on the breastplate of righteousness. Our feet must be covered with the gospel of peace, and we must take the helmet of salvation, Praise God! It is through salvation we are covered with the precious blood of Jesus. This spiritual clothing is our armor, which is our protection much like the Roman soldiers were covered when they went into battle. We too have our armor provided for us to fight the spiritual battle that is raging. God did not leave us defenseless, but he gave us everything that we needed to be more than conquerors through Christ Jesus.

Our weapons that we go into battle with are all spiritual. We are told to "above all, to take the shield of faith, wherewith we shall be," not may be, "but shall be able to quench," or put out **all** not some, but "**all** the fiery darts of the wicked one." Our faith is a defensive and offensive weapon, and we are told to above all to take and use the shield of faith, because without faith none of the others weapons will work. Without faith, we cannot become saved or receive salvation. Without faith even prayer will not work. Hebrews 11:6 says, "Without faith it is impossible to please God." Therefore above all, we must always take and use our shield of faith, which is our protection, as well as our weapon against our enemy, the devil and his army of demons. Our next weapon is our sword of the Spirit, which is the word of God, and in Hebrews 4:12, we are told that "the word is sharper than any two-edged sword," and we know that Jesus is the Living Word. Praise the Lord! In the scriptures, we can see that Jesus defeated satan's plots in the wilderness with the word. (Luke 4:1-18) We too must first get the word inside of us so that we can use it to fight with. Those who already have the word inside of them must begin to speak it out loud. In Ephesians 6:10-18, God's word tells us of the importance of wearing the whole armor of God as well as **praying in the Spirit for all saints.**

Jesus said in John 6:63, "The words that I speak unto you, they are Spirit and they are Life." Because the Holy Spirit lives inside of us, when we speak God's words in faith in Jesus' name, those words we speak are Spirit and Life also! Praise The Lord! God's word is our sword. It's what we as believers should fight with. We should be taking authority over the devil and his demons in the name of Jesus. We must be bold warriors. We are not to fear the devil or to run from him, but say to him "I order you in the name and in the power of the blood of Jesus to be bound and to loose my son, wife, husband, whoever, in the name of Jesus! I order you to go where God has set for you in the name of Jesus, and not return in Jesus' name!" (Matthew 18:18) We must speak faith words to whatever the problem is. If it is sickness, lay hands on yourself or loved ones and order that sickness to leave in Jesus' name and not to return. Now, when the believer takes authority over the enemy and wins the battle, or the enemy retreats, what happens next? Reinforcements arrive to pick up the battle where the defeated forces failed. You'd better believe the devil will send more attacks to the believer, perhaps even stronger than before. But we must continue to pray without ceasing, and use the name of Jesus. Romans 8:31 says: "What shall we then say to these things? If God be for us who can be against us?"

Praise God, we have another weapon which is the **angels of God.** The word lets us know that they are our ministering spirits that are sent forth to help us. In Psalms 34:7, the word tells us that "the angel of the Lord encampeth round about them who fear him, and delivereth them." There are different types and ranks of angels, and the word of God lets us know that some are warring angels, who are sent forth to help us fight our battles. Angels take their orders from God and they hearken to the voice of his word when spoken in faith by God's people. So, we as God's children can and should ask God to send forth his angels to protect and help us and our loved ones each day and night. **Almighty God's people should consistently plead the blood of Jesus Christ and use the keys of the kingdom which are binding and loosing.**

Another important weapon of the children of God is **praise and worship of Almighty God.** What an honor and a privilege we have to be able to praise and worship Almighty God! Amen! Isaiah 61:3 tells us "to put on the garment of praise for the spirit of heaviness." And as the word tells us in Ephesians 6:13, "Wherefore take unto you **the whole armor of God,** that ye may be able to withstand in the evil day, and having done all, to stand." Don't fall asleep, or get lazy, or tired of praying. Continue to do battle with the enemy, continue the good fight of faith! Praise God! Amen!

6

God Is Love And He Dwells In You - The Believer

THE LOVE WALK is exactly what it says. The word tells us that God is Love. Love is who God is. Love is a part of his very character, his very nature. Love is a fruit of the Spirit. To walk, means to continue to move. God is calling each of the members of the body of Christ, to walk in love, and to enter into a higher level and dimension in him. His desire is that his people walk, talk, think, feel, and act like him, Almighty God, who is Love.

I John 4:16 says, "And we have known and believed the love that God hath to us. God is Love, and he that dwelleth in love dwelleth in God and God in him."

Some people may ask, if God is love, and we dwell in him, and God is in the believer, then why is there, strife, and divisions among some who are members of the body of Christ? Why is there prejudice among Blacks, Whites, Hispanics, and in all races, in some that are members of the body of Christ? Why are there all types of sins in the body of Christ? The answer is that many in the body are not obedient to do the whole word of God and are not yet walking and moving consistently in the love of Almighty God. It's a choice to make a quality decision to obey God's commandments of love. As we obey God's holy word, we gain the victory over the enemy of our souls, satan, and enter into receiving various parts of our **Total Salvation Gift**, who is **Jesus**.

When we accept Jesus as our Savior, it is then that we receive the greatest gift or part of **Total Salvation, Jesus Christ.** Yes, God entered into our spirit as the third person of the trinity or Godhead, the Holy Spirit. We became saved or born again when we called on the Lord Jesus Christ according to Romans 10:9-10. Jesus said in John 14:6, "I am the way, the truth, and the life: no man cometh unto the Father, but by me." When a person makes the most important decision of his life to ask Jesus to save him, he is immediately born again, transferred from satan's kingdom of sin and death to God's kingdom of life eternal, and is baptized into the body of Christ (not water baptism). Unfortunately, many Christians never go further to receive all of the benefits as a result of Jesus shedding His precious, holy blood on Calvary's cross for them. Some of these areas are healing which includes spiritual, emotional, physical, financial, social as well as the restoration of relationships, both marriages and friendships. This names a few areas available once a person is saved. Hosea 4:6 says, "My people are destroyed for lack of knowledge."

When we obey God's word, we will reap the blessings. It is not name it claim it. God desires that we have a personal one-on-one relationship with him, Jesus the Lover of our souls, Amen! Read Isaiah 1:18-20, v/19 says, "If ye be willing and obedient, ye shall eat the good of the land." Each Christian must do God's word!

As we choose to obey and do God's word, our Victory, who is Jesus, will show up. He will show up as healing, deliverance, prosperity or whatever area of **Total Salvation that is needed.** The word salvation means so much. In the Hebrew the word salvation is defined as **Yeshuwah** – something saved, deliverance, aid, <u>victory</u>, prosperity, health, help, salvation, save (saving health welfare). The Greek word for salvation is **Soteria**. It means rescue, safety, deliver, health, salvation, save, saving. The words for salvation in both the Hebrew and Greek are very similar. Each definition represents a portion of what Jesus shed his precious blood for and who he is. Amen! God desires that we as believers enter into the fullness of his love gift, Jesus Christ, our **Total Salvation.**

After becoming saved or born again, God desires that we walk in love. In doing so, we will obey his two commandments to us.

Matthew 22:36-40, tells us that when Jesus was questioned by the Pharisees, there was a lawyer that asked, v/36 "Master, which is the great commandment in the law? v/37, Jesus said unto him, Thou shalt love the Lord thy God with all thy heart, and with all thy soul, and with all thy mind. v/38, This is the first and great commandment. v/39 And the second is like unto it, Thou shalt love thy neighbor as thyself. v/40 On these two commandments hang all the law and the prophets."

We have been given these two commandments by Jesus. If we make a quality decision to obey these commandments of love, then all the Old Testament commandments will be obeyed. We will not allow any idols in our lives because we will be in love with Almighty God. He and he alone will be <u>first</u> in our lives! We will not commit adultery or fornicate. We will not murder physically or emotionally, realizing a person can murder others with his tongue. (read James 3:2-10) When we choose to walk in love with the <u>help</u> of <u>Almighty God,</u> our tongues will be tamed. Our words will be words that encourage, bless, and edify. Our words will build up others as well as ourselves. We must begin to speak God's words of Spirit and Life over our spouses, children, jobs, homes, friends, over every area. As we continue to walk in love, speak, and do the whole word of God, we should also expect to see the miraculous. We should expect to see God show up and manifest himself as our Victory, as Jehovah-Shalom, the Lord our Peace, Jehovah-Rapha, the Lord our Healer; for, Jesus is our **Total Salvation** and his names are who he is and wants to be in we who are his people. Amen!

WHAT DOES SALVATION MEAN?

> **The Word Salvation Encompasses Everything That Is Good Which Comes From God. James 1:17 says, Every good gift and every perfect gift is from above, and cometh down from the Father of lights, with whom is no variableness, neither shadow of turning.**

Salvation - Hebrew - yeshuwah - something saved, deliverance, health, aid, victory, prosperity - health, help, salvation, save (saving health), welfare

Salvation - Greek - soteria - rescue, safety, deliver, health, salvation, save, saving.

The word Salvation means Jesus.

Luke 2:25-26: States that the prophet Simeon was looking for the birth of Jesus Christ. **Luke 2:26** states: "And it was revealed unto him by the Holy Ghost that he should not see death before he had seen the Lord's Christ." Simeon knew immediately when Jesus was brought to the temple for the dedication by his parents. Simeon took the baby Jesus in his arms and blessed him , and Simeon the prophet said "For mine eyes have seen thy Salvation."

Jesus Christ paid the price for Total Salvation and He is Our Total Salvation

Luke 3:6 States that John the Baptist said: "And All Flesh Shall See The Salvation Of God."

The greatest and most important part of SALVATION is the miracle of the new birth, or being born again. This takes place when a person accepts Jesus Christ as their Savior at which time they become a member of the family of Jesus Christ, Amen.

John 3:16 states: "For God so loved the world that he gave his only begotten Son, that whosoever believeth in him should not perish but have everlasting life."

7

No Greater Love Than This (Jesus) (God Is The Best Giver Of All)

PRAISE THE LORD! We, who are the children of Almighty God, are truly blessed in so many, many ways, whether we realize it or not. God blesses us because he and he alone can wake us to start a new day. He and he alone is the one who provides our daily bread, both the physical food, as well as the spiritual food, the word of God. I could go on and on to list how blessed we are and indeed he always blesses us real good. Amen! And yes, even those who are not saved which are not the children of God, reap many of God's blessings even though they often do not acknowledge it and give God the glory. The word of God tells us in Matthew 5:44-45 that we, as the children of God, are "to love our enemies and bless those that curse you and to pray for those that despitefully use you and persecute you, that ye may be the children of your Father which is in heaven; for he maketh his sun to rise on the evil and on the good and sendeth the rain on the just and the unjust." God's mercies are new every morning even though the unsaved do not realize the blessings, the goodness, and the mercies of Almighty God. As his believers, who are God's people, we should acknowledge his blessings and give him thanks each and every day, even before we get out of the bed. He should be the first person that we speak to. Amen! We should tell the Lord that we love him, appreciate him, and thank the Lord that we are his and that he is ours. To God Be The Glory! Amen!

As Christians, born again of the Spirit of Almighty God, we have received the greatest love gift of all in the entire world. No one could give us any greater gift and this gift was free. Jesus Christ is the gift that we did not work for or earn in any way. Truly we are blessed. If you have not yet received this free love gift, today is the day of salvation. Jesus is at the door asking to come into your heart to save you. It's your decision to receive the free gift of salvation, Jesus Christ. He is the first and greatest gift of the **Total Salvation** package. Amen!

In looking at giving, Father God and Jesus Christ are the greatest givers of all. Giving is so important as well as receiving. Giving will destroy yokes in Christians lives as each is yielded to the Lord, and are obedient to do the whole word of God. For example, to become saved or born again, although Jesus paid the price for us to be saved as well as for our **Total Salvation,** we had to do something. We had to **believe** and **receive** the free gift of salvation. For example, if I told our son, "Your Dad and I bought you a new suit", he would believe it and get really happy. We could tell him we had it and where it was. Although he believed us, if he never came to get the suit even though it was paid for and it was his, it would never do him any good. He could believe that we had bought the suit for him all he wanted, but if he never received it, he would never benefit from the suit. In actuality, even though he believed it was his, he would never reap his blessing. Likewise, with the unsaved who believe that Jesus Christ died for them , if they put off accepting Jesus and die before receiving him as their Savior, they will miss their blessing. Even though they may believe Jesus died for them, they still will spend eternity in hell because they never received the best gift of all, <u>**Jesus Christ.**</u>

There are spiritual laws just as there are natural laws. The law of gravity is an example of a natural law. If a person jumps off an hundred story building, they will fall; and unless God supernaturally intervenes, that person will most likely die. Also, in the spiritual arena there are spiritual laws at work.

Father God wanted his children back and he wanted a harvest. Because the first Adam sinned, every person that came into the world after Adam and Eve were in sin. Their legal father is the devil. Therefore, in Genesis 3:15, God spoke his words of Spirit and Life to Adam and Eve, the devil or satan, and to all of God's creations. God spoke a prophecy, "I will put enmity between thee and the woman, and between thy seed and her seed; it shall bruise thy head, and thou shalt bruise his heel." Letting them know that **Total Salvation** was on its way. God's best love gift to the world, Jesus Christ, would one day come to redeem mankind through the shedding of his holy and precious blood on Calvary's cross. Remember, it is a choice each person makes to choose to accept or to reject Father God's love gift, Jesus Christ, as their Savior. Amen!

Almighty Father God sowed Jesus into the earth, expecting to reap an increased harvest of what he sowed. He sowed or planted his best love gift, Jesus, in this earth. Jesus was God's seed that he sowed, so that he could reap an abundant harvest of more sons. For example, if a farmer wants an apple tree he takes a seed or a little sapling tree and plants it. Then he must wait a season, meaning a period of time for that tree to become fully grown and begin to bear fruit. When it is planted, the farmer must do things. He makes sure it has adequate water. He pulls the weeds, and perhaps even fertilizes it to help it grow properly while he waits for his harvest. If he planted an apple tree, he's not expecting the apple tree to bear pears, or bananas or something else. He planted apples; therefore, he expects and knows that he will reap a harvest of many, many apples from just the one seed that was planted. From the one apple tree, just think how many hundreds of apple trees can be produced. Why? Because now he has an even bigger harvest. The seeds are in his harvest of apples. **(See Visual of INCREASED HARVEST- SEEDS)**

Father God knew that if he sent Jesus, in the fullness of time, which was God's appointed time for Jesus to come, die and be resurrected, he would reap a harvest of born again people, from sowing his only begotten son Jesus Christ. God gave the greatest love gift, Jesus, who was God manifested in the flesh, and because of giving or sowing Jesus in the world, Father God continues to receive an abundant harvest.

Multitudes upon multitudes of people are being taken from the devil and are becoming sons of Almighty God, Amen! It's a spiritual law, and it works in every area of one's life. Whatsoever a man soweth that shall he also reap. If you sow death, you reap death; if you sow life, you reap life. (Read Galatians 6:1-10). Galatians 6:7-8 states, "Be not deceived, God is not mocked, for whatsoever a man soweth that shall he also reap. For he that soweth to his flesh shall of the flesh reap corruption, but he that soweth to the Spirit shall of the Spirit reap life everlasting." Some of the works of the flesh can be found in Galatians 5:19-21 and the fruit of the Spirit in Galatians 5:22-23. What type of fruit of the flesh are you bearing? Are you bearing fruit of the Spirit that all believers are commanded to bear? As we yield to God to obey his word to walk in love, he causes us to bring forth the fruit of the Spirit. This is accomplished as his people allow God to do a work in each. Amen! I thank God for his mercy, his grace, and the blood of Jesus. Praise God, one does not have to continue to reap the rewards of the flesh, which leads to destruction and death. When a Christian sows to the Spirit he will reap life everlasting.

Yes, God is the best giver of all, but as his children, we too are to be like Almighty God, our Father, who is the best giver. When we give, it is then that we are blessed in our giving and it releases blessings from God to come to us. I will use myself as an example. For years, I have ministered to others in the areas of healing, deliverance, preaching and teaching by the Spirit of God and I give God the glory! If the people I minister to had other needs, such as dishes that needed doing; bathrooms that needed to be cleaned, I would serve them in these areas as well as bring them a meal I prepared. Many times, I would not only minister to their spiritual needs, but I also ministered to their physical needs! Before Christmas, a lady came and cleaned my whole house, including our bathrooms. My husband and I had been so busy ministering to others I had not had time to clean like I wanted to. We had about thirty people coming to dinner. Praise the Lord! I reaped a harvest that I had sown throughout the years. I love to give and as my earthly dad always said to me, "you can't out give God. God's bank never goes broke." In looking at the other side, I missed a blessing several years ago. The same lady who cleaned for me, wanted to cook meals for me and my family because she knew how busy I was. It had been a secret desire of my heart to have someone cook for me and my family, but I had never told her this. When she offered, I refused this blessing. I did not receive it. For years, I'd been a giver, but I had difficulty receiving from others. Praise God! Now I better understand God's spiritual laws and the importance of not only giving, but also receiving. I have come to understand the scripture that says, "The liberal soul shall be made fat; and he that watereth shall be watered also himself." (Proverbs 11:25). Many times we miss God's blessing because of a lack of knowledge of God's word, pride or various other reasons.

We must sow seeds to reap our harvests. Reaping does not happen over night. You can destroy your seed. One way is with your mouth. Words of doubt, fear and unbelief can destroy your harvest. But you can hasten it with faith filled words. The wealth of the sinner is laid up for the just. Proverbs 13:22 declares, "A good man leaveth an inheritance to his children's children; and the wealth of the sinner is laid up for the just." The greatest inheritance that a parent can give is a spiritual inheritance. Amen! Giving, as I have already shared, is not just the giving of finances, although that is a must. We should also give our time. No one can pay a person for their time. Amen! We can give in various areas such as our prayers, talents and gifts physical and spiritual. God expects us to believe him for the harvests when we sow. Don't look at a particular vessel thinking your harvest is coming this way or that; look to God. Amen! It all comes from God, regardless of who he may choose to use. Amen! There was a time when I would give God a dollar or a few dollars and thought I was obedient. When I found out what God's word said, I immediately began to tithe because I loved God and wanted to please him and to do his whole word. I did not realize before then that the book of Malachi said I was robbing God; therefore, I was already cursed with a curse. But because I loved God and wanted to please him, and to obey the whole word of God, I began tithing and have ever since. Even though tithing to God was never taught, as far as I can remember, at the church I was once a member, I have always loved to give to others. When I give, I am the one who gets blessed. After we give ten percent of our income to the church where we are fed, then we are to give offerings to the church. If God speaks to sow into someone's life or other areas, we can; but the tithe belongs to God and goes into the storehouse or the church you are attending. Amen! If you don't have a home church, then sow it where God directs, where the whole word goes forth until he directs you where he wants you to be planted, so you can grow. Amen! (Read Malachi 3:8)

In Proverbs chapter 3, God tells us not to forget his law. We know that Jesus calls the believer to the Love Walk, (Matthew 22:37-40). If we truly love God, we will do his whole word. Proverbs 3 further states that we are not to forget God's law but keep his commandment. If we do, verse 2 tells us of blessings that will be reaped; which are length of days, time to accomplish what we need to do each day, long life, and peace, things we all need that money cannot buy. Verse 3 tells us to not let mercy and truth forsake us, for when we extend mercy and truth to others and allow it to dwell in us richly, verse 4 tells us we will find favor and good understanding in the sight of God and man. All of this is a part of the Love Walk. God extends mercy to us every day and he has given us his truth, which is his word, to live by and to guide us. When we let God's mercy and truth rule in our lives, the blessings of favor and understanding follow us. Proverbs 3:5-6 tells us to "Trust in the Lord with all thine heart, and lean not unto thine own understanding, in <u>all</u> thy ways acknowledge him, and he shall direct thy paths." God's word further calls us to not be wise in our own eyes, but to fear the Lord and <u>depart</u> from <u>evil</u>. <u>Do not</u> do things the way of the flesh. God calls the believer to the supernatural way of doing things, to a higher level in him. We are eagles. Eagles don't do things like many other birds. Many times they fly alone. We, as God's eagles, don't think and act like the world. If need be, we eat lunch alone so we can be away from the dirty jokes or gossip. Amen!

God further tells us how to be blessed and how to reap God's supernatural blessings. We are to acknowledge and trust God, do his whole word, walk in love, fear him and depart from evil or sin. As we do these things, we find that obedience will bring <u>forth health, to our body, and nourishment to our bones</u>, (Proverbs 3:8) amen.

In Proverbs 3:9-10, the word reminds us again to honor the Lord with our substance, and the **firstfruits of all our increase**. If you are blessed with a bonus on the job or any financial gift, you should give God the firstfruits of that blessing, realizing it comes from God. It is only ten percent he asks for, so we can be blessed. Amen! In verse 10, God tells us why, so that our barns shall be filled with plenty, and our presses shall burst out with new wine, more and more blessings. Psalms 115:14 is also a good scripture to stand on if you're a doer of God's word. Amen! To God Be The Glory! Praise God! The Lord shall increase you more and more, you and your children.

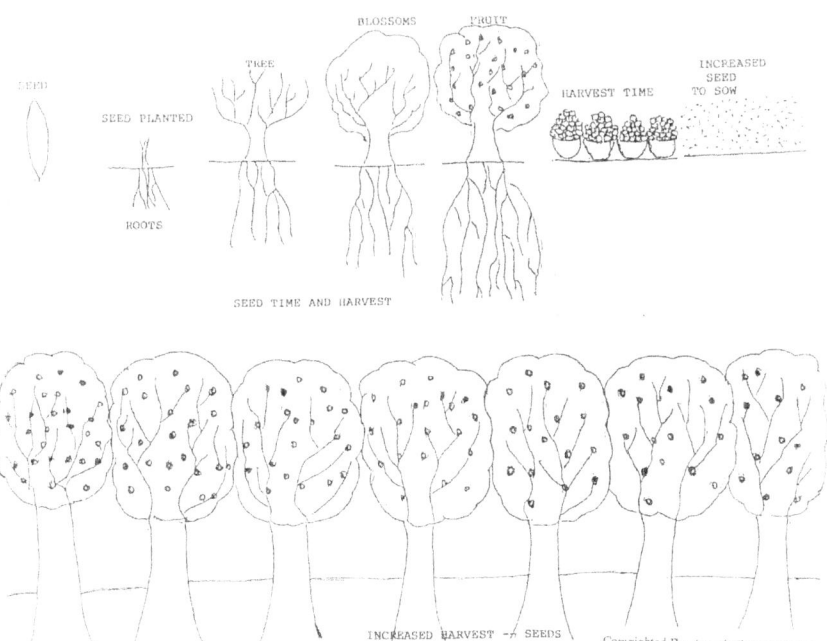

KEYS TO RECEIVE YOUR HARVEST---- YOUR INHERITANCE
Copyrighted By Apostle Crystal M. Naylor

	Day	Month	Year	Years
SEED	T	I	M	E	===

HARVEST Of What Was Sown ---Planted
Giving Of Love, God's Word, Healings, Finances, Etc.

It Takes **TIME** To See, Or To **Reap** Whatever **SEEDS** You Planted Usually. The Person Like A Farmer Must Take Care Of The **Seeds That They Sow**

HOW?

1. By Watering Their Seed's With The Word Of God

2. By Staying In Faith As They Speak Aloud God's Word's Of Spirit And Life And **Not** Speaking Negative Words.

3. By **Not** Agreeing With Others Who May Try To Steal Their Coming Harvest By Speaking Against God's Words—(It Will Destroy Your Seed And Your Harvest Will Not Arrive.)

4. By Thanking And Praising God For The Manifestation Of Your Harvest/ That Which You Have Sown In Faith And Are Believing God For.

5. When The **HARVEST** Arrives—Always give God The Glory By Sharing With Others About Your Victory, And What God Has Done, Is Doing, And Will Do.

8

Healing Of Spiritual Emotional, Physical, Social And Financial Hurts Through Obedience - Walking In (Love) And Doing God's Whole Word

I PRAISE GOD for my victory, and for the victory of every member of the body of Christ. We have been given the victory because Jesus paid the price through the shedding of his precious blood when he was beaten with many stripes by the soldiers, and when he was crucified on Calvary's cross. In John 10:18, Jesus said that no man took his life, and that he had the power to lay down his life and power to take it again. We have the victory in every area of our lives, we who are believers, saved, born again sons of Almighty God. It does not matter how we feel. What matters is what God's word says which is TRUTH. God's words are Spirit and Life and they are able to change facts. Jesus said in John 14:6, "I am the **Way** the **Truth** and the **Life;** no man cometh unto the Father, but by **Me."**

The scripture says in John 1:1, "In the beginning was the Word, and the Word was with God, and the Word was God." Jesus Christ is the Living Word who was with God the Father from the beginning, along with the Holy Spirit in heaven. Father God loved mankind so much that he sent his only begotten Son, Jesus Christ, to become clothed in flesh and born of a virgin on earth. Jesus loved mankind so much that he shed his holy blood to redeem mankind. Thereby paying for man's **Total Salvation** and making a way back to Father God for anyone who accepts Jesus Christ as one's Savior. In John 14:6, Jesus clearly tells us that he is the Way which lets us know that we can't even get to Father God unless we first go through Jesus, who is the Way. Amen! That is why we pray in Jesus' name always. Only through the precious shed blood of Jesus can we come before Almighty Father God!

God wants us to understand, realize and know that nothing, including sickness, disease, lack of anything, friends, finances, husband, wife, children, barrenness, poverty, hurts, sexual molestation, physical or emotional abuse, divorce, lies, nothing is more powerful, or greater than Jesus Christ, the Word of God. The Living Word is Jesus and Jesus is the Living Word. Even the disease of aids or anything that you can think of is not greater than Jesus, who is the Living Word.

Jesus said in Luke 18:16, "Suffer little children to come unto me, forbid them not : for such is the kingdom of God." Jesus was telling his disciples to let the little children come to him so he could lay his hands on them, for such is the kingdom of God. In Matthew 18:4, Jesus told his disciples, as well as us today, who is the greatest in the kingdom of heaven. "Whosoever therefore shall humble himself as this little child, the same is greatest in the kingdom of heaven." Just prior to this, he had said, "Unless you be converted, and become as little children, ye shall not enter into the kingdom of heaven." The word converted in the Greek is strepho, meaning to turn quite around, or reverse, turn self about. Jesus was telling us that we must be changed in our thinking and actions. We must become as a little child. Consider how a child thinks. If you, as a parent, tell your child, "when you come home from school today, I'm taking you to the ice cream parlor to buy you an ice cream cone", that child will be excited, expecting to go with his dad or mother to get ice cream after school. They know you will do it because of who you are. You are his parents, the ones that he loves, trusts, adores, obeys and believes in. Jesus wants us to see that as God's people, we each must become as a little child and trust him in this way also. We don't have to have all the answers ourselves. All we have to do is trust and obey Jesus by putting our trust in the Living Word, who is Jesus. The word of God is Life. The words on the very pages of the bible are alive, but it will not do us any good until we believe like a little child that nothing is too difficult for Almighty God. Christians must remember that God will do nothing outside of his holy, alive word. When we make the quality decision to become as a little child and trust God and do things God's way, then our hearts become tender and our minds are converted, changed, and ready to receive from Almighty God. Amen! Pray and ask God to give you a tender, teachable heart towards him and the things of God and he will. Amen! Just believe him and trust him like a little child. You will begin to enter the kingdom of heaven, on earth now, as well as one day shortly when we are raptured to meet the Lord in the air. The kingdom of heaven is also a physical place, the third heaven, where God lives, and where saints go to live after leaving this earth. The kingdom of heaven also refers to the blessings of God. It refers to Jesus, who is the one that bestows blessings upon us, Praise the Lord! Jesus is our **Total Salvation**. Amen! John 1:1 says, "In the beginning was the Word, and the Word was with God, and the Word was God." Jesus is the <u>Word</u> and the Word is <u>Jesus</u>. The Word of God is life and Jesus is <u>Life</u>.

Although the word in our bible is alive, we must read the word daily (or eat it, and meditate on it). In order to gain its benefits, we must ask how does this apply to our lives? What does it mean? We should ask the Holy Spirit to illuminate God's word to us as we read and meditate upon it. We must speak God's words in faith, which are Spirit and Life over whatever the problem may be. Even if there is not a current problem, the word spoken in faith consistently can prevent a problem from arising many times.

Exodus 15:26 reveals one of Almighty God's covenant names, Jehovah Raphah, the Lord our Healer. The Hebrew definition for healer is to mend, to cure (cause to heal), physician, repair thoroughly, to make whole. In Exodus 15:26, God told his people, whom he had delivered by his mighty hand from the bondage of slavery by the Egyptians, that if they would listen to him and obey his commands, **that He would be their Jehovah Raphah, the Lord that healeth thee.**

God spoke the prophesy in Isaiah 53:5 hundreds of years before Jesus was born through the prophet Isaiah which states: that **with the stripes of Jesus we are healed**. This was referring to the fact that Jesus would one day take on his body all sicknesses and diseases for mankind. God saw the work on Calvary's cross as finished. As Revelation 13:8 tells us, in the mind of God, Jesus had already been slain from the foundation of the world. Praise God! Before Jesus was ever birthed into the earth, Father God saw the sin debt paid and humanity healed. In the New Testament, Peter, who was one of Jesus' apostles, saw what happened to Jesus. He was beaten with many stripes and every sickness and disease was placed on his body so that mankind could be redeemed, and go free. Romans 5:8 tells us, "But God commendeth his love towards us, in that, while we were yet sinners, Christ died for us." The choice however, is up to every person to accept or reject Jesus and all he provided through his death and resurrection, **Total Salvation**. Hallelujah! I Peter 2:24 says, "Who his own self bare our sins in his own body on the tree, that we being dead to sins, should live unto righteousness, by whose stripes **ye were healed."** Peter knew it was already done. He was there when Jesus said on the cross, "It is finished," Amen! God wants us to realize that Jesus is the Living Word and the Living Word is Jesus. They are one and the same. Jesus said in John 14:6, "I am the Way, the Truth, and the Life, no man cometh unto the Father, but by me." The word of God is alive. It is the way for us to receive life. The word tells us that, God's words are life **(the Hebrew word for life is chay - alive)** unto all those that find them and health **(the Hebrew word for health is marpe - curative, medicine, deliverance, cure, yielding, remedy, sound, wholesome, healing)** to all their flesh. Proverbs 4:22 says, "For they are life unto those that find them, and health to all their flesh."

In both the Old and New Testaments, God tells us that his word is alive, living, and if we will put it into our hearts and obey (do his whole word), it will be health and medicine to **all** our flesh. Praise God! One little dose won't do. A dose of the word every now and then is not enough. We must consistently fill our hearts with the word of God. Why? It is life, health, medicine, a cure for all our flesh. That means every problem that has arisen, or will arise, can be changed by the word of God, which is truth. Amen! We must believe, receive, and act on the whole word of God consistently. Let me give an example of how God's word works. A few years ago a young lady had an abortion. Afterwards, she was told by the doctors that she would never be able to have another child. She tried to commit suicide. I talked over the telephone to this young lady, who said she was a Christian but was not living a holy life. I encouraged her with the word of God and she asked the Lord for forgiveness of her sins. I shared with her that God could heal her womb so that she could have children. I prayed for healing for her and for a miracle to occur in her life. I found out several years later that indeed she had become pregnant again. I praise God for his love, his mercy and his grace. I also thank God that when she became pregnant this time, she did not have an abortion and take the life of her unborn child.

It is important to be planted where you can receive the whole word of God and be watered properly so that you can grow and be healed and delivered and receive **Total Salvation**, who is **Jesus Christ**. God desires that you also work in the church in which he has ordained for you to be planted. It is there that you can grow properly, as well as contribute your talents and gifts in your local church for God's glory.

If you are saved and wondering how to start on the road that God has for you, first repent of any and all sins. Then begin to hear, read and apply the word of God consistently to your life. As you apply the word of God to your life, you are putting what you have heard and read into action. Continue to hear the anointed word of God, for as Romans 10:17 says, "So then <u>faith cometh</u> by <u>hearing</u>, and <u>hearing</u> by the word of God." We must continue to hear the word of Almighty God, do it, as well as apply the word consistently in our lives. As we do these things, the desired godly changes will be manifested. Amen!

Jesus is the Living Word and he is all powerful. God's written word is also alive and powerful. It is necessary that we eat or read and digest God's words from the bible daily. God's word is medicine. It is also important to remember that Proverb 4:22 says, "For they (God's words) are life, unto those that find them and health to all their flesh."

(The hebrew word for health is marpe - medicine, cure, remedy, etc.) God's word is medicine, a cure, and a remedy to all our flesh.

It is important for believers to read, hear, and do the whole word of God, which includes walking in love daily. As we do God's word, healing and whatever part of Total Salvation is needed, will be ministered to the whole man, spirit, soul and body. This will take place by believing and acting on God's whole word. Amen! Indeed God's word is true and it will work for you. Through walking in love and obedience, healing of spiritual, emotional, physical, social, and financial hurts will be manifested in your life.

THE LOVE WALK
Jesus - The Word - All One And The Same

John 1:1 - In the beginning was the WORD, (JESUS) and the Word (JESUS) was with God, and the WORD (JESUS) was God.

JESUS = LIVING WORD

LIVING WORD = JESUS

JESUS = TRUTH

TRUTH = JESUS

Exodus 15: 26 - I am the Lord that healeth thee (Jehovah Raphah) Hebrew word for heal, healeth - (raphah).

I am the Lord your cure, physician, healer, repairer, the one who makes you whole.

Hebrew - raphah - to mend, to cure, cause to heal, physician, repair, thoroughly make whole.

Isaiah 53:5 - But he was wounded for our transgressions, he was bruised for our iniquities: the chastisement of our peace was upon him; and **with his stripes we <u>are</u> healed.**

I Peter 2:24 - Who his own self bare our sins in his own body on the tree, that we, being dead to sins, should live unto righteousness, by **whose <u>stripes ye were healed.</u>**

Greek word for healed - iaomai - to cure, heal, make whole

I Peter 2:24 - By whose stripes ye were cured, healed, made whole.

To God Be The Glory!

The Word Of God

Spiritual

Matthew 6:33 - But seek ye first the kingdom of God, and his righteousness; and all these things shall be added unto you.

Matthew 22:37-39 - Jesus said unto him, Thou shalt love the Lord thy God with all thy heart, and with all thy soul, and with all thy mind.
38: This is the first and great commandment.
39: And the second is like unto it, Thou shalt love thy neighbour as thyself.

John:13:34-35 - A new commandment I give unto you, That ye love one another; as I have loved you, that ye also love one another.
35: By this shall all men know that ye are my disciples, if ye have love one to another.

Proverbs 4:7 - Wisdom is the principal thing; therefore get wisdom: and with all thy getting get understanding.

Proverbs 16:33 - The fear of the LORD is the instruction of wisdom; and before honour is humility.

Proverbs 16:3 - Commit thy works unto the LORD, and thy thoughts shall be established.

Health And Healing

Isaiah 53:5 - But he was wounded for our transgressions, he was bruised for our iniquities: the chastisement of our peace was upon him; and with his stripes we are healed.

I Peter 2:24 - Who his own self bare our sins in his own body on the tree, that we, being dead to sins, should live unto righteousness: by whose stripes ye were healed.

Psalms 118:17 - I shall not die, but live, and declare the works of the LORD.

Wealth

Psalms 84:11 - For the LORD God is a sun and shield: the LORD will give grace and glory: no good thing will he withhold from them that walk uprightly.

Psalms 35:27 - Let them shout for joy, and be glad, that favour my righteous cause: yea, let them say continually, Let the LORD be magnified, which hath pleasure in the prosperity of his servant.

Proverbs 13:22 - A good man leaveth an inheritance to his children's children: and the wealth of the sinner is laid up for the just.

Protection

Psalms 91:1-16 -
1: He that dwelleth in the secret place of the most High shall abide under the shadow of the Almighty.
2: I will say of the LORD, He is my refuge and my fortress: my God; in him will I trust.
3: Surely he shall deliver thee from the snare of the fowler, and from the noisome pestilence.
4: He shall cover thee with his feathers, and under his wings shalt thou trust: his truth shall be thy shield and buckler.
5: Thou shalt not be afraid for the terror by night; nor for the arrow that flieth by day;
6: Nor for the pestilence that walketh in darkness; nor for the destruction that wasteth at noonday.
7: A thousand shall fall at thy side, and ten thousand at thy right hand; but it shall not come nigh thee.
8: Only with thine eyes shalt thou behold and see the reward of the wicked.
9: Because thou hast made the LORD, which is my refuge, even the most High, thy habitation;
10: There shall no evil befall thee, neither shall any plague come nigh thy dwelling.
11: For he shall give his angels charge over thee, to keep thee in all thy ways.
12: They shall bear thee up in their hands, lest thou dash thy foot against a stone.
13. Thou shalt tread upon the lion and adder: the young lion and the dragon shalt thou trample under feet.
14: Because he hath set his love upon me, therefore will I deliver him: I will set him on high, because he hath known my name.
15: He shall call upon me, and I will answer him: I will be with him in trouble; I will deliver him, and honour him.
16: With long life will I satisfy him, and shew him my salvation.

Protection

Psalms 37:18-19 - The LORD knoweth the days of the upright: and their inheritance shall be for ever.
19: They shall not be ashamed in the evil time: and in the days of famine they shall be satisfied.

Isaiah:54:17 - No weapon that is formed against thee shall prosper; and every tongue that shall rise against thee in judgment thou shalt condemn. This is the heritage of the servants of the LORD, and their righteousness is of me, saith the LORD.

For Our Children

Psalms 115:13 - He will bless them that fear the LORD, both small and great.
V14 - The LORD shall increase you more and more, you and your children.
V15 - Ye are blessed of the LORD which made heaven and earth.

Proverbs 11:21 - Though hand join in hand, the wicked shall not be unpunished: but the seed of the righteous shall be delivered.

Proverbs 22:6 - Train up a child in the way he should go: and when he is old, he will not depart from it.

Isaiah 54:13 - And all thy children shall be taught of the LORD; and great shall be the peace of thy children.
V14 - In righteousness shalt thou be established: thou shalt be far from oppression; for thou shalt not fear: and from terror; for it shall not come near thee.

Isaiah 59:19 - So shall they fear the name of the LORD from the west, and his glory from the rising of the sun. When the enemy shall come in like a flood, the Spirit of the LORD shall lift up a standard against him.

Isaiah 59:20 - And the Redeemer shall come to Zion, and unto them that turn from transgression in Jacob, saith the LORD.
V21 - As for me, this is my covenant with them, saith the LORD; My spirit that is upon thee, and my words which I have put in thy mouth, shall not depart out of thy mouth, nor out of the mouth of thy seed, nor out of the mouth of thy seed's seed, saith the LORD, from henceforth and for ever.

Romans 10:13 - For whosoever shall call upon the name of the Lord shall be saved.

9

Breaking Generational Curses Through Love (Jesus)

Galatians 3:12-14

PRAISE THE LORD because the word of God is alive. The word is quick and powerful, and sharper than any two-edged sword. It is able to cause the enemy, satan and all of his cohorts, to flee when a believer speaks and stands on God's word in faith, knowing that God inside of a believer is greater than the enemy or whatever he sends his way. (I John 4:4) God has equipped the believer with many spiritual weapons, including the blood of Jesus and his word. Revelation 12:11 tells us that the saints or believers overcame him, by the blood of the Lamb and the word of <u>their</u> testimony. What have you been saying lately? What is your testimony? Jesus died and arose from the grave to give us **Total Salvation,** which includes the first and greatest gift of becoming saved or born again, however, it is up to every person to choose or reject this gift. As a part of **Total Salvation**, Jesus also paid for our victories in this life, for one of his covenant names is Jehovah Nissi or the Lord our Banner, who is our Victory. But like everything, we must believe it and receive it. There is also something else we must do. To give an example, if someone purchased a lovely gift for you and you never accepted the lovely gift, then you would never enjoy the benefit of it. The same is true for every believer for every area of their lives. God has given us spiritual and physical laws and we must use them properly for them to work in our daily lives.

In considering generational curses, we know that the curse began in the Garden of Eden when Adam and Eve disobeyed God. Everything was cursed. Their bodies began to die. Sickness and disease began, the ground was cursed and thistles began and more. Even the animals were cursed because a serpent chose to listen to the devil and to disobey God. It was their choice, just as it is our choice today, to obey God or not to obey him. Every believer should choose to yield their members to righteousness and not unrighteousness.

God warned Adam and Eve. He told them not to eat of the tree of the knowledge of good and evil, but they could eat of every other tree in the garden, even the tree of life. Because of the original sin, generational curses were passed down from bloodline to bloodline. I praise God for Jesus Christ. Jesus loved you and I so very much that he paid the price for our sin debt and for every curse that came upon mankind. You may say, well why am I sick? Why don't I have sufficient finances? Why this or why that? We must realize that the problem is not God. Jesus has already paid the price for our **Total Salvation**. Amen! The problem always lies with God's people somewhere. To list a few reasons, it might be because of the lack of knowledge of God's word. It may be that a Christian is hearing the whole word but is not doing it; or not being consistent in doing the word of God. It could also be that the person is not hearing the whole word of God. They may be in a church that believes and preaches the importance of becoming saved, which is the first, and most important part of salvation, but they don't believe in healing, which is one of the supernatural gifts of God. Or perhaps they do not teach or believe in tithing or some other part of Total Salvation. Maybe you feel that you have a lack of faith, or you are in fear, sin, or you are not tithing. The list of reasons continues, but I thank God for his love, mercy, and grace and that indeed he looks upon our hearts. No, it does not mean he winks at sin, but he knows whether or not we have a sincere desire to make a change. God knows whether we are allowing him to help us change areas of our lives that need to be dealt with. Amen! Even in the Old Testament,

God promised his people, if they obeyed him, that he would be Jehovah Raphah to them, their Healer, their Physician. He would thoroughly make them whole and that none of the curses that came on the Egyptians would come on them. Read Deuteronomy 8:1-4, 16-18 and Exodus 15:26. Deuteronomy 30:19 states, "I call heaven and earth to record this day against you, that I have set before you life and death, blessings and curses; therefore choose life, that both thou and thy seed may **live."** God wants us to prosper in every area spiritually, emotionally, physically, financially and socially, and to have godly families and harmonious relationships in every area of our lives. This does not just fall on God's people. Each person has an important role to play in receiving God's promises.

In Isaiah 53:5, the Word of God tells us, "But he was wounded for our <u>transgressions</u> (Hebrew - Pesna - rebellion, sin trespass, revolt), he was bruised for our <u>iniquities</u>, the chastisement of our peace was upon him, and with his stripes we are healed." God called the things that were not in Isaiah 53:5 as though they already were. The prophet Isaiah prophesied this scripture by the Spirit of God hundreds of years before Jesus was birthed, and thousands of years before we were born. God saw the sin debt as already paid for our victory, our **Total Salvation.** Praise the Lord he also saw us as already healed!

Galatians 3:12-14 tells us: "And the law is not of faith: but, the man that doeth them shall live in them." When a person did not keep the law in the Old Testament, there was a punishment to be received from the hands of men. Verses 13 and 14 tell us: Christ has redeemed us from the curse of the law, being made a curse for us (even the curse that was a result of the sin of Adam and Eve); for it is written, cursed is every one that hangeth on a tree: v/14 that the blessings of Abraham might come on the Gentiles through Jesus Christ; that we might receive the promise of the Spirit through faith. Because Jesus Christ has paid the price through the shedding of his precious blood, we have been redeemed from the curse of the broken law.

Praise God, as believers, we should shout for joy for all that Jesus has done for us! We are entitled to the blessings of Abraham as well as those in the New Testament. What a great heritage we have, but it is through faith that we inherit the promises of God. Just as it took faith for us to believe and receive Jesus as our Savior, the same is true for the rest of our **Total Salvation** gifts. It is through our <u>faith in action</u> that we obtain our inheritance, in the here and now. Hebrews 11:1 says, "Now faith is the substance of things hoped for, the evidence of things not seen." Faith is tangible, it is a substance. When it is manifested visibly, it is the proof or evidence.

An example in the physical of faith could be a married couple that is both healthy and fertile. When the husband and wife decide they want a child, they pray and make love or come together sexually. The male has the sperm and the female has the egg. At the right time, the sperm is released and joins the egg. A union takes place, a child is conceived and the fetus begins to grow; whether they feel the fetus grow or see it take place, it has happened. The sperm and egg can represent our faith. Nothing happens until our faith is released to God, then something takes place (**evidence is on the way** - see **visual example of faith**). When the child is born, then we see the evidence of the substance (the sperm and egg) that joined together which began to form nine months before. (**See Visual of Hearts**)

In the spiritual realm, one of the ways that curses or blessings come forth is determined by what Christians speak and do. Another factor is if the person is obeying God's word or not, and whether he is walking in love or not. In John 14:21-23, Jesus says if a man loves me he will keep my commandments. V/21 "He that hath my commandments, and keepth them, he it is that loveth me: and he that loveth me shall be loved of my Father, and I will love him and manifest myself to him." God manifests himself in healing, finances, and other ways, when we keep the love commandments completely. When Christians do the <u>whole word of God</u>, which includes tithing as stated in Malachi 3:8-12, God promises to rebuke the devourer (satan) for us. God will rebuke satan and not allow the curse to come as we stand in faith on God's promises to his believers.

Not forgiving others is also an area that the devil tries to entrap Christians. He does not care who he entraps. He just wants to get God's people to not forgive because he knows that it will break the line of blessings and answered prayers for God's people. (Read Mark 11:22-26) Also, refusing to forgive someone can lead to bitterness.

(Read Hebrews 12:14-15). Not forgiving can open the doors to various curses, as well as sickness and disease.

(**See Visual of Tree**) - God calls His people trees throughout the Word of God. There are times that the believer brings the curse upon themselves by the words that proceed from their mouths. (That tickled me to death, it scared me to death, take care - why not talk blessings?) In Matthew 12:36-37, Jesus said, "But I say unto you, that every idle word that men shall speak, they shall give an account thereof in the day of judgment." It is time that Christians become FVIPs, people of Faith, Vision, Integrity, and Pure Hearts. Almighty God desires that each become people of faith that are quick to agree with HIS word, people like Joshua and Caleb and most of all like Jesus Christ. V/37 says, "For by thy words thou shalt be justified, and by thy word thou shalt be condemned." The curse is broken and destroyed by the power of God's anointing. God's words, consistently spoken in faith, will change the facts because God's words are anointed words of Spirit and Life. They are Truth! Therefore, any existing facts are subject to change when we apply God's words of truth and life to them in faith and as we walk in love and do the whole word of God consistently. Amen!

REDEMPTIONS PLAN

Hebrews 12:2 –"Looking unto Jesus the author and finisher of our faith, who for the joy that was set before him endured the cross, despising the shame, and is set down at the right hand of the throne of God."

Father God and Jesus Christ are our examples. They are the **Greatest Givers** of all.

Father God knew that in order to reap an abundant harvest of more sons he had to **(Sow=Give) his only begotten son, Jesus Christ, into the earth.**

Father God and Jesus fully expected to receive many sons because of **(Sowing=Giving).**

God so **loved** the world that he **gave** his only begotten Son, that whosoever believeth in him should not perish but have everlasting life. (**John 3:16**)

Jesus Christ took on flesh to Redeem Mankind and he **(Gave=Sowed) his life willingly.**

Father God had one seed = Jesus Christ his only son.

Father God and Jesus Christ reaped and are continuing to reap an abundant harvest of many sons, and daughters, those who are born again.

"Now faith is the substance of things hoped for, the evidence of things not seen." *Hebrews 11:1*

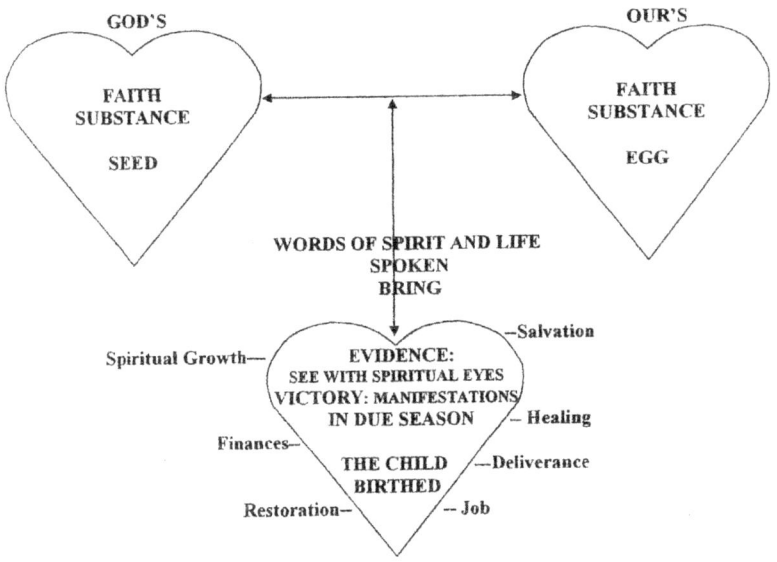

"Death and life are in the power of the tongue: and they that love it shall eat the fruit (blessings or curses) thereof." – *Proverbs 18:21*

Matthew 12:34-36 – v/36 "But I say unto you, That every idle word that men shall speak, they shall give account thereof in the day of judgement."
Idle – inactive, barren, useless, unemployed, not working on your behalf.

We can abort God's blessings or we can help them come forth.

"Even so faith, if it has not works, is dead, being alone." – *James 2:17*

"A wholesome tongue is a tree of life:" – *Proverbs 15:4*

"And let us not be weary in well doing: for in due season we shall reap, if we faint not."- *Galatians 6:9*

By Apostle Crystal Naylor - Copyrighted

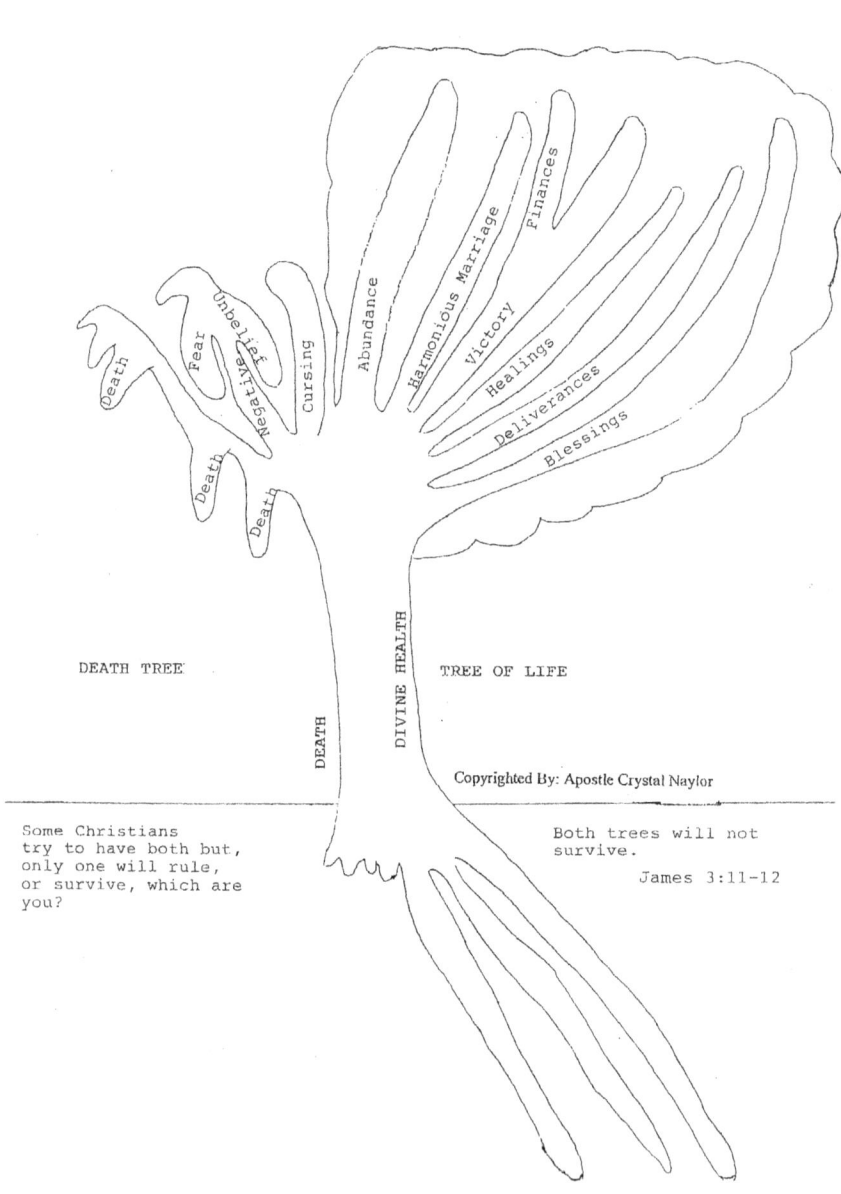

VICTORIOUS! GLORIOUS! CHURCH! ▪ 87

Deuteronomy 30:19 - I call heaven and earth to record this day against you, that I have set before you life and death, blessing and cursing; therefor <u>choose life</u>, that both thou and thy seed may live.

CHOOSE?

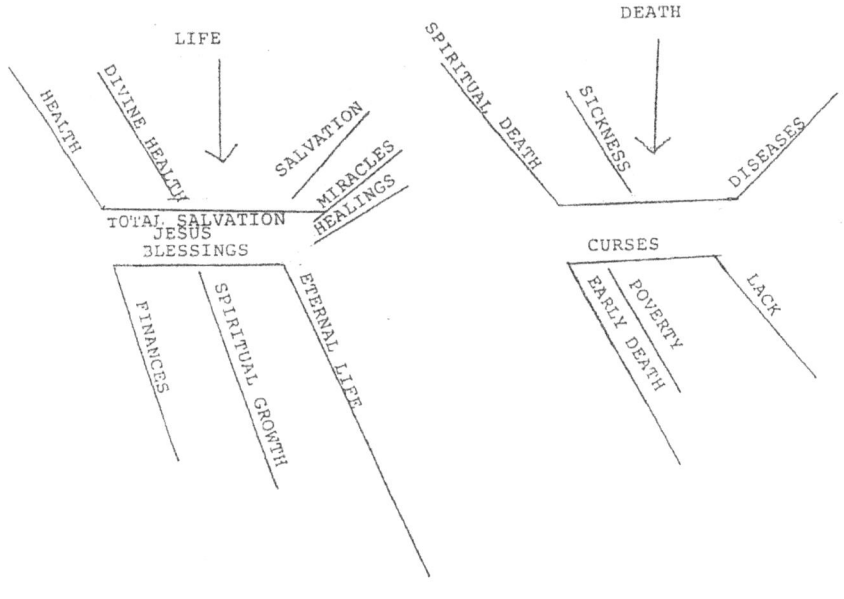

Breaking Generational Curses Through Love (Jesus) - Part II

Praise God! For truly with God, who is Love, all things are possible to those that dare to believe and trust him. Amen! What man says is impossible, or dead, or dying, through the power of Almighty God, can be brought to life even as Christ Jesus was raised from the dead. Perhaps you have been given a death sentence by a bad report from a test, or a negative doctor's report. With God, all things are possible! Perhaps you lack finances or your child is on drugs, remember with God all things are possible to those that believe! We must choose whose report we will believe. Yes indeed, there are things we must do and say. Paul said we are to put on the "whole" armour of God. After standing on God's <u>word</u>, which are the promises of God that have been sealed with the precious blood of Jesus that cannot be broken, we must continue to stand. We must continue to trust and believe God regardless of what our eyes see or our ears hear. Knowing that God is faithful and in due season, in the fullness of time, God's time, he will manifest himself in our situation. In John 14:21, Jesus said, "He that hath my commandments, and keepth them he it is that loveth me: and he that loveth me shall be loved of my Father, and I will love him, and will "<u>manifest</u>" <u>myself</u> to him." We are to be obedient to do God's word and always walk in love. Jesus said, we are to love God as commanded in Matthew 22:37, with all our heart, soul and mind. We then are to love our neighbors as ourselves (Matthew 22:39). We will not break any of the Old Testament commandments if we purpose in our hearts to do these two love commandments.

Jesus also said in John 15:12, "This is my commandment, that ye love one another, as I have loved you." We know that Jesus loved man so much that he laid his life down for us and we must begin to lay our lives down for the body of Christ in prayers and deeds. Many times we must let our desires and plans go to do God's will and be used to bless someone else, even if the person is not yet a member of Christ's body, as God by His Spirit directs us. Jesus said in John 13:34-35, "A new commandment I give unto you, that ye love one another as I have loved you, That ye also love one another. By this shall all men know that ye are my disciples, if you have love one to another." A major key to breaking generational curses is to walk in love. That is why God the Holy Spirit, through the Apostle Paul, said in I Corinthians 13:13, "And now abideth, <u>faith, hope, charity</u> (or love) these three; but the greatest of these is charity (or love)." Amen! God, who is love, dwells in every born again believer. The believer has every fruit of the Spirit, which is the very nature and character of Almighty God himself and the greatest fruit of all is love. Love is in every born again child of God. Each born again person must purpose in his heart to allow the nine fruit of the Holy Spirit to come forth in their lives. Amen!

As we allow God to conform us into the image of his Son, Jesus Christ, the works of the flesh begin to die. The carnal must die. For the word in Romans 8:6 tells us, "For to be <u>carnally minded</u> is death, but to be <u>spiritually minded</u> is <u>life</u> and <u>peace."</u> Romans 8:13 says, "For if you live after the flesh, ye shall die; but if ye through the Spirit do mortify the deeds of the body, ye shall live."

There is the natural man, the person that does not have the Spirit of God inside of him, the unsaved (I Corinthians 2:14). Then there is the carnal man, the person who has accepted Jesus and is saved but has many grave clothes on. He looks, walks and talks like the world at times. The carnal Christian also tries to combine his walk with the world and God. He is led by his flesh instead of by the Spirit of God. (I Corinthians 3:1-4) There is also the spiritual man, the person that is born again. Although he is in the world, he knows that he is not of the world and he reflects Jesus Christ in what he does and says. His lifestyle also reflects Jesus Christ. The Christian that is a <u>spiritual</u> man is led by the Spirit of Almighty God rather than the flesh. Amen! To God Be The Glory!

The Lord desires that every born again Christian, regardless of their age or the period of time that they have been a member of his body, grow up spiritually. He does not want his people to remain babies. (Read I Corinthians 2:9-16 and I Corinthians 3:1-9)

God wants us to realize that he is never the problem. Jesus said in John 10:10, "The thief cometh not but for to steal, and to kill, and to destroy." Jesus wants us to know that he is the one who blesses. Jesus said, "I have come that they might have life, and that they might have it more abundantly." Praise The Lord! The word of God in 1 John 3:8

tells why Jesus came and what Father God's purpose was for sending Jesus. It states, "For this purpose the Son of God was manifested, that he might destroy the works of the devil." To God Be The Glory! Amen! We only need to read the word of God to see the works of the devil. Jesus was always about his Father, Almighty God's business of destroying the works of the devil, and bringing people more abundant life. Jesus opened blinded eyes, spiritually and physically. He cast out demons, performed miracles, healed the sick, and he preached and taught the <u>gospel</u>, or <u>good news</u>. Jesus Christ was destroying the works of the devil. The final victory was accomplished on Calvary's cross when he died and arose three days later victorious over death, hell and the grave. I Corinthians 15:55-57 says, V/55 <u>"O death where is thy sting? O grave where is thy victory? V/56, The sting of death is sin and the strength of sin is in the law. V/57, But thanks be to God, which giveth us the victory</u> through our Lord Jesus Christ." Amen! To God Be The Glory!

Today the born again believers are God's ambassadors in the earth, and we each need the empowerment of the baptism of the Holy Ghost! After Jesus' resurrection, he walked on this earth in his resurrected, glorified body for forty days and was seen by many, as recorded in Acts 1:2-4, Mark 16:9-14, and I Corinthians 15:6. Before Jesus ascended to heaven, he told his disciples to wait to be empowered by the Holy Ghost. On Pentecost, those who were obedient received this promise as recorded in Acts 1:8 and Acts 2:1-6. Today as Christians we too need to receive this same empowerment by the Holy Ghost. Amen! In Matthew 11:12 Jesus said, "the kingdom of heaven suffereth violence; and the violent take it by force." It is up to us, the believers, to take back what the devil has stolen or is trying to steal because Jesus has already paid the price for our **Total Salvation**. That's why I John 4:4 states, "Ye are of God little children, and have overcome them (demon spirits) because greater is He (God) that is in you, than he (satan and his demons) that is in the world." To God Be The Glory! Amen!

The word of God lets us know that Jesus took our sins, sicknesses and diseases upon himself at Calvary's cross (Isaiah 53:5 and I Peter 2:24). The word also tells us that Jesus took every curse on himself so we could walk in his blessings for us. We must enforce what Jesus has done for us. For instance, if you had a security alarm on your car, it's up to you to set it and make sure that it's functioning. In the spiritual realm, the word of God lets us know that we have angels. (Hebrews 1:14, Psalm 34:7, Psalm 91:11, Psalm 103:20) The angels of God hearken to his word. I remember years ago when I first saw angels. They were dressed in all white, talking around a tree in our backyard. I later came to realize they were <u>not</u> busy then because I did not know the importance of speaking God's words that are Spirit and Life. Psalm 103:20 tells us, that God's angels hearken to the voice of his words. Amen! Likewise, demons are moved by the sword of the Spirit which is the word of God. God's words of Spirit and Life are a mighty weapon when spoken in faith against the devil and his demonic spirits. Only humans have the God ordained privilege to use God's words. Words are powerful. James 3:2 tells us, "For in many things we offend all. If any man offend not in words, the same is a perfect man, and able to bridle the whole body." Verse 10 says, "Out of the same mouth proceedeth blessing and cursing. My brethren, these things ought not so to be."

In the word of God, God often refers to his people as trees. God's desire is that as his trees, we bear good fruit, the fruit of the Holy Spirit. As we purpose to walk in love, it is then that we are quick to forgive others, and repent and allow God to work in us and through us to bring forth his very nature: love, joy, peace, long suffering, gentleness, goodness, faith, meekness and temperance. (Galatians 5:22-23)

Each Christian needs to ask, as God's trees, what type of fruit am I bearing. Is it a mixture of the works of the flesh as listed in Galatians 5:19-21: adultery, fornication, uncleanness, lasciviousness, and the list continues. Galatians 5:16 says, "This I say then, walk in the Spirit and ye shall not fulfill the lust of the flesh." Amen! As you consciously choose to do things God's way and walk in the Spirit, and allow the nine fruit of the Holy Spirit to be manifested in your life, then the works of the flesh, which are the very nature and character of the devil and his demons, will leave. Thereby <u>many generational curses are broken as you choose to walk in love towards God and your fellow man.</u>

When you walk in love, it does not mean you do not stand up for what is right in the face of sin. In Galatians 5:21 and 26 it speaks of envy. Envy is a sin that cannot always and immediately be seen at times. In the bible, we see this sin in the life of King Saul. King Saul was envious of David and wanted him dead. He even tried to kill David with a javelin while David was trying to be a blessing to him. Because Saul had sinned against Almighty God, an evil spirit had been sent to torment Saul. David played an instrument to help give deliverance to Saul for a period of time. Saul was jealous of David who had slain the giant. The people began to sing and dance saying, "Saul hath slain thousands and David ten thousands." (I Samuel 18:6-12) Saul continuously tried to kill David. Many times, there are "Sauls" in our lives, who are envious of us for various reasons. How should we react? Does it cause you to be in unforgiveness? For example, someone lies about you because of envy, mistreats you, and gives a job to someone else who is less deserving. The reasons for envy are endless, but the devil and his cohorts (demons) are always behind the action. Unfortunately, the works of the flesh are seen in some members of the body of Christ, and this should not be so. Galatians 5:26 says, "Let us (the believers) not be desirous of vain glory, provoking one another, envying one another." Hebrews 10:24 tells us that we should "provoke one another unto love and to good works." Praise God. As you are obedient to do God's word, to continuously walk in love and to forgive others, you will see more and more of God's power released to break more and more generational curses. To God Be The Glory! Praise God! Amen! Through **Love**, who is **Jesus,** as an individual chooses to walk in love, he becomes victorious over the devil in whatever way he may come. His life will also demonstrate the love of Jesus Christ which dwells in every member of the body of Christ.

Breaking Generational Curses Through Love (Jesus) - Part III

We have seen throughout God's holy word, the importance of walking in love continuously. It is a weapon that the devil hates because it releases the power of God in the believer's life. Praise God!

Galatians 5:6 tells us that "faith worketh by love." In Matthew 22:37-39, Jesus tells us we must love God with our heart, soul, and mind and love our neighbors as ourselves. In Galatians 5:22, love is listed as the first fruit of the Spirit. In I John 4:16, the word tells us that God is Love and he that dwells (remains) in love, dwells (remains) in God and God in him. Amen! In I Corinthians 13:13, it tells us that although one day certain things shall vanish away that faith, hope and **charity** (which is **love**) shall abide and of these three, **charity** is the greatest. Amen! God wants his people to get this truth deep within us so that we will become consistent doers of the whole word of God. Amen! Why? So that we will demonstrate to one another, in the body of Jesus Christ, that we really do love God and each other. As we walk in love, this love will overflow to not only God and the body of Christ, but to those who are unsaved as well. They will know that we are truly Christians because we are doing God's word as followers of God. In Ephesians 5:1-2, the word of God clearly tells us, "Be ye therefore followers of God, as dear children; And walk in love as Christ also hath loved us, and hath given himself for us an offering and a sacrifice to God for a sweet smelling savour." We are to lay down our lives for one another in love. This is done as we encourage others, pray for others, give to and bless one another in whatever way God directs us. We also must reach out to the unsaved. Jesus told his disciples in John 13:35, "By this shall all men know that ye are my disciples, if ye have love one to another."

When you make the quality decision to walk in love, you are quick to forgive and quick to repent. One of the fastest and most subtle ways to open the door to the devil and to bring curses into the lives of believers is through not forgiving someone. There are times that a believer may be wronged in some way by another believer or even an unsaved person. An example may be of an individual that tells a lie about you. Perhaps the person said something that you did not say and you have no way to prove you never said it. You may confront the individual about the lie and they may still say you said it, when only you and God know the real truth about the situation. You know that you have done nothing wrong and so does the devil. God would have us to forgive such an individual and pray for him.

The devil, of course, would like Christians to allow their flesh to rule and to not forgive. If you don't forgive, then every time you see the person you will be reminded of what they did and you will get a little angrier, to the point you may begin to talk about the person. If you as the wounded person continues to refuse to forgive, eventually bitterness will take root in you. Hebrews 12:14-15 tells us, "Follow peace with all men, and holiness without which no man shall see the Lord. Looking diligently lest any man fail of the grace of God, lest any root of bitterness springing up trouble you, and thereby many be defiled." Not forgiving is sin, and it leads to bitterness and it will trouble you. A bitter person is most miserable and those who come into contact with a person that is bitter are defiled many times themselves. They are defiled by the bitter person's attitude, their words and actions. Being in the presence of someone who is bitter is not pleasant at all, and they often have an unpleasant odor. The opposite is true when you are in the presence of a person who is on fire for Jesus, who is walking in love. There is a sweet fragrance from them, and you just love being in their presence.

God's word also tells us in Mark 11:26 that if we don't forgive others, Father God will not forgive us. In Matthew 5:23-24, Jesus said, "Therefore, if thou bring thy gift to the altar, and there rememberest that thy brother hath aught against thee; Leave there thy gift, before the altar, and go thy way; first be reconciled to thy brother, and then come and offer thy gift." Forgiveness is so important to the child of God because it releases them from bondages of the devil. It also releases the other person that offended them in some way when he chooses to repent and walk in love.

Hosea 4:6 tells us that God said, "<u>My people </u>are destroyed for lack of knowledge." God does not want his people ignorant of the devil's devices. He teaches us through his word, which is truth, which will change every situation as we are consistently obedient to do the whole word of God. Amen! God is never the problem. Amen! The curses, regardless of what they may be in a believer's life, have already been taken by Jesus Christ. Galatians 3:13-14 says, "Christ **hath redeemed** us from the curse of the law, being made a curse for us, for it is written, Cursed is everyone that hangeth on a tree: that the blessings of Abraham might come on the Gentiles through Jesus Christ: that we might receive the promise of the Spirit through faith." Through faith, we enter the first and greatest part of **Total Salvation,** who is **Jesus,** when we choose to accept Jesus as our Savior. Praise God, there is so much more. Although Jesus became a curse for us, we must enforce the victory at Calvary's cross in our lives. Satan will try to bring temptations to God's people even as he did to Jesus while Jesus was on this earth. Praise God, we like Jesus when he was in the wilderness, must use the sword of the Spirit against satan and all of his cohorts/demons. James 4:7 says, "Submit yourselves therefore to God, resist the devil and he will flee from you." As we obey God's word, we submit ourselves to God. As we speak God's words of Spirit and Life to satan as Jesus did, he will flee for a period of time because satan does not give up. Therefore, we must never give up. Praise God, because God in us is "greater than he (the devil) that is in the world." (I John 4:4) We must be even more consistent and persistent than the devil and all his cohorts/demon spirits. Amen!

As Holy Ghost baptized, Spirit filled believers, we have been given the power, "exousia" power, "authority", to use the name of Jesus. We have also been given the "dunamis" power, "miracle working power" by Jesus Christ to cast out the devil or demons, in Jesus' name. Jesus said in Mark 16:17-18, "And these signs shall follow them that **believe;** In my **name** shall they cast out devils, they shall speak with new tongues; They shall take up serpents, and if they drink any deadly thing, it shall not hurt them, they shall lay hands on the sick, and they shall recover."

The word of God tells us, we are to be as wise as serpents but as harmless as doves. When it comes to demonic forces, we are to pull down strongholds through the power of Almighty God, who is (the Strongest Man) Jesus Christ, and in the name and the power of the blood of Jesus Christ! Amen! Jesus shed his precious blood and arose from the dead triumphantly over the enemy of our souls. Hallelujah! Now it is up to every believer to enforce the victory given to us as Jesus' believers (Mark 16:17-18).

Covenant Promises of God

I John 1:9 - If we confess our sins, he is faithful and just to forgive us our sins, and to cleanse us from all unrighteousness.

I Peter 2:24 - Who his own self bare our sins in his own body on the tree, that we, being dead to sins, should live unto righteousness: by whose stripes ye were healed.

Isaiah 53:5 - But he was wounded for our transgressions, he was bruised for our iniquities: the chastisement of our peace was upon him; and with his stripes we are healed.

Psalm 118:17 - I shall not die, but live, and declare the works of the Lord.

Psalm 115: 13-14 - He will bless them that fear the Lord, both small and great. The Lord shall increase you more and more, you and your children.

Isaiah 49:25 - But thus saith the Lord, Even the captives of the mighty shall be taken away, and the prey of the terrible shall be delivered: for I will contend with him that contendeth with thee, and I will save thy children.

I John 5:14, 15 - And this is the confidence that we have in him, that if we ask anything according to his will, he heareth us. And if we know that he hear us, whatsoever we ask, we know that we have the petitions that we desired of him.

Find the covenant promise that best meets your needs in the word of God and stand on God's word in faith, as you believe, and confess them consistently. Amen.

Breaking Generational Curses Through Love (Jesus) Part IV

Praise God, we serve the Mighty God who is infinite. He has no beginning and he has no end. He is Almighty God or El Shaddai. He is the all sufficient one, who gives nourishment. God desires that we come to him to get whatever it is that we need in faith, knowing that he is Faithful. Praise God! Revelations 19:11 tells us that his name is "Faithful and True." Amen! There are many ways we can stop the victories and the blessings of God from reaching us, which are all tied to believing and doing the word of God. If there is a problem, it is not God. A lack of knowledge will hinder you. A lack of faith or love will hinder you, for Galatians 5:6 tells us that **faith works by love.** Amen! It is very important to continue to stand on God's word in order to receive his promises.

In Daniel chapter 9, we find Daniel, who was a godly man, prayed for his people the Jews, who were in captivity. He prayed for both their sins and his, even though there is no record of him sinning. Daniel pleaded for the forgiveness of his people even as Moses did for his brethren who had sinned against Almighty God. Chapter 10 of Daniel records that Daniel fasted and prayed for three weeks before he heard from God. Daniel was determined not to give up until he heard from God. We must do the same. In Daniel 10:11, the angel called Daniel a man "**greatly beloved.**" He explained to Daniel that from the very first day that Daniel began to fast and pray that he was heard, but the Prince of Persia, a demonic spirit, withstood God's angel for 21 days, keeping him from coming to Daniel with the answer to his prayer. It was not until one of the Chief Princes of God's angels, Michael, came to help the angel of God, that the messenger angel was successful in reaching Daniel. Galatians 6:9 says, "And let us not be weary in well doing for in due season we shall reap, if we faint not."

Ephesians 6:10 -13 tells us, "Finally my brethren, be strong in the Lord and in the power of his might. Put on the <u>whole</u> armour of God, that ye may be able to stand against the wiles of the devil. For we wrestle not against flesh and blood, but against principalities, against powers, against the rulers of the darkness of this world, against spiritual wickedness in high places. Wherefore take unto you the whole armour of God, <u>that ye may be able to withstand in the evil day,</u> and having done all, to stand." Praise God, how do we stand? We stand clothed in the <u>whole</u> armour of God. We should never leave home spiritually naked. If no one else knows we are not clothed in God's armour, the devil and his demons know. We must use the armour God has given to his believing children, Amen! In verses fourteen and fifteen, it tells the Christian to stand having his loins girt with truth, and to have on the breastplate of righteousness and his feet shod with the preparation of the gospel of peace. Verse sixteen says <u>above</u> <u>all</u>

take the shield of faith wherewith ye shall be able to quench **all** the fiery darts of the wicked. Amen! We need every piece of God's armour on daily, regardless of what comes our way. We must always fight the good fight of faith, realizing that the Captain of the Lord of Host, Praise the Lord, is Jesus Christ. Jesus is the Captain of all his angels Praise God. "If God be for us who can be against us?" (Romans 8:31) Amen! Therefore, as Ephesians 6:13 tells us, "having done all", continue to stand. Where? On God's words which are true and will never ever fail. If we don't waiver or give up, the manifestation of God, who is **Jesus**, our **Total Salvation** will show up and be manifested in our situations, Amen! Jesus became a curse for us. The curse of the broken law in the Garden of Eden is still in the world. We see the effects of sin everywhere. Even Jesus Christ was not exempt from temptations of the devil. He was tempted in the areas of the pride of life, the lust of the flesh and the lust of the eyes. Jesus used his own words of Spirit and Life, against satan. He had to enforce his own authority by speaking his words. Christians must do the same. Today, Jesus has given his people the right and the authority to use his name as well as the power to destroy the works of the devil through the spoken word of God. Another key to victory is when a believer is baptized with the Holy Ghost and power, even as Jesus was baptized. (Luke 3:21-22, Luke 4:1, Luke 4:14).The baptism of the Holy Ghost empowers a believer to do the greater works that Jesus said we would do. In John 14:12 Jesus said, "Verily, verily I say unto you, he that believeth on me, the works that I do shall he do also: and greater works than these shall he do; because I go unto my Father." Jesus also said in Acts 1:8, "But ye shall <u>receive power</u>, after that the Holy Ghost is come upon you: <u>and ye shall be witnesses</u> unto me, in both Jerusalem, and in all Judea, and in Samaria, and unto the <u>uttermost parts</u> of the earth."

As believers, we are indwelt by the Spirit of God inside of our spirit. Therefore we cannot be possessed by a demon spirit. Only an unsaved person can be possessed by demons. It is so very important that Christians get God's word into their spirit. Psalm 119:130 lets us know that the entrance of God's word gives light and it gives understanding. The light of God's word will reveal any dark areas in the believer's life. The word of God will also teach us who we are in Christ Jesus. As you grow in the word, you can put the devil and his oppressing demons on the run! The word will reveal areas where a Christian is not walking in love. It will reveal to the Christian that has an open heart, anyone that he or she has not forgiven. As you are obedient to forgive, it is then that bondages are broken in your life and you are released of many things. We must always remember Jesus, who is our example, forgave even while he was being mocked and crucified on Calvary's cross. If we don't forgive others whether it is our fault or not Father God will not forgive us. (Mark 11:25-26) If we don't forgive, not only will our prayers be hindered, but it will cause that unforgiving person to become bitter, (Hebrews 12:15). Not forgiving is one reason an individual may not receive the promised blessing from Almighty God; however, there are many other reasons as well. Whatever the reason is that hinders an individual, it is all tied to not obeying the first commandment of love which states in Matthew 22:37, "Thou shalt love the Lord thy God with all thy heart, and with all thy soul, and with all thy mind." If we truly love God, we will obey his <u>whole</u> word. Amen! As we do God's word consistently, it closes doors to the enemy of our soul, the devil. Just as God is no respecter of persons, the devil is not a respecter in that he does not care who he destroys or how he does the job of destroying. God, who is not like the devil, extends his love and mercy to **all** who will receive his Son Jesus as their Savior.

Galatians 3:13-14 tells us that Jesus has redeemed us from the curse of the law being made a curse for us. Jesus used the word (the sword of the Spirit) against the devil. We also must put the word of God to work on our behalf as well as on the behalf of others as God directs us. Jesus has given us the right and authority to use his name and he has given us the power over demons. Amen! (Mark 16:17-18 and I John 4:4) So let's use the word of God, which is the sword of the Spirit as Jesus did. As we do, we will see demons flee! Through the power of God's word and as we willingly submit to do God's word consistently, <u>we will see many generational curses broken through the power of the anointed word of God, as we continue to walk in love</u>. Amen!

FAITH SPEAKS

TO REAP YOU MUST SOW

Death and Life are in the Power of the tongue and they that love it shall eat the fruit there of.   Proverbs 18:21

Salvation   Healing   Financial Increase   Favor   Love – Total Salvation

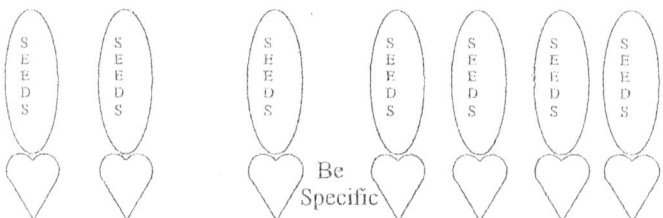

Be Specific

Put God's Words In Your Mind- To Get It Into Your Heart
Scriptures – Promises Of God = Inheritance = Our Covenant = God's Will

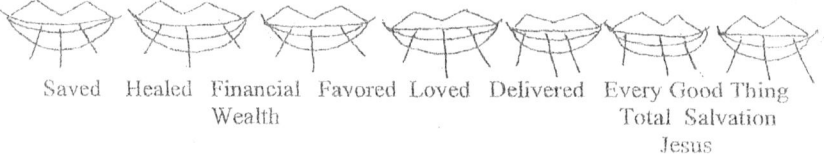

Saved   Healed   Financial   Favored   Loved   Delivered   Every Good Thing
                 Wealth   Total Salvation
                                                             Jesus

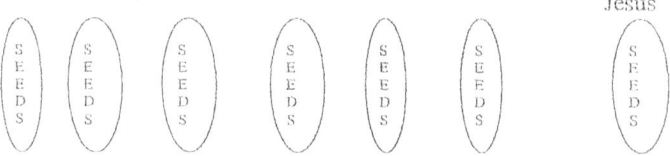

When God's (Seeds) Words Are <u>Spoken</u> In Faith Consistently
Good Seeds Are Planted And The Desired HARVEST Will Come

Copyrighted By: Apostle Crystal Naylor

Breaking Generational Curses Through Love (Jesus) Part V

Praise God, for indeed we already have the victory because **Jesus** is our **Total Salvation** and everything is in him. One definition in the Hebrew for salvation is victory and Praise God, Jesus is our victory or Jehovah-Nissi. Amen! Praise God, his banner over us is love, for he is LOVE. Amen! II Corinthians 2:14 states, "Now thanks be unto God, which always causeth us to triumph in Christ, and maketh manifest the savor of his knowledge by us in every place." Amen!

Although Jesus has already been made a curse for us, as stated in Galatians 3:13, whether receiving healing deliverance, or the greatest miracle of all of **Total Salvation**, which is to become born again; we have a part to play. The curse is still in the world which includes sickness and disease, sin and so much more. The devil and his demon spirits hate believers. The devil even tried to tempt Jesus at his weakest point after he had prayed and fasted for forty days. The devil comes to every born again believer to try to tempt us, to try to build strongholds or to keep the existing strongholds in tact.

When a person becomes saved through the precious blood of Jesus, most times the strongholds or generational curses, may not leave that person immediately. Why? Because even though that individual has become saved or born again, the devil does not want him free. The new birth took place in the man's spirit but the mind must be renewed by God's word, Romans 12:1-2. The devil hates that the person is now saved; therefore, many times the temptations will become even more intensified. Sometimes the illness or sickness, in one's body will even worsen. We can still Praise God for the **VICTORY**! We can thank him for our **TOTAL SALVATION** because that's how God sees you and I. He sees every born again believer in the body of Christ, as more than conquerors and overcomers. Praise God, as we read, hear, and do God's word, strongholds will be broken. Amen.

Every time we are freed from a stronghold of satan, we are to remain free in that area and move on to destroy other strongholds through the power of God in our lives. Amen! Galatians 5:1 tells us, "Stand fast therefore in the liberty wherewith Christ hath made us free, and be not entangled again with the yoke of bondage." In other words, once you are freed or receive the victory in a particular area, don't go back to that sin, don't open doors to allow the curse back on you. Don't allow the enemy in anyway to rope you and tie you up again with his strongholds, in Jesus' name! Amen!

A demon cannot possess a born again man because God indwells the spirits of his people; however, Christians can be oppressed. I Praise God, because the **Strongest Man (Christ Jesus)** indwells every born again believer; therefore, they can be delivered from being oppressed by demons. Hallelujah! A demon's first choice is to possess a person, but if he cannot possess an individual, he will try to oppress a person. A demonic spirit's next choice is to possess animals, and its last choice is to inhabit things or objects. God wants us to be as wise as serpents but as harmless as doves, Amen! In Luke 8:26-40, the word of God tells us that Jesus went into the country of the Gadarenes and that Jesus found a man that had many demons. When the man with the demons came into the presence of Jesus, a demon cried out, v/28 "What have I to do with thee Jesus, thou Son of God most high? I beseech thee, torment me not." Here we see that the demonic spirit that possessed that man immediately recognized Jesus and spoke through the man. The demons did not want to leave this man and be cast into the deep. They (the demons) besought Jesus that he would allow them to enter into the swine and Jesus allowed the demons to enter the swine, which were many. Luke 8:33 states: "Then went the devils (demons) out of the man and entered into the swine, and the herd ran violently down a steep place into the lake, and were choked." Although the swine died, the demons did not because they are eternally damned spirits. There were those that saw what happened. They saw how Jesus had cast the demons out and the man that was once possessed, was sitting at Jesus' feet in his right mind. Hallelujah! V/36, "They also which saw it told them by what means he that was **possessed** of the **devils** was healed."

While Jesus was on the earth, he was about the Father's business. I John 3:8 tells us, "For this purpose the Son of God was manifested, that he might destroy the works of the devil." We only need to look into the world around us to see the works of the devil. Nowhere do we see Jesus putting sickness, disease, poverty or any such thing on people. Instead Jesus does the opposite. He brings life and life more abundantly. Jesus clearly tells us in John 10:10, "The thief cometh not, but for to steal, and to kill, and to destroy: I am come that they might have **life** and that they might have it more abundantly." Amen!

In Luke 11:14-20, Jesus cast a dumb spirit out of a man and the man was able to speak. There were some that saw Jesus do this and accused him of casting out devils or demons by beelzebub or satan. Jesus told them in so many words that he cast them out by the finger of God and that the kingdom of God has come upon them. How sad that they did not recognize nor receive Jesus. Many that Jesus had been sent to refused him. When we minister, we must realize that there may be times when we may not be received, but we must continue to always walk in the love of Almighty God. Amen! In Luke 11: 24-26, Jesus said that when an unclean spirit is gone out of a man, "he walketh through dry places seeking rest and when the demon finds none, it returns to the body it left that has been swept, and garnished or **delivered**." **Deliverance** is a part of **Total Salvation**. This demon then takes seven spirits more wicked than himself and they enter into the man that was once delivered. The state of this man is worse than the first. After a person has been delivered it is so important to eat the whole word of God. Just as we feed our natural bodies, we must feed our spiritual man. As Christians consistently feed their spirits, there will be no room for demons to return to bind a child of God through oppression. Remember, a born again child of God can not be possessed, but oppression by demonic spirits is possible. Actually, it is more important to feast on God's word than on natural food. God's word is life, health, medicine and so much more if we'll eat it in faith. The man that Jesus spoke of in Luke 11: 24-26, obviously was not sitting at the feet of Jesus or in the word to maintain his victory in this area of **Total Salvation** (deliverance). The example that Jesus gave, shows you and I how important it is to hear, read, speak and do God's word consistently. Amen! Praise God for Jesus Christ, who is our **Victory** and **Total Salvation.**

When ministering deliverance, remember to use the keys of the kingdom of heaven which are binding and loosing. (Matthew 16:19) Christians have been given the authority to use the name which is above every name to bind the enemy in the name and in the power of the blood of Jesus Christ. Amen! (Revelation 12:11) **Jesus Christ is the Strongest Man** who has already spoiled and defeated the devil. Amen! Praise God! "Greater is He (**Jesus Christ**) in you than he (the devil and his demons) that is in the world." (I John 4:4) AMEN!

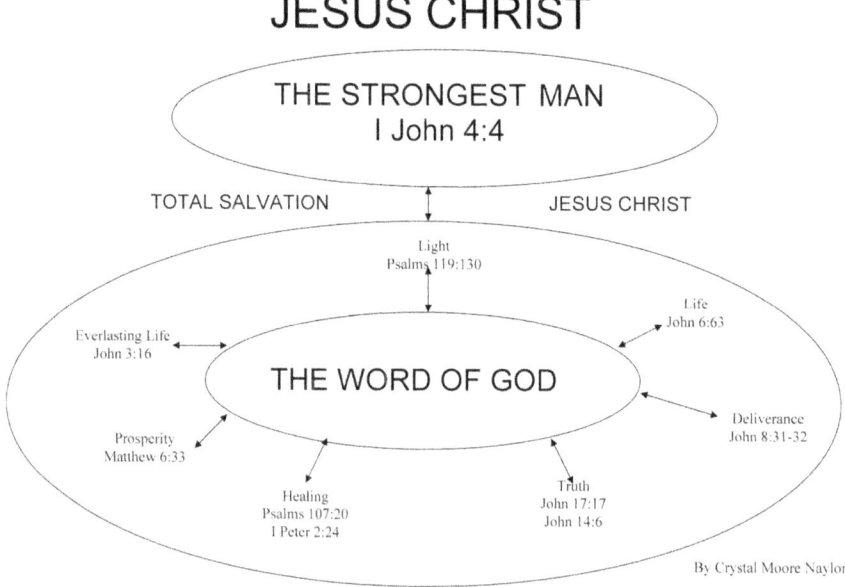

VICTORIOUS! GLORIOUS! CHURCH! ▪ 105

Some Strong Holds

The strongman or controlling demon and some manifestations
Only one demon can possess an unsaved person, but many can oppress a saved or unsaved person – (Mark 5:2-13)
It is important to stay filled with God's words, speak life, and obey God's word consistently – (Luke 11:24-26)

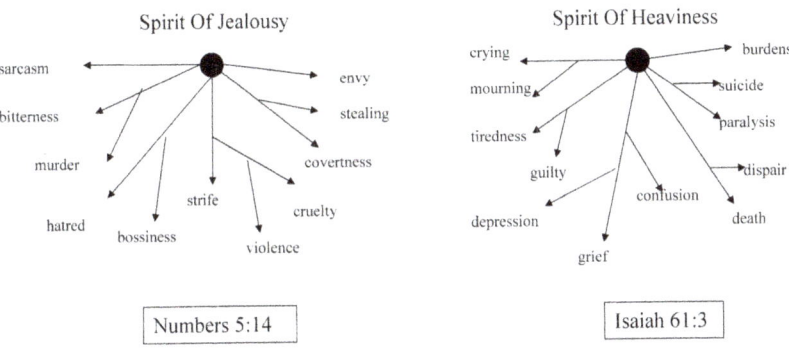

Some Strong Holds

The strongman or controlling demon and some manifestations
Only one demon can possess an unsaved person, but many can oppress a saved or unsaved person – (Mark 5:2-13)
It is important to stay filled with God's words, speak life, and obey God's word consistently – (Luke 11:24-26)

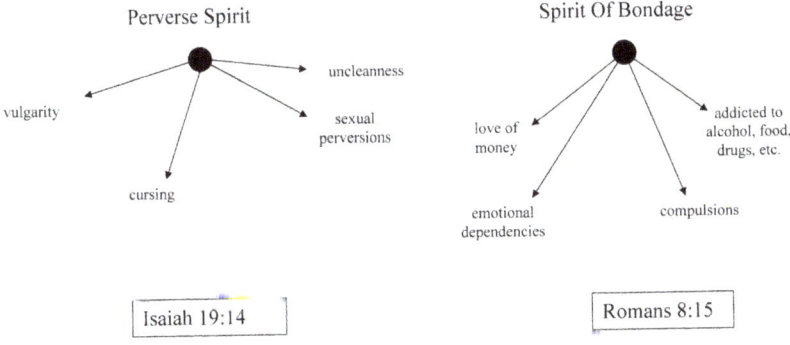

10

The Greatest Of All Is Love

JOHN 3:16 TELLS us, "For God so **loved** the **world**, that he gave his only begotten Son, that whosoever believeth in him should not perish, but have everlasting life." Praise the Lord for his love for us and all of mankind. I thank God for Jesus' obedience to pay the sin debt to redeem our souls. Amen! John 15:13 tells us that Jesus said, Greater love hath no man than this, that a man lay down his life for his friends. In v/14 Jesus said, "Ye are my friends, if ye do **whatsoever** I command you." Yes, Jesus loved you and I so much that he was crucified and arose from the dead so that whosoever accepts him as their Savior could have eternal life. Amen! Once a person receives the free love gift of becoming saved, he enters into the first and most important part of **Total Salvation**. We also receive a special assignment. Once we are born again or saved, we become ambassadors in this earth for the Lord. II Corinthians 5:17-21 tells us, "Therefore if any man be in Christ, he is a new creature: old things are passed away; behold all things are become new. v/18 And all things are of God, who hath reconciled us to himself by Jesus Christ, and hath given to us the ministry of reconciliation; v/19 To wit, that God was in Christ, reconciling the world unto himself, not imputing their trespasses unto them; and hath committed unto us the word of reconciliation. v/20 Now then, <u>**we are ambassadors for Christ,**</u> as though God did beseech you by us, we pray you in Christ's stead, be ye reconciled to God. v/21 For he hath made him to be sin for us, who knew no sin; that we might be made the righteousness of God in him." Hallelujah!

What a great honor and privilege to be commissioned by God himself to be his ambassador in the earth. This is one reason it is so important to seek to have a very intimate and personal relationship with Almighty God. As we do, we are seeking to know him, and not seeking what we can get from him. It compares to a child who gives us a hug or a kiss just because they love us; that blesses us. There are some children that will only hug or kiss their parent because they want something. God wants us to love him from a pure heart for who he is to us. It's not for what we can get, but because we love him. If our hearts are pure, we will want to know him and be like him. Yes, it's a gradual, ongoing process that as the relationship builds and God's people yield more and more to him, their needs and desires will change. This will become more and more evident in Christians' lives who become more intimate with the Lord on a daily basis. Matthew 6:33 tells us, "But seek ye first the kingdom of God, and his righteousness, and all these things shall be added unto you." As believers put God and his word first place consistently in their lives, they will become more and more like Jesus and the things that they will have a need of, as God sees fit, will be added unto them. Praise the Lord!

As God's ambassadors, we should always be **FVIP** people, people of **F**aith, **V**ision, **I**ntegrity, and **P**ure Hearts. We should begin to talk, look, act and even begin to think like God. As we do, we will begin to lay down our lives for one another in the body of Christ as well as those that are not saved as God directs us. We will begin to see each individual as a soul that has been created by Almighty God and therefore very important to him. People will become more important to us as we enter new levels of **walking in love**. We will become more compassionate and not just think about ourselves but also think about those around us. Our sphere of vision will increase as we see the world as a field of souls; a field of souls that are unsaved who need Jesus, even if they don't realize it yet. We will see souls that have accepted Jesus Christ as their Savior but they are not on fire for God. We will see souls that are lukewarm or backslidden. Matthew 7:13-14 tells us, "Enter ye in at the strait gate: for wide is the gate, and broad is the way, that leadeth to destruction, and many there be which go in thereat; v/14 Because strait is the gate, and narrow is the way, which leadeth unto life, and few there be that find it." As ambassadors of reconciliation, we are to take the message to the backsliders that they have been reconciled to God and that he loves them but that he expects and even demands that his people live a life style of holiness. I Peter 1:15-16 says, "But as he which hath called you is holy, so be ye holy in all manner of conversation; v/16 Because it is written, Be ye holy; for I am holy." Hebrews 12:14 says, "Follow peace with all men, and holiness without which no man shall see the Lord." As believers, we must choose to live our lives unto God through his power. God will enable us to be holy. We will be different from the world, so that many in the world will be drawn to Jesus, and enter the narrow gate that leads to eternal life. Amen! Jesus said in John 15:14, "Ye are my friends if ye do whatsoever I command you." In John 14:23, Jesus said "If a man love me, he will keep my words." No, we can't live holy in our own strength, but through the power of the Holy Spirit in us as we choose to yield to God we can live holy. He is the one who will help us walk in victory and walk in love. Amen!

When we are truly in love with someone, we want to make that person happy in this natural realm. The same is true when our relationship is right with Almighty God. We will not want to deliberately disobey him by not obeying the whole Word of God nor will we want to unintentionally miss God either. Why? Because he is number one in our lives; therefore, what his Word says is important to us because we recognize his Word as God himself speaking to us. We realize this regardless of how it comes to us, whether it's through our reading the word for ourselves (and we should daily) or by an anointed man or woman of God that's preaching and teaching the word Amen! Therefore, when we receive God's word, we will be quick to act on it and do it because we want to make God happy and because it's life to us. We know that it has the power to conform us into the image of Jesus Christ. This should be very important for every born again person that has been commissioned as ambassadors in this earth.

As we become more like Jesus, spiritual things will become more important to us than the physical, because we realize that this place is not our true home. We realize more and more that heaven is where our home is and our passport is Jesus Christ. Our focus will be on

people. Although everything one day will perish, souls are eternal and everyone will either spend eternity with God in heaven or be eternally dammed to hell and finally to the lake of fire. That's why we must begin to focus on the eternal things, realizing that the greatest of all is **LOVE, JESUS,** who is our hope of glory. As God's ambassadors, he's depending on his body of believers to realize that the fields are white and ready to harvest. Christians must realize that we are God's hands, feet, mouths, we are his body in the earth. God desires that his body share the good news that man has already been reconciled to Father God through the precious shed blood of Jesus. As co-laborers of God, one sows the seed, another waters, but only God can give the increase (I Corinthians 3:6-7).

God's word tells us that the harvest is "plentiful but the laborers are few." Therefore, we should pray to the Lord of the harvest that he may send forth laborers into his harvest, (Matthew 9:38). The greatest of all is <u>love</u>. Jesus loved us so much that he laid down his life for us. If we love Jesus, we will certainly care about what he cares about. Jesus desires that his people be his ambassadors for him in this earth. Amen! We <u>must</u> have a <u>heart</u> of <u>compassion</u> and a deeper love for <u>souls</u>. We must not be so caught up with this world that we don't see further than the issues facing us. We must be **FVIPs,** people of **faith**, **vision**, **integrity** and **pure hearts** that will enter into higher levels of **Total Salvation**, who is **Jesus**. Amen!

God's desire is that we have a willing and obedient heart, then he can use us. In John 21, after Jesus' resurrection, the disciples went back to fishing. They fished all night and caught nothing. Jesus told them to cast their nets on the right side of the ship and they would find fish. The disciples were obedient and they caught so many fish that they were not able to draw the net for the multitude of fish. Jesus desires that his people let down the net to catch many, as well as catch fish one by one, to win souls for the kingdom of God. As we do, we must allow the unsaved to see what Jesus looks like. He is Love. As we lay down our lives in obedience to God, we demonstrate that The Greatest Of All Is Love.

Throughout the word of God, we see Jesus as King, Apostle, Prophet, Priest, Evangelist, Teacher, Shepherd and more. He is also seen as a servant as he continuously ministered to the needs of others. Jesus told his disciples in Matthew 23:11, "But he that is greatest among you shall be your servant." Even after Jesus' resurrection, we see him preparing a meal for the disciples who had fished all night. After the disciples dined with Jesus, Jesus asked Simon Peter if he loved him more than the others. Peter answered, "Yea Lord, thou knowest that I love thee." Jesus told Peter, "Feed <u>my lambs.</u>" (John 21:15). Jesus asked Peter a second time if he loved him. Peter answered, "Yea Lord, thou knowest I love thee." Jesus told Peter, "Feed <u>my sheep."</u> In V/17 Jesus asked Peter a third time if Peter loved him, this time Peter was grieved and answered, "Lord thou knoweth all things; thou knowest that I love thee", Jesus said unto him, "Feed <u>my sheep."</u>

Jesus is asking each member of his body, do we love him? Do we love him more than pride, more than food, more than our spouse or our children, more than money or a job? Do we love him more than life? Are you willing to lay down your life for Jesus to demonstrate that the greatest of all is Love? Is our love for God, to do his will, above our own? Do we have love for members of the body of Christ that may have hurt us or that are hurt? Do we have enough love to share Jesus with the unsaved that need Jesus? **The Greatest Of All Is LOVE!** Will you demonstrate your love for Almighty God, both today and until he takes you home?

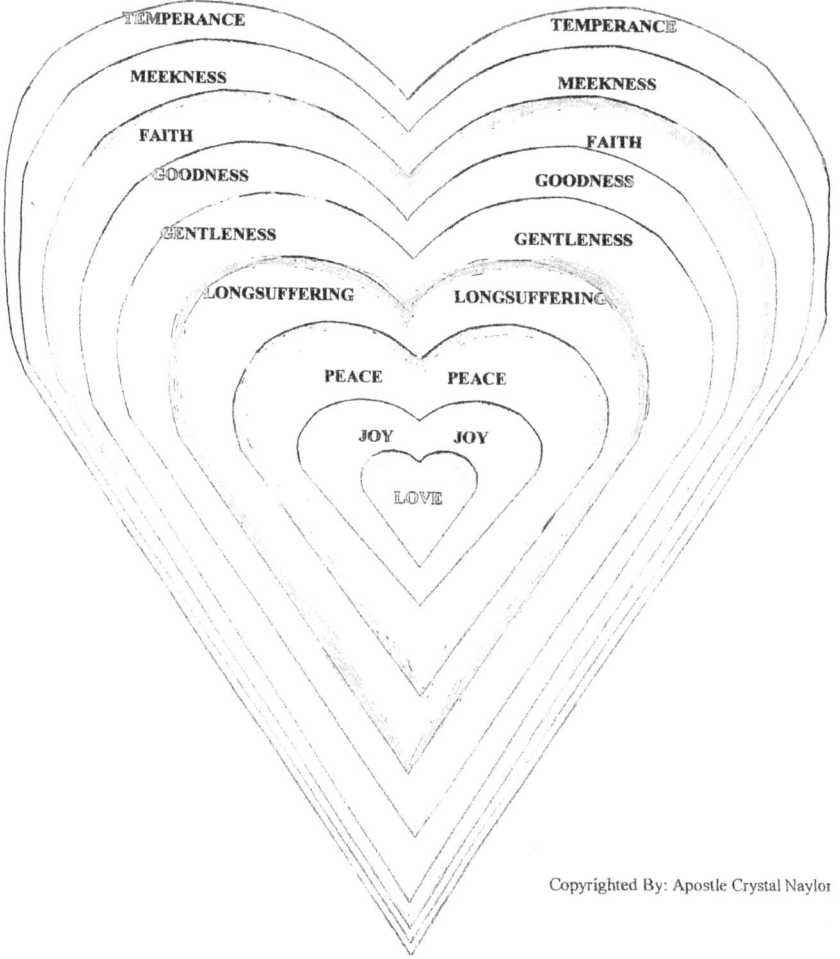

Intimacy With God

<u>Galatians 5:16</u> - This I say then, Walk in the Spirit, and ye shall not fulfil the lust of the flesh.

Fruit Of The Spirit	Flesh
Love	Hate
Joy	Sadness, Defeated
Peace	Confusion
Longsuffering, Patience	Impatient
Gentleness, Kindness	Rude, Harsh, Mean
Goodness	Badness, Wickedness, Evil
Faith	Doubt, Unbelief, Fear, Negative
Meekness, Humility	Pride, Boastful, Unteachable
Temperance, Self Control	Lack of Self Control, No Restraints

<u>Galatians 5:25</u> - If we live in the Spirit, let us also walk in the Spirit.

> **The more intimate a believer is with God,
> the more easily the fruit of the Spirit
> are manifest in that believer's life**

<u>Romans 8:1</u> - There is therefore now no condemnation to them which are in Christ Jesus, who walk not after the flesh, but after the Spirit.

11

See My Glory - See Me

PRAISE THE LORD! Indeed if we are able to see God's glory, then indeed we have seen Jesus. The word of God speaks of the glory of God or God's glory in both the Old and the New Testaments.

In the Old Testament, one of the words for glory is kabod that refers to the presence of God. It means glorious, splendor, honor and glory. In the New Testament one of the words for glory is the word doxa. It is defined as dignity, honor, praise, worship or glory. Throughout God's word, we see the presence of God referred to as the glory of God.

I believe that Adam and Eve were clothed with the glory of God which comes from the inside out and can be seen at times upon God's people today who have a committed and personal relationship with Almighty God. In Genesis 2:25, the word of God says, "And they were both naked the man and his wife, and were not ashamed." Adam and Eve were in perfect fellowship with God and spent time in his presence daily as he came down to talk with them. Adam and Eve certainly had to be covered with God's glory. We know that once they disobeyed God, their eyes were opened and they knew they were naked, and they were ashamed. When sin came into their lives their fellowship with God was broken and much of God's glory departed from them.

In Exodus 34:29-35, Moses had gone up to Mount Sinai a second time to get the commandments from God because he had broken the first set in reaction to the Israelites' disobedience. God's word tells us that Moses' face shone with the glory of God from being in his presence. The people were afraid to look on Moses or to come near him. Moses had to cover his face with a veil in order to speak to the people because of the glory of God that shined on his face

God used Moses in a mighty way. He was a prophet of God as well as a shepherd or pastor of God's people, the Israelites. God used Moses to bring the Hebrew people out of Egypt, and he gave Moses the pattern of the tabernacle. Everything concerning the tabernacle had to be made according to God's plans.

In the Old Testament, there are many types and shadows that pointed to Jesus. The tabernacle and its furniture also pointed to Jesus, including the ark where the glory of the Lord rested. God manifested his presence in the Old Testament as a pillar of fire and as a cloud. Exodus 13:21 says, "The Lord went before them by day in a pillar of a cloud, to lead them in the way; and by night in a pillar of fire, to give them light; to go by day and night: V/22, He took not away the pillar of the cloud by day, nor the pillar of fire by night, from before the people." When the glory cloud stopped moving, the Israelites would stop and make camp, at which time the priests would erect the tabernacle in a courtyard that measured seventy-five feet in width and one hundred fifty feet in length. Around the outside of the courtyard, a linen fence was put up on sixty posts that were seven and a half feet in height. At the eastern end of the courtyard, there was a gate that measured thirty feet wide that the priest and Levites passed through. In Exodus 25:1-8, we see that the Lord called his people to make an offering willingly to be used to build God's sanctuary. V/8, "And let them make me a sanctuary that I may dwell among them." Today, Jesus dwells inside of every born again Christian in the person of the Holy Spirit. God's word says in Romans 8:9, "But ye are not in the flesh, but in the Spirit, if so be that the Spirit of God dwells in you. Now if any man have not the Spirit of Christ, he is none of his." Praise God! We who are born again are truly blessed because God himself, in the third person of the Trinity, dwells in us. To God Be The Glory! Amen! Every born again believer has the **glory** of **God** inside of them, Amen! To some, this truth may be a revelation, but God wants his people to realize just how very important each of us is to him. Believers are so important that God has blessed us with placing himself inside of us. He wants Christians to realize and appreciate this great honor. Amen! Indeed, it is a privilege, and an honor to be the tabernacles of the Lord. Tabernacle means dwelling place. As God's mobile tabernacles, we must die daily. The Old Testament tabernacle pointed to the New Testament tabernacle, the body of Christ today. Even as Abraham willingly offered up Isaac, his only promised son, we too must be willing to lay down our lives. It's not that we must die physically, but we must allow those weights, those sins, that would try to beset us to die. We must allow God to daily do a vital work in our lives to change us more into his likeness, his <u>glory</u>. As we do, we will become <u>living sacrifices</u> to God that are pleasing and acceptable to him. As we willingly go to the altar repenting of sins, more of Jesus will arise in us. As we walk in love, more of God's glory will be seen in our lives

On the outside of the tabernacle was the brazen altar where animals were slain and offered up to God on behalf of the priest and the twelve tribes of Israel that is believed to have numbered into the millions. There was also a laver that was filled with water which was used by the priests for cleaning before they entered into the holy place inside the tabernacle, the inner court. Praise God, this lets us know that as Christians we are cleansed by the holy word of God. Ephesians 5:25-26 tells us that "Christ also loved the church and gave himself for it. That he might sanctify and cleanse it with the washing of water by the word." God's word is many times referred to as water. As we consistently read, meditate, memorize and study God's word, it washes us. We need to be washed daily.

In the Holy Place, there were three items. The **Golden Lampstand** was located on the south side of the Holy Place and was made of beaten gold with a central stem and six other stems or branches that extended from the base of the lampstand. Oil had to be poured into it which was a symbol of the Holy Spirit and then it was lit by the priest to provide light in the tabernacle. Praise God, when light comes, darkness leaves. Psalms 119:105 says, "Thy word is a lamp unto my feet and a light unto my path." John 1:4 says, "In him (Jesus) was life and the life was the light of men." We know Jesus is the Light, but in Matthew 5:14, Jesus calls his people the light of the world, and indeed we are when we allow his glory, Jesus' light, to shine forth through us. Psalms 119:130 says, "The entrance of thy words giveth light; it giveth understanding unto the simple." As the light from the golden lampstand provided light in the tabernacle, God in us provides light for others.

In the tabernacle on the north side of the Holy Place was the **Table of Shewbread.** It was made of acacia wood overlaid with gold. On the table were twelve loaves of bread representing the twelve tribes of Israel. This also pointed to Jesus. Jesus said "I am the living bread which came down from heaven: if any man eat of this bread, he shall live forever: and the bread that I will give is my flesh, which I will give for the life of the world" (John 6:51). In John 6:35, Jesus said "I am the bread of life: he that cometh to me shall never hunger; and he that believeth on me shall never thirst." In the Old Testament, only the priests were allowed to eat the showbread which pointed to Jesus Christ, the Lamb of God. Praise God, today every believer is allowed and commanded to eat the Lamb who is Jesus Christ, the Living Word, and our Bread of Life. As the people of the Lord regularly eat the bread at the Passover meal (Holy Communion meal) in remembrance of Jesus, this symbolizes Jesus' body, which was broken for them. Also as God's people feed their spirits on the word of God consistently, they can receive health and healing.

In front of the veil that separated the Holy Place from the Most Holy Place or Holy of Holiest was the **Altar of Incense.** It was made of shittem wood and was overlaid with pure gold. Incense was placed upon this altar by the priest. This incense pointed to Jesus who is a sweet smelling savor to Father God. It also pointed to the body of Christ. As we obey God's whole word and follow God as dear children and walk in love, we too become a sweet smelling savor unto Almighty God. As we minister to others, both saved and unsaved, in love with a pure heart, the glory of the Lord is revealed through us to others, and our lives permeate with a sweet smell. As we walk in love, we point others to Jesus and bring the fragrance of Jesus into the lives of others. Ephesians 5:1-2 states, "**Be ye therefore followers of**

God as dear children: And walk in love, as Christ also hath loved us, and hath given himself for us an offering and a sacrifice to God for a sweet smelling savor." I believe that the altar of incense also points to the prayers of the saints that rise up to God. Amen!

The **Veil** was the curtain that separated the Most Holy Place, where the presence of God rested over the mercy seat. The high priest was only allowed to enter into the Most Holy Place behind the veil once a year to make atonement for his sins and those of the Israelites. Before the high priest could enter, he had to first be prepared according to God's command to him. If he tried to enter without doing it God's way, he was slain. Praise God, today there is no longer a veil between man and God. We can come to Father God in prayer because of the precious blood of Jesus Christ! We, like the priest, cannot come into the presence of Father God any kind of way. Only when we repent of our sins and appropriate the precious blood of Jesus, can we "come boldly before the throne of grace, that we may obtain mercy, and find grace to help in time of need." (Hebrews 4:16) Praise God, when Jesus was crucified on Calvary's cross, the veil in the temple was torn from top to bottom, letting us know that the wall of partition between God and man had been done away with because of Jesus, who reconciled us to God the Father through his precious shed blood. Amen! Hallelujah! (Ephesians 2:12-18).

Behind the veil was the Ark of the testimony that housed Aaron's rod that budded, the golden pot of manna, and the tablet of the commandments given to Moses by God. Over the ark of the testimony was the **Mercy Seat** of pure gold. Two cherubims of gold were made and placed at each end of the mercy seat (Exodus 25:17-21). Above the mercy seat, the presence of God dwelled. The ark pointed to Jesus, who is our ark of the covenant. "For all the promises of God in him are yea, and in him, Amen, unto the glory of God by us." (II Corinthians 1:20) To God Be the Glory! Amen! So let each of us that are members of the body of Jesus Christ, continually yield ourselves to Almighty God. Let us consistently walk in love so that the glory of God may be revealed in our lives and flow through each of us as never before, so that God will be glorified in Jesus' name. Amen!

12

Total Salvation – Jesus – God's Will Fulfilled

Includes Glorified Bodies Given At The Rapture

INDEED OUR GOD is awesome. Father God is bigger than infinity plus infinity times infinity to the mega plus power; plus whatever is bigger than that we know or don't know, Amen! Praise God! Father God is Daddy, to those who are born again of the Spirit of Almighty God.

Almighty God wants every born again believer to know the truth of how big he is so that when problems, trials, times of test and temptations arise, we will realize and recognize that he is our Mighty God and that **with God <u>all</u> things are possible,** if we only believe. Father God also wants his children to not only realize who he is but also who his son Jesus Christ is, as well as the Holy Ghost. Father God, Jesus, and the Holy Spirit are all God; but each has a different role or function. **God the Father** is the **Administrator**; **God the Son, Jesus Christ** was sent as his **Ambassador**; and **God the Holy Spirit** is the **Anointing** that gives the believer the unction to function.

To state it another way, **Father God** is the **Visionary**; **Jesus** is the **Victory** (and because of Jesus the believer is the victor today whether they realize it or not); and the **Holy Spirit** is the **Velocity and power**. The Holy Spirit gives us what we need to get the job that we are called by God to do, completed. Or we can say that **Father God** is the

Director; **Jesus** is the **Designer;** and the **Holy Spirit** is the **Developer**. As we yield to the plans of the **Director**, (**Father God**) for our lives, the **Designer** (who is **Jesus**) will cause us to be conformed into his image as we yield to him by the power of the **Holy Spirit** (who is the **Developer**). The Holy Spirit dwells in every believer. In Colossians 1:26-27, the word says, "Even the mystery which hath been hid from ages and from generations, but now is made manifest to his saints: To whom God would make known what is the riches of the glory of his mystery among the Gentiles; which is **Christ in you the hope of glory."** Romans 8:11 tells us, "But if the Spirit of him that raised up Jesus from the dead dwell in you, he that raised up Christ from the dead shall quicken your mortal bodies by his Spirit that dwelleth in you." Praise God! God the Holy Spirit lives inside of every born again believer! The Holy Spirit is the one that quickens (meaning to make alive, give life). He made Jesus Christ's mortal body become immortal and eternally alive from the dead. Amen! Romans 8:11 tells us that the very same Spirit that quickened or made Jesus Christ's body arise from the dead will quicken the mortal bodies of believers. God the Holy Spirit, who is the third person of the Trinity, receives directions from Jesus, who receives directions or commands from Father God and the Holy Spirit does it. **God** the **Holy Spirit** is the **Anointing**; he is the **Developer** and he is the **Velocity** in the life of the believer. Amen! I Corinthians 15:51-53 says, "Behold I shew you a mystery, we shall not all sleep, but we shall be changed, in a moment, in a twinkling of an eye, at the last trump, for the trumpet shall sound, and the dead shall be raised incorruptible, and we shall be changed. For this corruptible must put on incorruption, and this mortal must put on immortality." Jesus Christ through the quickening **power** (the **Dunamis** – the Greek word for miracle working power of the Holy Ghost or Holy Spirit) was resurrected with an immortal body. At the time of the Rapture, every saint who has died whose spirit has gone to heaven will one day come with Jesus in the air to receive their glorified resurrected immortal bodies from the grave. Praise God, we who remain that are alive shall be raptured or caught up to meet the Lord in the air, and we too shall by the dunamis power of God, have our mortal bodies changed to glorified immortal bodies like Jesus Christ. Amen! To God Be The Glory!

I Thessalonians 5:9 tells us, "For God hath not appointed us to wrath, but to obtain salvation by our Lord Jesus Christ." **Jesus** is our **Total Salvation**. In **Jesus** we have everything. Amen! Once a person enters the first level of salvation, which is accepting Jesus as their Savior, this opens the door to receive so many other levels of salvation from **the Lord.** We must always remember that the greatest gift and miracle of all is that of becoming saved which occurs when one accepts Jesus Christ as their Savior! Amen! One day so very, very, very, very soon, God's will, will be fulfilled; and believers that have continued to do God's word and walk consistently in love will be raptured from this earth. Amen! I Thessalonians 5:8 tells us, "But let us, who are of the day, be sober, putting on the **breastplate** of **faith**, and **love**; and for a **helmet**, the **hope** of **salvation."** Christians should be looking forward to the appearing of our Lord Jesus who is our very, very, very, very Soon Coming King. Amen! The word rapture does not appear in the bible, but the words "caught up" do appear. Praise God for that day! Hallelujah! God's will is being fulfilled! And will be fulfilled when God's people who are like the five wise virgins are raptured or caught up to meet the Lord Jesus Christ in the air. The rapture is another part of **Total Salvation.** At the time of the **Rapture**, salvation of these mortal bodies will take place. I Corinthians 15:54-57 tells us, "So when this corruptible puts on incorruption and this mortal shall have put on immortality, then shall be brought to pass the saying that is written, Death is swallowed up in victory. O death, where is thy sting? O grave, where is thy victory? The sting of death is sin; and the strength of sin is the law; But thanks be to God which giveth us the victory through our Lord Jesus Christ." Amen.

The mystery indeed has been revealed, Christ in us, the hope of glory. The same Spirit that raised Christ from the dead shall quicken the bodies of God's born again sons, and daughters, **Jesus Christ's Victorious! Glorious! Church!** The Lord himself shall descend from heaven with a shout, with the voice of the archangel, and with the trump of God: and the dead in Christ shall rise first: "Then we which are alive and remain shall be caught up together with them in the clouds to meet the Lord in the air: so shall we ever be with the Lord." (I Thessalonians 4:17) Praise God! To God Be The Glory! Amen!

13

Come And Dine

"**THIS IS THE** day that the Lord has made; we are rejoicing and glad in it." Amen! To God Be The Glory! God is calling his body as never before to display his glory in the earth, to manifest who he is. Amen! In order for us to come forth and show forth the glory of God, in order for us to fulfill God's victorious, glorious destiny for our lives, we must **come and dine**. The call is "**come and dine**", to feast spiritually on the word of God, which is more necessary now than ever before.

God has called his people to be his reflections in the earth. We who are his born again children are to reflect what our Daddy looks like. When we have our relationship right with Almighty God, we realize that he is our Daddy God. Even if you don't have a relationship with your physical father, once you become born again, you have a spiritual Daddy, who is Almighty God. Your heavenly Father is greater than any earthly daddy could ever be. Praise God! No matter how good your earthly daddy is, no matter what he does, he will never be able to compare to our Daddy God, Almighty God. Praise the Lord! Almighty God wants us to know who we are spiritually, and who he is. He is the Creator of everything seen and unseen. Praise God! He also wants us to realize who our elder brother is. Jesus Christ is the second person of the Godhead who is our Savior, our Elder Brother, and our Total Salvation. It is also time for Christians to realize to whom we belong. Praise God! Jesus is our Savior. He is the one who paid the price for us, to redeem us from the curse of the broken law, to redeem us from eternal damnation and hell. Jesus paid that price, Praise God, and there is no way we can come to the Father except by Jesus Christ. When Jesus went back to heaven, he sent us the Holy Ghost, who is the Comforter. Jesus said "And I will pray the Father and he shall give you another Comforter, that he may abide with you forever" (John 14:16). Praise God! The Holy Spirit is the one that comes along side of us to help us, to lead us, to empower us, to guide us and to direct us in all truths. He is the one who comes and indwells every individual that accepts Jesus as their Savior. Praise God, we are blessed when we become the born again children of God. So it's time as never before for the people of God to realize who they are in Christ Jesus. It is also important to realize that the greater one dwells in we who are born again, in the person of the Holy Spirit. It is time to realize whose we are. We belong to God. Think about it, we belong to God Almighty, Hallelujah! We belong to Elohim, God the Father, God the Son and God the Holy Spirit. Praise God! The Lord wants his people to receive his glory because he's pouring out his glory as well as his fire. Praise God!

The glory of God is for us to be able to go and do his great and mighty exploits and to show who he is in the earth, and to reflect him. The fire of God is coming to bring forth a cleansing in the people of God. In order for that cleansing to take place, we must yield to God. We each must decide to yield to God and say, "Yes, Lord, I want to be fit for your use." Almighty God wants us to walk in the fear of God and in the love of God. When we walk in the fear of the Lord, and in the love of God, it is then that we will not want to sin and we will begin to sin less and less. We will do this because we will want to please our Daddy God. Think about an earthly daddy whom you love. Don't you want to please him because you love him? When I think about when our grandchildren visit us, they want to do things for their granddad, and I. We realize that they do it out of a heart of love, and I am sure that they do the same thing for their dad and mother out of a heart of love. The same is true for Christians that are yielded to God, we are eager to demonstrate our love for our Daddy God in various ways. We love God and we fear him, therefore we are not going to do things to displease him deliberately. We obey God out of holy fear and because we love him, Hallelujah! The word of God tells us in Psalm 111:10, "The fear of the Lord is the beginning of wisdom and a good understanding have all they that do his commandments." It is imperative that Christians have a reverential fear of God. If you don't have a fear of God, you need to pray and ask God to give you a deep fear of him. Having a holy fear of God does not mean that you are afraid of God. He wants us to come boldly before him. He wants us to realize that he is our Daddy, that he is our Creator, and that he loves and cares about everything that concerns his family, and yes he is the Righteous Judge. Praise God, he does judge sin. He is a jealous God, but he is also a God of love. Praise God! We don't have to be afraid of him. When we develop that personal intimate relationship, we will know the importance of how much he loves us and we will begin to love him more deeply and on a higher level. In Matthew 22:35-40, a lawyer asked Jesus, "What is the greatest commandment? Jesus replied, "Thou shalt love the Lord thy God with all thy heart, with all thy soul and with all thy mind." This is the first and greatest commandment. And the second is like unto it, "Thou shalt love thy neighbor as thyself." Then he goes on and tells them that "on these two hang all the laws and the prophets." So Jesus is stating that the most important thing is to love God. How many will say today, "Oh, I love God." I am sure that most people, who are born again children of God, will say I love God. Some in the body of Christ proclaim to love God, however they won't do his commands, they will not obey him. The word of God tells us in John 14:23, "If a man loves me he will keep my words." If we truly love God, we are going to do what he tells us to do, even though it might mean sacrificing something the flesh wants to do. If it is against the word of God or against the will of God, we need to let that thing go. Amen! As we **come and dine** regularly on God's word, it helps us to obey God's commands.

    We are God's ambassadors. He has already ordained that every born again child be an ambassador in this earth. What does an ambassador do? An ambassador represents his country. We are to represent heaven. An ambassador represents the leader of his nation. We are to represent God. He is our Leader. In order for us to effectively represent Almighty God, the first thing we must do is to **come and dine**.

What God is calling us to is better than any meal you can get at a restaurant or any meal that you can cook. It's not a physical meal. It is a spiritual meal. We must feast on the word of God. We must daily sit at the feet of Jesus. We must daily eat of his holy word. We must stay attached to Jesus. It is critical, as never before, that we stay attached to Jesus Christ. The word of God tells us in John 15:1-2 that Jesus said: "I am the true vine and my Father is the husbandman. Every branch in me that beareth not fruit he taketh away: and every branch that beareth fruit he purgeth it, that it may bring forth more fruit." When we are attached to Jesus, we shouldn't let anything come to separate us from the True Vine, who is Jesus Christ, Praise the Lord. John 15:3-4 says, "Now ye are clean, through the word which I have spoken unto you. Abide in me; and I in you. As the branch cannot bear fruit of itself except it abide in the vine; no more can ye, except ye abide in me." In the natural, when a branch is severed from the tree that it was once attached to, the branch will begin to shrivel up, and the leaves will begin to turn brown. The evidence, of the death that took place at the time the branch was separated from the tree, is not immediately seen. However, the death of the branch took place immediately when it was severed from the tree. So too, it is with anyone that does not remain attached to Jesus. We can't afford to be separated from him. Praise God, for we need to stay attached to Jesus Christ, the True Vine, so that we can bring forth much good fruit. As we stay attached to him, Praise God, we need to **come and dine** consistently on the word of God, so that we can continue to grow spiritually and bear much good fruit in our lives, Praise God!

Just like a fruit tree cannot bear fruit if it is not taken care of properly, the same thing is true for the born again children of God. This is why we must consistently dine on God's words. If you don't take care of a tree; by fertilizing it, watering it, pruning it and keeping it in the correct environment, it will eventually die. Like wise, God's people must stay attached to Jesus Christ who is the True Vine, and stay in his word so that spiritual separation or spiritual death will never take place. When we **come and dine**, to feast on the word of God, we are built up. It is then that we come to know who we are and whose we are in Christ Jesus. Praise God! It is then that we come to realize that we have purpose on this earth where God has placed us, which is to be about the Father's business. We must dine and stay attached to the True Vine, and feast on the word of God, to blossom and bear much good fruit. When Jesus called his disciples, they all were doing various things. When each of them stopped what they were doing to follow Jesus, it was then that they began to grow spiritually. It was when they answered the call to **come and dine** that the disciples were blessed and fulfilled. It was when they answered the call of Jesus. It was not until they stayed with him, watched him, followed him, and listened to him that they were actually dining at the feet of Jesus. As the disciples came and dined; they were being built up. They were being taught so they would know what to do when they would go to minister, Praise God! Hallelujah! Jesus was their teacher. The disciples saw Jesus healing, they heard him teaching and they saw him casting out demons. They were dining and sitting at the feet of Jesus which caused them to grow spiritually as they remained attached to the True Vine, Jesus Christ.

The same thing is true for Christians today, as each one gets into the word of God with a teachable spirit, spiritual growth will occur and the Christian will begin to bear good fruit. Today we have the bible, God's written word, that we can dine and feast on. When we look into the word of God, we are sitting at the feet of Jesus. We are seeing what Jesus is speaking to us. Through the word of God, we grow up spiritually. Through the word of God we are cleansed, we are purified. Through the word of God, we learn what God's word commands us to do. Each person must choose to obey the word of God. Praise God! The anointing of God can be increased as we **come and dine** on the word of God, and are consistently doers of the word of God.

David knew about dining at the Lord's table. In Psalms 23, he said "Thou preparest a table before me in the presence of mine enemies." David knew his God in a very intimate way. He was a worshipper. He danced before God. He sang and wrote songs to God out of a heart of love. David was able to say that the Lord preparest a table before me in the presence of mine enemies. The reason he was able to say that was because he had a personal relationship with his God. That's why even as a little shepherd boy, he was able to slay the giant with only a sling shot and stone. Knowing your God comes from spending time with him. It comes from consistently dining with him. It comes from sitting at his feet to be fed by God and to hear from him. David knew that God was his Total Salvation. At God's table, there is his wisdom, his joy, his peace, his grace, his love and much more to partake of. God has a table prepared for you, so why not **come and dine**. Each person decides whether they will eat or not eat, or how much they want to eat. God does not give you junk, he doesn't give garbage, nor does he give warmed over food to eat. Almighty God gives his people his best, which are his words of Spirit and Life.

Because David knew his God, he knew his ways. Therefore, when the enemy showed up, he knew God had a table prepared before him. If the enemy of sickness and disease come, we can say, "Lord, I thank you, that you are my Healer." We can say to the sickness and disease, "No you don't, I bind you satan and I bind you sickness and disease, in Jesus' name; and I command you to loose me and go in the name of Jesus Christ." Hallelujah! Jehovah Raphah has already paid the price as I Peter 2:24 says, "Who his own self bare our sins in his own body on the tree, that we, being dead to sins, should live unto righteousness: **by whose stripes ye were healed."** If you were healed, you are the healed of God. Hallelujah! Isaiah 53:5 says, "But he was wounded for our transgressions, he was bruised for our iniquities: the chastisement of our peace was upon him; and **with his stripes ye are healed."** Isaiah prophesied hundreds of years before Jesus' birth, that we are already healed. Praise the Lord! In I Peter 2:24, Peter was looking back at the cross when he said, **" with his stripes ye were healed."** So we must let that enemy of sickness and disease know. "Yes Jesus has already paid the price." The table that is prepared before God's people is healing and health. Therefore, we put the enemy of sickness and disease on the run in the name and the power of the blood of Jesus Christ. As we speak his words, we are using the sword of the Spirit. Amen!

If the enemy of lack comes up, we can say, "Lord I thank you that I am prosperous, and I say to lack that God is my Provider. I thank you that you supply my every need according to your word." In Philippians 4:19, you declare, "But my God shall supply all your needs according to his riches in glory by Christ Jesus." "So Lord I thank you that you are my Provider, that you are Jehovah - Jireh. I thank you Lord that my needs are met. Praise the Lord!"

If the enemy of heaviness or a depression spirit tries to bring sorrow to make you feel down-hearted and cast down, you can say, "I thank the Lord that the word of God has been prepared on the table of Philippians 4:4." The word of God says there, "Rejoice in the Lord always: and again I say, Rejoice." And therefore because I rejoice, the joy of the Lord is my strength according to Nehemiah 8:10. Why? Because you have come and dined on the word of God; and you have used the sword of the Spirit, which is the word of God against your enemies of heaviness or depression. Therefore, the Lord has prepared a table before you in the presence of your enemies. Hallelujah! As we eat God's word, we are able to put the enemy on the run with the word of God. This is why it is so important for you to go to church regularly and sit under the word of God. Hebrews 10:25 says, we must **come and dine** in the house of God especially where the whole word goes forth. It says "Not forsaking the assembling of ourselves together, as the manner of some is; but exhorting one another: and so much the more, as ye see the day approaching." Praise God! You need a church where you will receive the good nourishing word of God, a church where you don't get dessert all the time. Many times children want candy, candy, candy. They can't wait to get to dessert. They only want sweets. But to grow, Christians need balanced meals. Each needs to come and feast, and sit under the anointed word that the Shepherd has prepared for them. Praise God! Then you decide, "Well am I going to believe, am I going to receive, am I going to act on this word?" God desires that you believe, that you receive and that you act on his word. As you do, you become more and more anointed to get the job done that God has ordained. Praise the Lord! The word "anointed" may be described as the power of God to accomplish a particular task, Praise God! It could be the call to Pastor; it may be the call to minister to the sick or the call to encourage. There is an anointing to do all these things, and more. We can do nothing in our own strength and that's why we must **come and dine** on the word of God. That's why we must not only **come and dine** at church service, but also on an ongoing daily basis. Praise God!

We need to have God pour himself into our lives through his word. Praise God! It is important to be in the church God has ordained for each individual, where the whole word of God goes forth so that each one will be able to fulfill God's ordained victorious, glorious destiny for their lives. God desires that you be a blessing to yourself, to those that are saved, as well as to those who are unsaved, Amen!

Years ago, a lady asked me to go to the hospital to minister to her sister. As I was going past a particular room, the Holy Spirit spoke to me. "I want you to minister to this lady." I looked in the room and saw an elderly woman sitting completely bent over. Her head was facing her knees. So we went in and I began to minister to her. As I laid hands on her, the power of God came into her body and she began to sit up. The lady that was with me also laid hands on her and we began to speak and to take authority over that demonic spirit that had her bent over and commanded it to go in the name of Jesus. Then I began to minister salvation to her. Every time we would get to the part to call on the name of Jesus, a demonic spirit would not let her speak. I stayed with her for awhile but she didn't get her complete deliverance. I went on to minister to the lady we had originally come to see. While I was there ministering to her, the Holy Spirit instructed me to go back to the first lady and minister to her again. Praise the Lord! I went back and ministered to her, to God's glory! In the name and the power of the blood of Jesus, that demonic spirit left her. She then shouted out the name of Jesus, Jesus, Jesus! She had accepted the Lord as her Savior. She was released. She was no longer bound. By the power of the blood of Jesus Christ and the Spirit of Almighty God, she was set free. That's what God wants us to do. Many times God will have us going to a place, and on our way, God may speak to us that there are others that need to be ministered to. But in order to be effective, we have got to first **come and dine**. We have got to first sit at the feet of Jesus. We must spend that quality time with Jesus and we must do things his way. It is very important to be obedient and do what God tells you to do, when he says do it. It is important to be obedient. Amen! If I had said, "I'll come back tomorrow", she may not have been there. She could have died. God knows what he wants to do through each one of his people. We have got to be yielded to the Lord and be obedient at all times. It is not without a sacrifice to us at times, but it is always more than worth it. Amen! To God Be the Glory!

God is no respecter of persons. Some of the people that we minister to may not look too nice. They may not smell too good; but God said he is no respecter of persons, then neither should we be.

Jesus called a man, named Levi, who was a publican or tax collector. During Jesus' day, tax collectors were very much disliked because they were very dishonest. But, Jesus called a publican named Levi to become a follower of his and Levi answered the call. Praise the Lord! In Luke 5:27-32 it says, "And after these things he went forth, and saw a publican named Levi, sitting at the receipt of custom: and he said unto him, follow me. And he left all, rose up and followed him. Levi made him a great feast in his own house: and there was a great company of publicans and of others that sat down with them. But their scribes and Pharisees murmured against his disciples saying, why do ye eat and drink with publicans and sinners? And Jesus answering said unto them, They that are whole need not a physician but they that are sick. I came not to call the righteous, but sinners to repentance." Praise God! This scripture lets us know Jesus came for sinners. So we should realize that Jesus' heart is the Father's heart. His heart is for those who are lost. He came to seek and to save that which was lost. Praise God! We can rejoice because the word of God says in Romans 5:8, "But God commendeth his love towards us, in that while we were yet sinners, Christ died for us." Praise God! We must never come to the point that we are not concerned for those who are unsaved, but we should have a heart for those that are lost.

In Matthew's gospel, chapter 21 and verse 31, Jesus said that the publicans and the harlots would go into the kingdom of God even before the scribes and the Pharisees, those who thought they were number one, those who thought they had it together, those who did not receive the message of Jesus. God is calling his people to **come and dine** today. He is calling us to **come and dine** so that we can do the great and mighty works that he says he has ordained for the body of Christ to do by the Spirit of God. He wants his people to show forth his glory. He wants us to show forth his agape love. When we do that, others see Jesus Christ demonstrated through our lives.

God wants we, who have accepted Jesus, to realize that we indeed are anointed. The word anoint means to smear or rub with oil. It also means to consecrate to an office or religious service. An example of that would be when David was anointed by Samuel. Samuel had the horn of oil with which he anointed him to serve as king. Praise God! God wants us to know that we are smeared, that his born again people are covered with God's anointing. The devil and the demons recognize this. In previous generations, some parents did not often go to the doctor when they or their child was ill with a cold. One old home remedy which was done was to take the fat from a lamb and smear it all over the body; and to cover the person with towels that had been heated in the oven. This is a physical example of being smeared with the oil of a lamb. God wants his people to know that we are covered spiritually, we are smeared with the anointing of Almighty God. Remember, the anointing is there to help a Christian to perform a particular task that God has ordained. Praise God! It is the power of Almighty God. The Lord wants his people to know that we are equipped. In order for that anointing to flow in the way that God wants, we have to walk in love and faith. We have to walk in forgiveness and we have to be willing to be used by Almighty God. Praise God!

As stated in Luke 4:16-18, Jesus Christ, the Living Word, came to Nazareth on the Sabbath. He went into the synagogue and read from Isaiah. He told them that he was anointed. He knew that he was anointed by God the Father. Jesus Christ was God's manifested Son in the flesh. He walked this earth as a man like you and I, but never sinned. Almighty Father God was Jesus' Father. Jesus Christ's blood was sinless because his blood came from his Father God. Jesus never sinned because he chose to redeem mankind back. Praise the Lord! He chose to do the will of the Father. Jesus chose not to sin. He was tempted in every area like you and I but never sinned. (Hebrews 4:15) Praise God!

Jesus said in Luke 4:18, "The Spirit of the Lord is upon me, because he has **anointed me** to preach the gospel to the poor; he hath sent me to heal the brokenhearted, to preach deliverance to the captives, and recovering of sight to the blind, to set at liberty them that are bruised, To preach the acceptable year of the Lord." Amen! To God Be The Glory. When Jesus read these words in the synagogue, he said that this day this Scripture is fulfilled in your ears. Jesus knew that he was anointed to do what God called him to do because he spent time with the Father. Hallelujah! He did what was necessary. We must **come and dine**. We must come and sit at the feet of Jesus. We must go into the presence of God. We must do whatever we need to do so that the anointing of God will flow to us and through us to make changes in our lives and the lives of others. Praise God! Jesus Christ is our example. When he walked this earth, he called the people to be fishers of men and he is doing the same thing today. He said that the works that he did, that his people would also do and even greater works. God wants his people to come forth to manifest his glory, to bring forth total salvation, to demonstrate his power in the earth, that he may be glorified! We must stay attached to the true vine. Acts 17:28 says, "For in him, we live, and move, and have our being; as certain also of your own poets have said, For we are also **his offspring."** Amen! Hallelujah! To God Be the Glory! **Come and Dine.** Let us each choose this day and everyday to come and dine, to be spiritually fed, so that each may go forth filled with Almighty God, filled with that which we need to minister to whoever he brings to our path. To God Be The Glory! Amen!

Come And Dine - Part II

God wants his people to realize that it is indeed time to **come and dine**. He has called his people to become mature and to receive every part of **Total Salvation**. The Lord wants his people to grow spiritually, Praise the Lord! Every Christian must choose to whom they are going to yield to, and how much of God's Total Salvation gift they want to receive. Each must choose whether they are going to yield to God for his plans and purposes for their life or whether they are not going to yield. The choice is up to every Christian, however, once we make the choice to yield to God's plans for our lives, it is then that the change begins to take place in our life. When a person becomes born again, only the spirit of that man is born again, which is where God comes and dwells. That is where the new creation takes place. As for the soul, which is where the mind, will, and emotions are housed, godly changes occur as the Christian consistently renews their mind through reading, studying, and doing the word of God (Romans12:1-2). As for Christians' bodies, they will never change completely until we receive our immortal bodies. This will take place when we have been raptured or caught up to meet the Lord in the air and this mortal puts on immortality. Then the body will be incorruptible, (1 Thessalonians 4:16-18). Until that time, there is a constant battle that is going on between the soul, the body and the spirit.

The spirit is what wants to rule and the spirit is what should rule. In order for the spirit to rule, there are certain things that each born again person must do. Each must decide to allow the spirit man to rule. As Christians choose to read and study God's word, it is then that the Christians' spirits begin to become stronger than the flesh, which has been in control the longest. This is because every Christian was at one time not saved. As Christians consistently **come and dine on the word of God,** it is then that they will feast at the table of God and eat the meal that God has prepared for them. It is also important to collectively assemble ourselves together in the house of God, to sit under the anointed word of God. As a person does this, it is then that their mind can also begin to be renewed, because it is being transformed by the preached and taught word of God. It is then that the body or the flesh, can begin to line up with the word of God. Before godly changes can occur, the soul which houses the mind, the will, and the emotions must be renewed through the word of God. After a person is born again some Christians remain carnal, **Romans 8:1-8, verse 8 says:** "There is therefore now no condemnation to them **<u>which are in Christ Jesus</u>**, who walk **NOT after the flesh,** but **AFTER the Spirit."** The reason that some Christians are carnal is because they have not brought their flesh under subjection to the word of God. If they were a fornicator before becoming saved, their flesh is still in control because they are not renewing their mind with the things of God; they most likely will fornicate again. For example, if they see someone who looks good to them they may say to themselves; hmmm, that person looks so good. They may even say to the person I like the clothes that you have on; and to themselves, hmmm, I wonder what's under those clothes? The carnal Christian may at times even try to act upon their ungodly thoughts and words. This is true for both males as well as females. The body that once fornicated will start to fornicate again. The soul will say, "go ahead; you can do that thing, nobody is going to know." Before you know it, the flesh is laying down in sin. It has moved from the thought to the action. This not only occurs in the area of fornication, it can be drugs, or any other works of the flesh, (Galatians 5:16-21). Galatians 5:16 states, "This I say then, walk in the Spirit, and ye shall not fulfill the lust of the flesh." God does not want a person to go the way of the flesh, which is to listen to the will of the mind that has not been renewed. The mind does not have to dictate to the flesh. It is important to feed the spirit man. Christians should spend quality time in God's word so that their minds can be renewed, and they can move from being carnal to spiritual. Each person once they have accepted Jesus Christ as their Savior is a new creation in Christ Jesus, and do not have to stay in the baby stage. Every Christian can grow up in the Lord. That is why it is so important for the members of the body of Christ to **come and dine**!

Our God always makes right decisions. He is the Lord of the right decision. Amen! Praise God! We should not argue with him about whatever he tells us in his word. Even though the body and soul may not like it, we must daily choose to **come and dine** on God's holy word. God invites us daily to read his word. God is beckoning us to daily get into his word, daily to praise him, daily to worship him, daily to walk in love, daily to walk in forgiveness, daily to do the things that Jesus did, to act like Jesus, and to even to talk like Jesus talked. Praise God! Amen! It is so important, that we feast on the word of God. Many times when God's people feast on the whole word of God, it is then that their healings come forth, their miracles come forth, and whatever part they need of **total salvation** comes forth! It is then that as we are doing the word, not only reading it, but acting on that word that the anointing of God is able to come into our lives and to flow not only into our lives for ourselves, but to flow through us to meet the needs of others. The anointing may be defined as the power that comes on a born again child of God to accomplish a specific task for the Lord's glory.

The Lord's anointing can come on a believer even to do things in the secular world for themselves, as well as to provide help to others. Primarily, it is to help you carry out your destiny that God has ordained for you so that you can glorify him in even greater ways. Although God's anointing blesses his people, the anointing is not only for we who are born again, but it is also to demonstrate God's glory for other people as well. The anointing destroys the yoke. Isaiah 10:27 states, "And it shall come to pass in that day, that his burden shall be taken away from off thy shoulder, and his yoke from off thy neck, and the yoke shall be destroyed because of the anointing." Christians should choose to yield to God so that the anointing will flow to them and through them. Praise God! Jesus is our example in his word , Jesus said it was necessary for even himself to be water baptized. Praise God! Jesus went to the Jordan River and John the baptist baptized him by immersion, because Father God had commanded it. The Holy Spirit also descended in the bodily shape of a dove upon Jesus Christ as he came up from the water of the Jordan River, and he received the baptism of the Holy Ghost. Jesus did not enter into his ministry until he received the baptism of the Holy Spirit. In Luke 4:1-2, it says that Jesus left the Jordan **being full of the Holy Ghost** and he was led by the Spirit into the wilderness to be tempted for forty days by the devil. While he was there, he did not succumb to the devil's temptations and he was victorious over the devil in every single area of temptation. Praise God! The word says that he went into the wilderness **in power** and he came **out in power.** Praise God. Jesus returned in the dunamis miracle working power. God's desire is that people be born again. Once a person is born again God doesn't want the born again person to stop at that first level of being saved; although this is the first and most important miracle of **total salvation.** When a person becomes saved, God desires that each born again person receive water baptism as well as the baptism of the Holy Spirit. The baptism with the Holy Ghost or Spirit occurs when the Holy Spirit comes upon the saved person who desires this baptism. It enables God's people to live a more victorious life in the Lord. Praise God. When a person receives the baptism of God the Holy Spirit he helps the believer by providing the additional anointing of God, or the dunamis or miracle working power as recorded in Acts 1:8.

Christians need to be able to minister out of the overflow. In Luke, chapter four we see Jesus beginning his ministry after being baptized with the Holy Spirit. He was then anointed for ministry. In Luke 4:14 the word says, "And Jesus returned in the power of the Spirit into Galilee: and there went out a fame of him through all the region round about. And he taught in their synagogues, being glorified of all." He then went into the temple and read from the book of Isaiah 61:1-2, knowing that the anointing, the power of Almighty God was upon him. Jesus read the prophecy concerning himself while he was in their synagogue on the sabbath day as recorded in **Luke 4:18-19, *"The Spirit of the Lord is upon me, because he has anointed me to preach the gospel to the poor; he hath sent me to heal the brokenhearted, to preach deliverance to the captives, and recovering of sight to the blind, to set at liberty them that are bruised", "To preach the acceptable year of the Lord."* Amen!** We see Jesus ministering with the additional power that God had placed upon him, which was given with the baptism of the Holy Spirit. If Jesus Christ needed to receive the baptism of the Holy Ghost, that should let the people of God know that the baptism of the Holy Spirit and the evidence of speaking in other tongues in needed. In **Acts 10:38**, Peter states: **"How God anointed Jesus of Nazareth with the Holy Ghost and with power**: who went about doing good, and healing all that were oppressed of the devil; for God was with him." Peter, an apostle, shared the gospel about Jesus Christ with Cornelius, a centurion. Cornelius, having heard the good news concerning Jesus Christ was saved. The Holy Ghost came upon Cornelius, who was a gentile, as well as those who were with Cornelius who believed the words which Peter spoke to them. They spoke with tongues. Following this, they received water baptism as recorded in Acts 10:14-48. In Luke 5:16, we see that Jesus, after ministering, withdrew himself into the wilderness and prayed. This lets us know the importance of spending quality time each day in prayer with God, Amen. Jesus knew the importance of staying in communion with the Father because he said, whatever the Father shows me that is what I do and whatever he tells me that's what I say. (John 5:19, John 8:28) The Lord wants us to have a special closeness with him. Praise God! It is time for the body of Christ to recognize and to realize that we each have been called by God for a specific destiny. May each member of the body of Christ be able to say like Jesus Christ, that the Spirit of the Lord is upon me because he has anointed me to fulfill my destiny in destroying the works of the devil. Praise God! We who are born again are the ambassadors of God and we are his witnesses. In John 14:12, Jesus said: **"Verily, verily, I say unto you, He that believeth on me, the works that I do shall he do also; and greater works than these shall he do; because I go unto my Father."** Praise God! We should be looking forward to doing the greater works. We should be about the Father's business.

After the resurrection of Jesus Christ, Jesus gave the gospel (good news) to a woman named Mary Magdalene whom he had cast out seven demons. He told her to go and tell the disciples that he was risen from the dead. When she went to them with the message of the good news gospel of Jesus Christ's resurrection, the disciples did not receive her words. Later when Jesus appeared to the disciples, he rebuked them for their unbelief and the hardness of their hearts. After that he gave them the great commission. The great commission wasn't just for his disciples at that time. It is for all disciples throughout all ages. Praise God! (Read Mark 16: 14-18) The Lord is no respecter of persons even as demonstrated when Jesus Christ chose Mary Magdalene to be the first person to carry the gospel after his resurrection to his disciples. The Lord is no respecter of persons, but he is a respecter our faith and obedience, amen.

In Luke 14, Jesus gives a parable about the servant that had been sent by his lord to go and gather people to **come and dine**, to come to a great feast. Today, the Lord is giving the invitation. The table is just about ready to be set in heaven. The invitation is going out on earth and God is sending the invitation to the born again believers. He is sending it to those who are not born again, to accept Jesus Christ as their Savior so that they too may **come and dine** in heaven at his great supper. Praise God! In Luke 14:16-24, we see that even though the great supper had been prepared, people made many excuses. We see the same thing today, however, God is calling us to go past the excuses and compel people to **come and dine.** Jesus Christ gave this parable in Luke 14:16-24: *"Then said he unto him, a certain man made a great supper, and bade many: And sent his servant at supper time to say to them that were bidden, Come; for all things are now ready. And they all, with one consent, began to make excuse. The first said unto him, I have bought a piece of ground, and I must needs go and see it: I pray thee have me excused. And another said, I have bought five yoke of oxen, and I go to prove them: I pray thee have me excused. And another said, I have married a wife, and therefore I cannot come. So that servant came, and showed his lord these things. Then the master of the house being angry said to his servant, Go out quickly into the streets and lanes of the city, and bring in hither the poor, and the maimed, and the halt, and the blind. And the servant said, Lord, it is done as thou hast commanded, and yet there is room. And the lord said unto the servant, Go out into the highways and hedges, and compel them to come in, that my house may be filled. For I say unto you, that none of those men that which were bidden, shall taste of my supper."*

We see that this master was upset and rightly so. He had prepared a great supper and the people were making all kinds of excuses why they couldn't come. The master said that of these that he had bidden, none of them were going to have part of his supper because he had given the invitation and they did not come. So he said to his servant, compel them to come. It was the poor, the maimed, the halt, the blind, who came to the great supper. There were many that had been rejected by man who came to the great supper. The word compel may be defined as to secure, or to bring by force, to have a powerful, irresistible effect. That's what God desires of his people, that we each have a powerful irresistible effect on the unsaved and the backslidden. When we share the word, some may not accept it, however we must not give up. We must continue to compel people concerning Jesus Christ in a loving way. We must be persistent because we know who has them bound. It is the devil. We must realize that we have the one who is the Irresistible One in us, which is Almighty God. Praise God! Amen! It is important to compel them, so they can come out of the devil's kingdom. Why? As we saw in this parable, the Lord wants his house filled and we can liken that unto the body of Christ. Father God wants the body of Jesus Christ to be filled. Praise God! He wants the people that are in satan's kingdom to come out, to be loosed, so they can come unto Jesus Christ, that his house can be filled. Amen! To God Be the Glory!

The word is now going throughout the world, to the saved, to the backsliders, as well as to the unsaved. God is calling all of his people to become his ambassadors, to carry the call to others, to **come and dine**. What a privilege and an honor. The Lord has prepared a feast. The feast is his anointed word, and it is up to each of us to share God's word. As we feast on the word of God individually, we answer the call to **come and dine**. When you assemble yourselves together in the house of the Lord where his word goes forth, the call to **come and dine** is answered again. It is when the word is received from the Lord's banquet table and applied in a believer's life that the Christian will become more like Jesus Christ.

In looking at the word of God, we see that Jesus fed the people spiritually and physically. There will be times when we will be asked to do the same thing. As we feed people spiritually, or invite them to feed on the word of God; we are compelling them to **come and dine on the spiritual word of God**. Amen! Almighty God wants his house to be filled. There is a great supper that is being prepared and soon that supper is going to be ready, which is the marriage supper of the Lamb. I believe it is a literal supper. It says in **Revelation 19:7-9:** *"Let us be glad and rejoice, and give honour to him: for the marriage of the Lamb is come and his wife hath made herself ready. v/8 And to her was granted that she should be arrayed in fine linen, clean and white: for the fine linen is the righteousness of saints v/9 And he saith unto me, Write***, Blessed are they which are called unto the marriage supper of the Lamb.** *And he saith unto me, these are the true sayings of God."* Amen! Hallelujah! This is the marriage supper of the Lamb that is being prepared. I am excited, just realizing that this time is fast approaching. We can see the signs throughout our country, and throughout the world, as God's prophecies are being fulfilled. We know that the return of Christ is imminent. What should Christians do? It should encourage and motivate Christians to **come and dine** more on the word of God. As Jesus Christ's ambassadors, each should give the call for others to **come and dine** as well. Amen!

Jesus also fed his disciples and others physically. On one occasion, Jesus appeared to his disciples after his resurrection when they were fishing. They had caught nothing all night long. Jesus told them to cast the net on the right side of the boat. They were obedient and the net was filled. When they came in, they found that Jesus had prepared a meal for them. He told them to **come and dine**. He then fed them physically. They had not been able to catch fish before because they had not heard from the Lord. We need to spend time with God so we can hear from him, so that we can truly be fishers of men. We need to hear his voice and to be obedient to whatever he tells us to do. The invitation to his disciples was to **come and dine**. Physically, Jesus had been with them; they had been dining and eating with him while he was here on this earth, during his earthly ministry. Jesus fed his disciples physically. After the disciples successfully caught fish, Jesus fed them physically, so that they would go forth and continue to carry the call to others to **come and dine**. He says the same to you and I today to, **come and dine**. Praise God! Today we are to go forth and carry that same call to others, so that they might become members of the body of Christ, that the house of the Lord may be filled. God desires that the body of Christ be filled and that they enter into heaven for that great supper, which is the marriage supper of the Lamb. Hallelujah! What a great victorious day that is going to be. As members of the body of Jesus Christ, this is the day that each member should be looking forward to. Amen!

14

Total Salvation And God's Glory (Don't Rob God)

GOD WANTS HIS people to realize that we are the generation that will see Jesus Christ rapture his own. We who are born again are the **JESUS GENERATION! Hallelujah!** The word of God tells us in Psalms 22:30, that God will have a seed that will serve him. We, who are the members of the body of Christ, are that seed. We are that royal seed that God has ordained for a time such as this, however God is saying to his people, "don't rob me." **Don't rob God!** He is not saying this to the world; he's saying it to his people. God desired, even in the Old Testament, that his people would not rob him. You may wonder who would rob God. Some of God's people still rob him today. This should not be so, certainly not among those who call themselves Christians.

God allows his people to choose to serve and obey him or not to serve and obey him. God is a gentleman and he is not going to make people do anything. We are not robots, God has given free will to man. When the Israelites were delivered out of Egypt, the word tells us that they were delivered by the mighty hand of God. Moses then went up to Mount Sinai. While Moses was gone, God's people, the Israelites, got into abominable sins. God told Moses "get down from here." He told him what was going on. In other words, God's people were robbing him. The people had started murmuring and complaining. When God's people murmured and complained against their leader, they were actually murmuring and complaining against God. They were murmuring and complaining because they felt Moses was taking too long. Moses was in the very presence of Almighty God, getting what God wanted to bring to his people, and they could not wait on God's timing. They couldn't wait on God's Shepherd, God's man, God's Prophet, God's mouthpiece, who was Moses; so they went to Aaron, who was the brother of Moses. They told Aaron we want gods like the heathens. (I'm paraphrasing here.) So Aaron had them break off their earrings of gold and melted them down. Their jewelry was made into a molten golden calf, which was an abomination, and it was robbing God. It was robbing God because he was to be their only God. It was robbing God because they used the very things that the Lord had caused them to receive from the Egyptians to build the idol of the golden calf.

The word of God tells us in Isaiah 42:8, *"I am the Lord: that is my name: and my glory will I not give to another, neither my praise to graven images."* The Hebrew word for glory, as stated in Isaiah 42:8, is defined as splendor, glorious, glory, and honor. God commands his people not to give his glory to another; nor to graven images. God was very upset with his people. They had not only made the golden calf, but they were saying in essence, "We don't want you any more God. We don't want the True and Living God, we want the idol god, the god we can make up ourselves." They decided that they were not going to obey the Shepherd whom God had spoken to them through, and they complained against Moses; which was another way they robbed God. When the Israelites did not honor the spiritual leader that God had given to them, they also dishonored Almighty God. Aaron gave the people what they wanted. A true shepherd will not give what you feel like you want. A true Shepherd is one who is following God and is going to give what God says to the congregation, much like Moses did. As Moses was getting the commandments from God, the congregation would not wait. So they went to Aaron to get what they wanted. When you are in green pastures, you are at a place where the whole word goes forth. This is a place where God's people can grow and come to know God's acts and his ways, which was what Moses was called to bring God's people into. Aaron made the golden calf that the people wanted and they were happy. They robbed God because they changed their allegiance. They said, "Okay, we don't want God;" they made an allegiance with the devil. They were saying: " We want the devil; we want the same god that the heathens worship." So that was what they did. Who do you think their guidance was from? Not Almighty God but from the devil. They robbed God when they took the gifts that God had given to them, gifts of gold that God had taken from their enemy. For hundreds of years, God's people had been in slavery to the Egyptians, a type of the world. God brought them out by his mighty hand, using his servant, the prophet Moses. They took the very gifts that God had given to them and gave them back to the devil when they made the golden idol. They robbed God by taking his gifts and making it an idol. Aaron also robbed God.

Exodus 32:5 tells us that Aaron built an altar before this idol. God's people were only to build altars before him. It says that Aaron built an altar, and the golden calf was before this altar and then he proclaimed that the next day was going to be a day of feast unto the Lord. Can you imagine how God and Moses must have felt as the people worshipped this idol. They had built a golden calf and had decided what they wanted. The people had created it for themselves. They were standing before the altar, which was supposed to be dedicated only to God; but now it had been dedicated to the god made by hands, out of the gifts that God has given unto them. The people were robbing God. Many times people think, "I have money, I have food." No, we have to realize who has given us these things. "I have talents, I have gifts." Who has given these talents, gifts and anointing to us? They are not for ourselves only; they are to be used for God's honor and his glory. God expected his people to use his blessings to glorify him, not to build an idol to worship. God expects his people today not to rob him either. When he blesses his people, he desires that it always be used for his honor and glory amen!

Total Salvation And God's Glory (Keep Your Vows)

Acts 3:19 says: *"Repent ye therefore, and be converted, that your sins may be blotted out, when the times of refreshing shall come from the presence of the Lord";* Praise God! We are now in the times of refreshing from the presence of the Lord. God is pouring out his Spirit upon all flesh and it is going to intensify in the closing moments of time. Praise God! God is calling for a holy people. He is calling for his **VICTORIOUS! GLORIOUS! CHURCH!** Praise God! He is calling his people to come out of sin. The Lord desires that his church reflect him. Although his church is in the world, we are not to be like the world. He is saying to do what I have commanded you to do in my word. He has a work for his body to do as never before. God is a vow-keeping God. He always keeps his promises. Praise the Lord! He expects we who are his children, to be like him and do likewise. The word "vow" in the Hebrew is "nadar." It means to promise, to do or give something to God. It means make a vow. Praise God! Some of the definitions of the word covenant are, compact made by passing between pieces of flesh, covenant, league. Praise God! God is a covenant-keeping God to his people. In the Old Testament, the Lord appeared to Abraham in Genesis 15:17-18 as a smoking furnace and a burning lamp. As the Lord passed between the sacrifices that Abraham had laid out before the Lord, this sealed the covenant. In the New Testament, we find that Jesus Christ was sent so that the people of God could have a new and better covenant. Jesus became the Living Sacrifice. No longer are animals slain because Jesus Christ was slain. His flesh was ripped open and his precious blood was shed. The purpose of that was to seal the covenant. Praise God! Jesus Christ provided a covenant that can never be broken. Amen! God will not break covenant and he does not expect Christians to break covenant. Once a person becomes a born again child of God, he is in covenant with God. Once a Christian enters into covenant with Almighty God, it is up to each person to keep their vows. Praise God!

In the Old Testament, the priests of God were to be holy unto God. They were ordained by God to do certain things for God. Each one of God's children today is also a priest, and is ordained to do certain things for him. Whether or not each person fulfills his destiny is his choice. The choice is up to each member of the body of Christ whether they are going to be obedient and willing to do what God is commanding. When a person does not obey there are consequences that he suffers. Those who are not obedient often lose their blessing. Isaiah 1:19 states: "If ye be willing and obedient, ye shall eat the good of the land." In the Old Testament, before the priests were allowed to enter into the tabernacle, they had to do cleansing processes, which God had commanded them to do before they entered the tabernacle. Only the high priest was allowed to go behind the veil to the Holiest of Holies, once a year to make atonement for himself, and for the congregation. When those of the tribe of Levi became priests, they realized that their position was a very holy and reverential position, and a very serious job that they were undertaking. When they took it, they were actually making a vow to God. They were saying, "Yes Lord, we are going to do it your way." They knew if they didn't do it God's way, that there would be repercussions.

Samuel, who was ordained by God to be a prophet and a judge, warned Eli of God's coming Judgement because of sin. During this time, the ark of the Lord was taken by the Philistines. Prior to the Philistines taking the ark of the Lord, it was housed in the Holiest of Holies. The presence of God hovered over the Ark Of The Covenant. Inside the ark were the commandments, which were given to Moses, along with Aaron's rod that budded, and a pot of manna. All of this was holy unto God, it belonged to God. When Eli was priest, both he and his two sons, who were priests, were in sin along with the people of God. Eli and his sons died and the Israelites lost God's hand of protection upon them and God's glory was not with them. It had departed therefore, they lost the battle with the Philistines and the Philistines took God's ark. The Philistines were a heathen nation. They thought that because they had the Ark of the Covenant, that God was with them. They did not realize what they had done, nor did they know what was going to happen to them. Had they known, they would have never taken what belonged to God. That teaches God's people the importance of not taking the things that belong to God. Christians are not to take his glory. Whatever God gives to a Christian can be shared with others, but the things of God are not to be touched unless he allows it. For example, if somebody is blessed with finances, you don't take their finances. God has blessed that individual. God can speak to that person to give it to you or not to give it to you. Praise God! If they are truly following God, they are going to sow it where God says. Amen!

After the Philistines had taken God's ark they set it before their idol god, an image which they had made. The next day when they got up, their idol was on the ground. They quickly set the idol up. The next day the idol had fallen over again. Its head had been cut off along with the palms of both its hands. God had done this. God was so angry with these people, that there was a plague that spread throughout Ashdod, which was where the ark was located. Many people died as a result of the plague. They lost their lives and not only that, but they had tumors on their bodies because they touched God's ark which was holy. They touched that which belonged to Almighty God. This teaches the importance of God's anointing, God said: "Touch not mine anointed, and do my prophets no harm." (Psalms 105:15) When you touch the things of God, "the anointing destroys yoke." (Isaiah10:27) The Philistines were of their father, the devil, so they were being destroyed. They did not have the right motives. God did not belong to them. They did not want God for the right reason; they just wanted what they thought they could get from him.

God is now intensifying his glory to be poured out upon all the earth. The word of God tells us that faith works by love. God is calling forth a holy people so that we will be able to receive, contain the glory of God, in greater measures, and release the glory of God. We who are born again have God inside of us, but the glory needs to flow through us. God is pouring it out even more upon his people, so we can go forth and do the greater works with the signs, the wonders and miracles. But he wants holy vessels that are fit for the master's use, vessels that are totally sold out to him, vessels that he knows he can trust, vessels that he knows that are **not** going to compromise, no matter what comes against them, no matter what the enemy might bring, vessels that will trust him and believe his word no matter what report comes. Almighty God is going to have such a people. Amen! To God Be the Glory! He is calling for his people to come forth as never before, because the glory of the Lord is risen. His glory is risen upon his people and it is going to arise even more. Praise God!

After the incident at Ashdod, the Philistines were so upset; they carried the ark to Gath. The people of Gath were smitten in their secret parts with tumors and many of them were slain. They then carried the ark to Ekron. All of these towns were places that the Philistines had taken from God's people. The people of God had broken their vow with Almighty God, resulting in the loss of the presence of God and his blessing. So God was saying to his people then, as well as to his people today, **"keep your vows"** that are made to the Lord. The Philistines were so upset because they were losing so many people. The plague of tumors was spreading among them, so they called their priest. They called the diviners and those that worked wickedness. Their priests told them that if they wanted to get this thing off of themselves, they should get some gold and make models of those plagues and make some images of mice and put them on a <u>new cart</u>. Don't give God any old thing; don't give him what you don't want. Don't give Almighty God just a little bit, but give him your best. Remember that Almighty God gave mankind his best when he gave us his son, Jesus Christ. That is what God is calling for today, for his people to give him their best. Whether it's our service or time, our talent or our money, we should give God our best, not the leftovers. He doesn't want the leftovers. Praise God! How would you feel if someone told you they had a coat for you and the coat was ragged, old, and dirty and they did not even want to wear it themselves. How do you think God feels? Father God has given us his very best love gift, his Son Jesus Christ, who paid the price to redeem mankind through the shedding of his holy blood at Calvary's cross. Thank you Jesus! Even the Philistine priests said, take this kine, which is a type of cattle that never had a yoke on it before. It hadn't worked or been used to labor before. They let it go to see whether it would go to where the Israelites were. Sure enough, it went right to the Israelites, to a field owned by a man named Joshua. In I Samuel 6:4-5, the diviners and the priests told the Philistines, after making five golden emerods or symbols of the tumors and mice of gold, to give the God of the Israelites the glory, so he might lighten his hand. In other words, he might show some mercy to them. When the ark arrived in Beth-shemesh, the Levites offered the kine or the cattle that had been sent, the gold that was on the cart, and everything unto the Lord. However, at Beth-shemesh, over fifty thousand of God's people were slain because they looked into the ark. They knew they were not supposed to touch it. They disobeyed God. This shows us that even today as God's people, it is still important to keep our vows to God and to obey him. We must keep our vows to God. We can't do things haphazardly or the way we want to do them. We can't say, "Oh I don't have to do that much; or I'll just do a little bit." No! God is a jealous God and a righteous God. Yes, he's a God of mercy, but he is also a righteous judge. After many of the people of Beth-shemesh were slain, they sent a messenger to Kirjath-jearim to come and get the ark of the Lord. It was taken to Abinadab and his son Eleazar, who had to be sanctified themselves so that they would be right before God, before taking care of the ark. For twenty years, the ark of the Lord remained in Eleazar's safe keeping. The favor of God rested on him, because he did things God's way. Praise God! It stayed with Eleazar until King David came to get the ark of the covenant. Praise God!

It is important to keep our vows to God because it demonstrates our love and respect for Almighty God. It allows God to bring forth his blessings in a greater way so that his glory will be able to fall upon his people in a mighty way, and flow through his people. We sing, "Fill us Lord with your presence", "We want more of you," "Let your glory fall." Do we really want God's glory to fall? **That's why he is calling his people to repent and be converted. The word tells us in Acts 3:19-21: "Repent ye therefore, and be converted, that your sins may be blotted out, when the times of refreshing shall come from the presence of the Lord; And he shall send Jesus Christ, which before was preached unto you: Whom the heaven must receive until the times of restitution of all things, which God hath spoken by the mouth of all his holy prophets since the world began."** The former and latter rain was prophesied of old, we are there. God is pouring out the former and the latter rain and it is going to intensify. It is important to be prepared for the anointings of God. Do you want

VICTORIOUS! GLORIOUS! CHURCH! ▪ 153

God to use you? Remember that it is important to keep your vows to Almighty God. Amen!

In I Samuel 7, we can see the importance of keeping vows to Almighty God. It had been twenty years since the ark had been returned and the people had been lamenting and crying out to God. In I Samuel 7:2-17, the word of God says: "And it came to pass, while the ark abode at Kirjath-jearim, that the time was long: for it was twenty years: and all the house of Israel lamented after the Lord. And Samuel spoke unto all the house of Israel, saying, If ye do return unto the Lord with all your heart, then put away the strange gods and Ashtraroth from among you, and prepare your hearts unto the LORD, and serve him only: and he will deliver you out of the hand of the Philistines. Then the children of *Israel* did put away Baalim and Ashtaroth, and served the LORD only." V/5 "And Samuel said, Gather all Israel to Mizpeh, and I will pray for you unto the LORD. And they gathered together to Mizpeh, and drew water, and poured it out before the LORD, and fasted on that day, and said there, we have sinned against the LORD. And Samuel judged the children of Israel in Mizpeh." So they put away the idols and in so doing, they got rid of the sin that was separating them from Almighty God and they repented and cried out to God. Then Samuel, the righteous leader of God, prayed for their souls. V/7-17, "And when the Philistines heard that the children of Israel were gathered together to Mizpeh, the lords of the Philistines went up against Israel. And when the children of Israel heard it, they were afraid of the Philistines. And the children of Israel said to Samuel, Cease not to cry unto the LORD our God for us that he will save us out of the hand of the Philistines. And Samuel took a sucking lamb, and offered it for a burnt offering wholly unto the LORD: And Samuel cried unto the LORD for Israel; and the LORD heard him. And as Samuel was offering up the burnt offering, the Philistines drew near to battle against Israel: but the LORD thundered with a great thunder on that day upon the Philistines, and discomfited them: and they were smitten before Israel. And the men of Israel went out of Mizpeh, and pursued the Philistines, and smote them, until they came under Bethcar. Then Samuel took a stone, and set it between Mizpeh and Shen, and called the name of it Eben-ezer, saying Hitherto hath the LORD helped us." (Ebenezer means stone of help) "So the Philistines were subdued, and they came no more into the coast of Israel: and the hand of the Lord was against the Philistines all the days of Samuel.

The cities which the Philistines had taken from Israel were restored to Israel, from Ekron even unto Gath; and the coasts thereof did Israel deliver out of the hands of the Philistines. And there was peace between Israel and the Amorities. (God made *their enemies to be at peace with them*.) And Samuel judged Israel all the days of his life. And he went from year to year in circuit to Bethel, and Gilgal, and Mizpeh, and judged Israel in all those places. And his return was to Ramah; for there was his house; and there he judged Israel; and there he built an altar to the LORD." We each need to have altars in our homes today. Families need to come together and not limit themselves to only going to church. Christian families need to take time for prayer together, time for praise and worship together in their homes, as well as take time to giving God the glory. Amen! To God Be The Glory! God was able to move on behalf of his people in the old testament when they renewed their vows to him, and gave him glory, when they repented of their sins. They got rid of the idols and chose to live holy before God. That's what God is saying to his body today, collectively throughout the world, get rid of any idols in your life. Christians that are really spending time with God, are all saying the same thing. He's calling his people to repentance because the great move of God, the revival, has started and it is going to intensify. The glory is falling and it is going to fall in a greater measure; and God is using members in his body who will yield themselves to him. Praise God! God wants to use his members of his body in greater ways. Make sure you are not going to be left out of this great move of God. Praise God! When God looked at the Israelites, he was pleased because of their repentance. When they repented the enemy was defeated, the cities were returned, and peace was restored.

Now we are going to look at vows in another area. God was married to his people in the Old Testament and is still married to his people today. When a person accepts Jesus as his Saviour, he becomes married to the Lord. Praise God! We become one with him. What happens when you get married? A husband and wife, become one. The same thing is true when we accept Jesus as our Saviour. The Lord is calling his body to stop committing spiritual adultery with other lovers. He doesn't want his people shared with idols. The dictionary meaning of "idol" is an image, material object, which can be a person or thing, which is worshipped as a deity. This is my definition, that which a child of God puts before God, or takes the place of God. It can be a hobby, a job, television, a game, a person, or something else. In addition to these it can be graven images in a person's home, job, or wherever the person may place it to worship the graven image. It could also be a person's ministry, laziness, food or sleep, to mention only a few other things which could be idols in a Christian's life. Some things may not be sin, but it becomes sin, when it takes God's place, and is put before Almighty God. Amen! You may ask, what about a hobby I enjoy? It can become a person's idol when it takes the place of God, even if the hobby is reading. You should not allow it or any hobby to consume you. It is important to obey God and spend time with him. Keep in mind that Christians' hobbies should be godly. Remember that whatever is an idol to a Christian is sin and may be called spiritual adultery. God is calling his people **not** to commit spiritual adultery with other lovers, such as idols. He's calling his people to be pure both spiritually and physically. He is calling his people to be morally pure. God says he is a jealous God. We have seen how jealous he was as we have looked briefly at the book of I Samuel. Whatever takes God's place in a believer's life is an idol; it is your lover. Just as vows are made when a man and woman are married, vows are also made when we accept Jesus as our Savior. When we say, "Lord, save me", we are saying, "Lord I am now yours, and I am not going to live the life I lived before." You may say, you can't clean yourself up, which is true, God knows that, and as you yield to him and get into his word, and do his word, he will help you. But you should be working towards keeping your vows. Some are not trying to keep their vows or are not living lives that please God by obeying God's holy word. In the Old Testament, when certain laws were broken, the persons would be stoned to death. Today we are in the period of grace. As Christians, although we are not stoned for the breaking of God's Ten Commandments, he still expects his people to obey them. When God's people keep his commandments of love that were given by Jesus Christ, each will come to a point in their lives that they will **not** break any of the ten commandments, and if sin is committed each should be quick to repent. Jesus said in Matthew 22:37-40, "Thou should love the Lord thy God with all thy heart, with all thy soul, and with all thy mind. This is the first and great commandment. And the second is like unto it. Thou shalt love thy neighbor as thyself. On these two commandments hang all the law and the prophets." If Christians would do it God's way to, (**walk in love**) they won't have to worry about breaking any of the ten commandments. Nor would they have idols before themselves, and they would not allow anyone or anything to take the place of God. It is so important to obey God's word.

For a person that's married, your spouse is your lover. It is well pleasing for a husband and wife to enjoy one another sexually in marriage. Marriage is ordained of God, and it is a holy ordinance of God. When you make your vow to your spouse, you are saying that you are going to love, honor, and cherish your mate. The wife is saying she's going to obey the husband as unto the Lord. But the word also says that you are supposed to submit one to another in the fear of God. (Ephesians 5:21) Praise God! Remember, Christians are to submit to God first of all. When you keep your vows to God, you are not going to commit physical adultery with someone else because you fear God, and you love God. That is why it is so important to have your relationship right with God, even if your spouse doesn't do what he or she is supposed to do. As believers, each individual should be doing what is right no matter what. Praise The Lord, Amen! You are to love, honor and cherish one another. The marriage vows are not to be taken lightly. Jesus stated in Matthew 19:5-9, "For this cause shall a man leave father and mother, and shall cleave to his wife: and they twain shall be one flesh?" *We who are born again are one flesh with Almighty God. God is in those who are born again. Praise the Lord!* Verse six states: "Wherefore they are no more twain, but one flesh. What therefore God has joined together, let no man put asunder. They say unto him, Why did Moses then command to give a writing of divorcement, and to put her away? He saith unto them, Moses because of the hardness of your hearts suffered you to put away your wives: but from the beginning it was not so. And I say unto you, whosoever shall put away his wife, except it be for fornication, and shall marry another, committeth adultery: and whoso marrieth her which is put away doth commit adultery." "What therefore God has joined together, let no man put asunder." The word says in Proverbs 5:15-23, "Drink waters out of thine own cistern, and running waters out of thine own well. Let thy fountains be dispersed abroad, and rivers of waters in the streets. Let them be only thine own, and not strangers' with thee. *Don't be sexually intimate with anyone other than your spouse.* Let thy fountain be blessed: and rejoice with the wife of thy youth. Let her be as the loving hind and pleasant roe; let her breasts satisfy thee at all times; and be thou ravished always with her love. And why wilt thou, my son, be ravished with a strange woman, and embrace the bosom of a stranger? For the ways of man are before the eyes of the Lord, and he pondereth all his goings. His own iniquities shall take the wicked himself, and he shall be holden with the cords of his sins. He shall die without instruction; and in the greatness of his folly he shall go astray." So we see what adultery can do, how it can cause a man or a woman to lose their soul, wind up in hell, when unrepented. Is it worth it? The greatest, most precious thing we have is our soul. We can thank and praise Almighty God for his love, his mercy, and his grace, and for the precious blood of Jesus Christ, which cleanses his repented and converted children.

The word of God tells us in Proverbs 12:4, "A virtuous woman is a crown to her husband: but she that maketh ashamed is as rottenness in his bones." So a virtuous woman is a blessing to God, and a man who has a virtuous woman for a wife, is truly blessed. Amen! Adultery is a violation of a vow made between a husband and wife and Almighty God. When the marriage covenant is made, the couple is making the agreement not only with one another together before Almighty God, but also with Almighty God, Amen! Sometimes when the marriage vow has been broken, the couple can have an even better marriage than before when both are willing to work with one another. It is also important that the one who broke the marriage vow is honest and repents to God and their mate and is willing to have their relationship with God and their mate restored. That is why God says in his word to not be unequally yoked with unbelievers. God is talking about marriage. He tells Christians that they are to be married to a believer. At times there have been those who have made the mistake of marrying unbelievers and then they live an unhappy life. Yes, it is true that an unbeliever can be led to the Lord, however in many instances, it is not without great hardship and great struggles. It is important for singles to keep their focus on God and wait for the mate God has for them. In the case where believers are already married to unbelievers, the word of God says, if that unbeliever is pleased to dwell with the believer, let them stay. The unbelievers are sanctified by the believers. The word of God in I Corinthians 7:12-16 states, "But to the rest speak I, not the Lord: If any brother hath a wife that believeth not, and she be pleased to dwell with him, let him not put her away. And the woman who hath a husband that believeth not, and if he be pleased to dwell with her, let her not leave him. For the unbelieving husband is sanctified by the wife, and the unbelieving wife is sanctified by the husband: else were your children unclean; but now are they holy. But, if the unbelieving part, let him depart. A brother or a sister is not under bondage in such cases: but God hath called us to peace. For what knowest thou, O wife, whether thou shalt save thy husband? or how knowest thou, O man, whether thou shalt save thy wife?" So the word of God is saying that if the unbelieving husband or wife is pleased to dwell with the believer, let them remain married. Sometimes, both people are unsaved when they marry, and later one becomes born again or saved and the other one doesn't become saved. In this case, the believer is still to remain with the unbelieving spouse if the unbeliever be pleased to dwell or remain with the believer. The word of God states I Corinthians 7:15-16, "But if the unbelieving depart, let him depart. A brother or a sister is not under bondage in such cases: But God hath called us to peace. For what knowest thou, O wife, whether thou shalt save thy husband? or how knoweth thou, O man, whether thou shall save thou wife?" *The believer is to be an example of Almighty God in this earth exhibiting Christ-like character, and in so doing it is possible that their mate will eventually become saved.* The believer should live a godly life before the unbeliever. A Christian should not compromise, nor should they violate their vows to God. God expects his believers to keep their vows and be faithful.

Males and females who keep vows are people of integrity. The word of God tells us in Proverbs 20:7, "The just man walketh in his integrity: his children are blessed after him." Amen! Proverbs 22:1 declares, "A good name is rather to be chosen then great riches, and loving favor rather than silver and gold." Our word is our bond. If we say, Lord yes I am going to keep my vow, Lord I am going to do what you tell me to do; God expects the vows that are made to be kept, and so do most people. A person who keeps their vows shows that they are a person of integrity. God is calling us to keep our vows to him in all areas. Whatever we do unto men, do it as unto the Lord. Colossians 3:17 says, "And whatsoever ye do in word or deed, do all in the name of the Lord Jesus Christ, giving thanks to God and the Father by him." To give an example, if you tell the Lord you will work in the nursery, that is a vow. It is also a privilege and an honor. If you have the privilege to work in a church nursery or with children in any capacity, realize that this is an honor, as well as a great responsibility. When working with children, the Lord can give you words of healing, deliverance, encouragement, and comfort to speak to their spirits. God's words are Spirit and Life. Amen! God is calling for his people to be faithful wherever they are. Always remember, your word is your bond. When you make a vow, keep it. It is important to do what you say. God says keep your vows. Because your helper did not show up, and it's your Sunday to sit under the word and you were looking forward to hearing it, it's important to keep a good attitude and still work in your assigned area. Are you going to throw in the towel? Are you going to get a nasty or bad attitude? No! Remember your vow that you made to the Lord that you would serve him. Colossians 3:23-24 declares, "And whatsoever, ye do, do it heartily, as to the Lord, and not unto men; knowing that of the Lord ye shall receive the reward of the inheritance; for ye serve the Lord Christ." It is important to keep your vows. It is also important to have a right attitude before your family, your pastor, members of the body of Christ, as well as before those who have not yet accepted Jesus Christ as their Savior. Praise

God! **Keep your vows.**

When you make a commitment or vow to God, it does not always have to be related to ministry. It could be on your job, in school or elsewhere. You may say, "Lord I'm going to do this for you, or I'm going to live holy. Perhaps you may say, Lord, I'm not going to be ashamed of you any more, I'm not going to compromise, or to go the way of sin anymore." Or perhaps you may say, "I'm going to come to church every Sunday." When you make vows to the Lord, sometimes you will lose friends, sometimes it will cause problems in a relationship. If you have an unsaved or backslidden spouse, it may cause various problems. It is time for Christians to be people of integrity. A person that keeps their word is a person that realizes that their word is their bond. They keep their vows when they do what they said they would do; and it should be with a good attitude.

It is also important to keep your vows concerning money. Money is very important to God. Money is important to establish God's kingdom in the earth. The word of God tells us in I Timothy 6:10, "For the **love of money** is the root of all evil: which while some coveted after, they have erred from the faith, and pierced themselves through with many sorrows." God's people are not to love money, and they are not to love the world or the things of the world. There's nothing wrong with having money. God desires that his people have money. However, he wants his people to keep their vows concerning money. The Lord wants to see how his people will use money. God wants to see whether his people are good stewards, and if they will do what his word says. He wants to see if they are consistent tithers and givers. God wants to know if he can trust his people concerning money. The Lord also wants to be able to trust his Christian people with others. Can he trust you with other people? For example, you promised someone that you would minister to them or help them with something. When it is time to fulfill your promise, you don't want to do it. So you tell the person that you can't make it or something came up. A person who does this has not kept their promise. It is time for God's people to be people of integrity who follow through and keep their vows. Amen! To God Be the Glory!

It is important for every Christian to yield to God and keep their vows. I will give you a personal example. When I answered the call to be a minister of the gospel of Jesus Christ, it was a matter of me saying yes to the Lord. I actually answered the call before I went to bible school. Although I knew God had called me, and that he had ordained me, it was not something that I really wanted to do. I feared God and I loved God. I said, "Lord, if this is really what you want me to do, I'll do it, but I need you to help me do it." I had no doubt that the Lord wanted me to enter the ministry, but I was very shy at that time. I would become very nervous when I had to speak before people. I also knew that it would be a great responsibility. Every Christian is called to ministry because all are called to be God's ambassadors from the youngest to the oldest, however all are not called by God to the five fold ministry.

God desires that we all be dedicated. He desires that all of his people have a love for those who are unsaved. He wants every Christian to be faithful and diligent. When I began to pastor, I knew that the Lord wanted me to lay down my life for his sheep, and I did. I do it out of a heart of love for God and his people. As God's under shepherd, he wants me to be an example of Jesus always. It means that I must keep things right at home with my husband and honor him as the priest of our home. I know the importance of keeping a good attitude and that I could not bring forth God's word with anger in my heart. I know that I am accountable to God. If somebody has done something to offend me, I know that I must get that thing right. The same thing is true with the body of Christ. Maybe you are ministering in the music area, or perhaps helping in the parking lot, you must make sure that you are keeping your vows. Your attitude must be sweet and your motives must be pure at all times. You should not come into the house of the Lord any kind of way. If you had an argument at home, don't come into the house of the Lord angry. It is important to get things right before you come in to the Lord's house. The devil does not care who he uses. He'll use your child, your neighbor, the dog or the cat. He will use anyone or anything he can to keep you from going to church and having a good attitude. Christians must realize the importance of getting themselves cleaned up and in right standing with God prior to going into praise and worship. It simply means we have to repent and ask the Lord for forgiveness. When God's people are in church they should be focusing on God and realize that they are on holy ground. As Christians, we should be thankful that we have a place to worship God freely in our country. There are Christian people in China and other countries who must worship the Lord Jesus Christ underground because they are being persecuted. Wherever believers worship the Lord, that place becomes the sanctuary of Almighty God, and is holy ground. Amen! We should be thankful whenever we are able to meet with other Christians and worship God collectively, wherever it may be. Praise God, we can rejoice because as Christians, we are God's mobile living sanctuaries that he has chosen to dwell in. We should be thankful that we can worship him in Spirit and Truth.

God is concerned about our attitude. He desires that his people have thankful hearts. He is concerned about us keeping our vows and doing that which he has called each of us to do from the youngest to the oldest. In Psalms 76:11 it says, "Vow, and pay unto the Lord your God: let all that be round about him bring presents unto him that ought to be feared." God's word tells us that we are to bring presents to the Lord. When Christians come into the house of the Lord, they should not come empty handed. They should bring something. They should bring their best gift for the Lord, Amen! As we saw in I Samuel 6:7-8, the Philistines gave their best. They didn't dare send the cart that carried God's ark back empty. Nor did they send back the old cart, but a new one. Neither did they attach cattle that had been worked or sickly. No, they sent their best, even though they were heathen people. Psalms 50:14-15 declares, "Offer unto God thanksgiving; and pay thy vows unto the most High: And call upon me in the day of trouble: I will deliver thee, and thou shalt glorify me."

If you want God's deliverance, God's victory, then follow the example of his people, the Israelites who repented. They gave up those things that were holding them, and separating them from God. They repented and paid their vows. They did what God said. They offered sacrifices. When we give offerings, we are bringing sacrifices to God as he calls us to do. Most Christians want the blessings, but each should bring sacrifices to God as well. Ecclesiastes 5:4-6 states: "When thou vowest a vow unto God, defer not to pay it; for he hath no pleasure in fools: pay that which thou has vowed. Better is it that thou shouldest not vow, than that thou shouldest vow and not pay. Suffer not thy mouth to cause thy flesh to sin; neither say thou before the angel, that it was an error: wherefore should God be angry at thy voice, and destroy the work of thine hands?" When you make a vow, you make a vow first of all to God. You might be putting your name on a piece of paper with someone else, but the vow is to Almighty God. He hears it and expects it to be fulfilled and completed. Christians should want to please God and to be in right standing before him. As the people of God obey him the blessings of God can flow in greater measures. Amen!

Proverbs 19:17 states: "He that has pity upon the poor lendeth unto the Lord; and that which he hath given will he pay him again." Proverbs 11:25 states: "The liberal soul shall be made fat: and he that watereth shall be watered also himself." Praise God! Increase comes from the Lord. If you want increase, then you must be a giver. God is the Greatest Giver and he is the believer's example. You must choose to pay your vows. Amen! The word of God tells us, as we pay our vows and do what the Lord would have us to do, that the times of refreshing from the presence of the Lord are going to come. One of the greek words for refreshing is revival. The glory of God is going to be poured out in such a way that even the heathen will take notice. God wants his people to see that he is a good God. He wants the unsaved to come to him. III John 1:2 states: "Beloved, I wish <u>above all things</u> that thou <u>mayest prosper</u> and <u>be in health</u>, even as thy soul prospereth." When the unsaved see that Almighty God's people are faithful people and that they are full of God's love, many will want the God that we love and serve. Jesus Christ said in John 13:35, "By this shall all men know that ye are my disciples if you have love one to another." God tells his people in Isaiah 42:8, "I am the Lord: that is my name: and my glory will I not give to another, neither my praise to graven images." Praise God! God is telling his people today not to have any idols. Amen! Christians are to make the Lord number one in their lives, and to pay their vows. Remember when Christians pay their vows in various areas, including financially, they are sowing seed, amen! **Pay your vows** is the word for today!

Now He that ministereth **(seed)** to the **(sower)** both minister bread for your food, and **multiply** your **seed sown**, and increase the fruits of your righteousness : II Corinthians 9:10

God (ministers or gives seed\money to the sower) **Sower** one who **plants** or **gives** into Gods kingdom.

Every good and perfect gift \ Total Salvation
SEED to the **SOWER**
My Best For Your Best
Tithes and Offerings For You LORD .

God multiplies seed sown
and increases the fruit of your righteousness =
conforms more into Gods image as you obey and do Gods word.

Copyrighted By: Apostle Crystal Naylor

Seed Time and Harvest Time

There is a time to sow seed and a time to reap your harvest from the seed you sowed.
 cultivate
You water your seed until the harvest comes with scripture consistently.

Sow or Give

Money – Finances
 Clothes
 Cars
 Bibles
 Toys
 Smiles

Reap Harvest

Money – Finances
 Clothes
 Cars
 Bibles
 Toys
 Smiles

Remember never eat your seed. Your seed is in your harvest and the 10th belongs to God, give your tithe to him. (Don't touch the tithe, it's HOLY and belongs to God), sow it!

Genesis 8:22
Malachi 3:8-18

Galatians 6:8-9 "For he that soweth to his flesh shall of the flesh reap corruption; but he that soweth to the Spirit shall of the Spirit reap life everlasting. And let us not be weary in well doing: for in due season we shall reap, if we faint not."

Matthew 6:33 "But seek ye first the kingdom of God, and his righteousness; and all these things shall be added unto you."

Love in Jesus Christ,
Apostle Crystal Naylor

15

Total Salvation And God's Glory

Do You Want My Glory?

DO YOU WANT my glory? That is the question that the Lord is putting before us today. God is pouring out his Spirit upon all flesh as never before. In the book of Joel, the prophet was prophesying of the day that we are currently in. This was many, many centuries ago, even before Peter stood up on the day of Pentecost and prophesied about the out pouring of Gods Spirit. God wants people to realize that he is indeed pouring out his **glory**, or **total salvation,** and each person must determine how much of his glory, how much of his **total salvation** they want to receive. Praise God! God is always a giver. It is up to each individual to receive.

In the word, we can see how God manifested his glory at different times, both in the Old and the New Testaments. God is calling his people today to receive the fullness of his glory, which God is pouring out by his Spirit. In the Old Testament, God's glory was manifested in different ways. In Exodus 16:10, God's glory was manifested in a cloud. The people of God were able to see this manifestation. In Exodus 24:17, the word of God tells us that the sight of the glory of the Lord was like a devouring fire on Mount Sinai. Although the Israelites were afraid of God's glory, Moses did not have any fear of God and his glory because he had a personal relationship with Almighty God. Much like Moses, when a person who has a lifestyle which is holy, and is walking in the ways of God, he too can know God's acts, as well as God's ways. God desires for his body, not only to know him for his acts; (the things that he can and does do for us), but to also know his ways, (his character, how he feels about things). The most important thing is to know him intimately, and to have a personal one on one relationship with him. When Moses came down from the mountain, his face shone. It shone so brightly that the people wanted him to cover his face. Why did his face glow? Moses face glowed because he had been in the very presence of Almighty God. He had been in the glory of God. Hallelujah! That lets you and I know the importance of getting in the word and having an intimate relationship with Almighty God. It is when we fellowship with him, worship him, that the Lord begins to reveal himself to us. It is then that we can actually go into the very presence of the Lord. When we go into God's presence, it is there that his glory is poured out upon us in a special way, and we are changed. We can never be in God's presence, sit at his feet and not be changed, and many times visibly changed. Often this change is seen on believers who have an intimate relationship with God. Many will say, "Oh I see a glow on you or around you, or your face is so bright, its glowing." Why, because that individual has been in the presence of Almighty God. The word for glory is kabod. There are many different words for glory, but this is the primary word that we are looking at. It means splendor, weight (in a good sense), it means copiousness or abundance, an abundance of his glory, gloria, gloriously, glory, honor, honorable. God is pouring out his glory in this end time hour. He has always manifested his glory to his people that would do the things that were necessary for his glory to show up. He is pouring out his glory as never before on his people.

In Exodus 33:18-23, when Moses returned to Mount Sinai, he asks the Lord to show him his glory. God told Moses that he could not look on his face, therefore, he put him in a cleft of the rock and he showed Moses his back parts as he passed by. Can you imagine how awesome God is? The power! The majesty! The honor! The glory! The splendor of Almighty God! He put his hand up as he went by and he declared who he was. God declared his very character, his very nature. He revealed his glory to Moses. Praise the Lord! Just think, Almighty God is our Daddy when we become born again. Amen! He is the author of everything seen and unseen. He loves us. He cares for us and cares about everything that concerns us.

In II Chronicles 5, it is there that we see that Solomon had finished the building of the temple and the ark of God was being brought into the house of the Lord! There were praises going up and the priests had sanctified themselves. God wants his people to prepare themselves for his glory today. In II Chronicles 5:11-14, it states, "And it came to pass, when the priests were come out of the holy place: <u>(for all the priests that *were* present were sanctified</u>, and did not then wait by course: Also, the Levites which were the singers, all of them of Asaph, of Heman, of Jeduthun, with their sons and their brethren, being arrayed in white linen, having cymbals and psalteries and harps, stood at the east end of the altar, and with them an hundred and twenty priests sounding their trumpets:) It came even to pass, as the trumpeters and singers were as one, to make one sound to be heard in praising and thanking the Lord; and when they lifted up their voice with the trumpets and cymbals and instruments of music, and praised the Lord, saying, For he is good; for his mercy endureth forever: that then the house was filled with a cloud, even the house of the Lord; So that the priests could not stand to minister by reason of the cloud: for the **glory of the Lord** had filled the house of God." There was singing, there was praising, there was music, and God was pleased. His glory was manifested in the presence of a cloud which was so strong that the priest could not stand to minister. It is important to realize that even today it is necessary for Christians to prepare themselves to come before God. We can not come any kind of way, if we truly want to get into his presence. God is asking the question, **do you want my glory?**

In the New Testament, there are examples of God's glory being manifested, as well as in the Old Testament. In the book of Acts on the day of Pentecost, there were one hundred and twenty obedient disciples who had waited for the promise of God's glory, which was the outpouring of his Spirit. They were where God told them to be, so they reaped the blessing. They reaped the harvest of the outpouring of God's Spirit. They reaped the blessing of his **glory.** Truly our God reigns, and he is worthy. God is pouring out his glory in this generation, as prophesied, as never before. God desires that his people yield to him, and obey his word so that they may receive his blessings, which includes his glory! After Jesus Christ's resurrection, he was on the earth for forty days in his resurrected glorified body. In I Corinthians 15:6, the word states that Jesus was seen by his disciples after his resurrection, and by over five hundred brethren before he ascended back to heaven. Ten days after Jesus' ascension on Pentecost, there were one hundred and twenty disciples, both men and women, that were waiting for the promise that Jesus had given them. Jesus told them that they needed to be baptized with the Holy Ghost to receive the power that they would need to be his witnesses. They had already received water baptism and they were saved, however they needed the additional power to do God's supernatural greater works that Jesus prophesied that many of his people would do as recorded in John 14:12. There Jesus said, "Verily, verily, I say unto you, he that believeth on me, the works that I do shall he do also; and greater works than these shall he do; because I go unto my Father." Jesus knew it was expedient for him to leave, to go back to heaven, to be on the right hand of Father God. He knew that this was necessary so that another Comforter, the Holy Spirit or Holy Ghost, would come upon those who desired to be baptized by God the Holy Ghost, as well as indwell every person's spirit who would accept Jesus Christ as their Savior. These are two separate experiences. In John 14:16-17, Jesus prophesied when he said, "And I will pray the Father, and he will give you another Comforter, that he may abide with you forever; Even the Spirit of Truth; whom the world cannot receive, because it seeth him not, neither knoweth him: but ye know him; for he dwelleth with you, and shall be in you." When God, the Holy Spirit, enters into a person's spirit, it is then that the person becomes born again or saved because they have accepted Jesus Christ as their Savior.

Jesus also knew the importance of the Holy Spirit coming upon his people to baptize them with the additional power. It was to give them the necessary power to do the greater works. The Holy Spirit was also sent from heaven to endue Jesus Christ with power as recorded in Luke 3:21-22. The word of God tells us that after Jesus was water baptized in the Jordan by John, the Holy Ghost descended in a bodily shape like a dove <u>upon</u> him. Following this, the word of God states in Luke 4:1, "And Jesus, **being full of the Holy Ghost,** returned from Jordan and was led by the Spirit into the wilderness. Being forty days tempted of the devil. And in those days he did eat nothing: and when they were ended, he afterward hungered." Praise God! Jesus was victorious over every temptation of the devil while he was in the wilderness. Luke 4:14 states, "And **Jesus returned in the <u>power of the Spirit</u>** into Galilee: and there went out a fame of him through all the region round about." It was then that Jesus began his earthly ministry.

In Acts 2, it is recorded that the hundred and twenty disciples waited for the promise of the Holy Ghost and power to come upon them. Jesus had told the disciples as recorded in Acts 1:8, "But ye **shall receive <u>power</u>, after that the <u>Holy Ghost</u> is come <u>upon</u> <u>you</u>**: and ye shall be witnesses unto me both in Jerusalem, in all Judea, and in Samaria, and unto the uttermost part of the earth." On Pentecost, after the Holy Ghost **came <u>upon</u> them**, the hundred and twenty disciples were all filled with the Holy Ghost and began to speak with other tongues, as the Spirit gave them utterance. This was a manifestation of God's glory that the disciples experienced. God's glory may be experienced and seen in different ways. It is also defined in different ways. To give a simple definition, I would say that the glory of God is God's manifested presence that comes to bring a change upon an individual or individuals or to bring about change in a situation or a circumstance. An example of **the glory of God** which is the presence of God bringing about change can be seen as recorded in Acts 10:37-39. The word says that Peter preached to Cornelius and his family. After Jesus was water baptized by John, Peter stated, "**God anointed Jesus of Nazareth with the Holy Ghost and with power**, who went about doing good, and healing all that were oppressed of the devil; for God was with him." As Peter spoke, the **Holy Ghost <u>fell on</u> all the gentiles** who were with Cornelius which heard the word. **They began to speak with tongues** and **magnified God.** Following this Peter said,

"Can any man forbid water, that these should not be baptized, which have received the Holy Ghost as well as we?" (Acts 10:44-47) Peter was referring to them receiving water baptism.

The manifested presence of God may be visibly seen or experienced in various ways. An example would be a rushing mighty wind as seen in Acts 2. The results of God's glory at times may be seen physically. And at times, felt or smelled. Another example of God's glory would be when a person becomes born again, which is the greatest miracle of all. It is then that this person experiences the miracle of God entering into their spirit. We can not see the Spirit of God as he enters into a person's spirit, but we know that it takes place. When the new birth takes place, it is an example of God's glory being manifested in a person by entering into their spirit man. Praise God! We can see the manifestations of what has happened outwardly when we see the good fruit coming forth in that individual's life. Another way that God's glory can be manifested is when a person who is addicted to drugs becomes delivered. When that person accepted Jesus Christ as their Savior, in many cases that addiction did not leave right away. The person still may look bound, and act bound, however, as he sits under the word and yields to God to obey his word, that bondage will leave. In some instances, no matter what the bondage is, whether it is drugs, alcohol, smoking, food addictions, etc., as soon as that person becomes born again, their deliverance is instantaneous, which is also a demonstration of God's glory in their life. Whether deliverance is immediate or over a period of time, it is still the glory of God being manifested to bring deliverance. The manifested presence of God may be sometimes visibly seen or experienced. Some examples seen in God's word are a rushing mighty wind, a devouring fire, and a cloud which was the presence of God that was so heavy the priests could not stand to minister. These are all examples of some of the different ways in which God's glory may be manifested. Sometimes we are blessed to see these manifestations. Sometimes we can actually sense them, and feel them in different ways, as God allows. Praise God!

Another example of God's glory being manifested was on the mount where Jesus was transfigured. There we see that Jesus was visibly changed. I believe this was pointing to the day that Jesus was going to be resurrected and receive his new body, his glorified body. Praise God! Three of his disciples were there with him to see Jesus' transfiguration. The Greek word for transfiguration is metamorphosis. The caterpillar is an example of metamorphosis, for after a period of time, it changes into a moth or butterfly. There is also a metamorphosis that takes place when a person becomes born again and accepts Christ as their Savior. The word metamorphosis means to change, to transfigure, or to transform. God's people are changed from glory to glory. II Corinthians 3:18 states, "But we all, with open face beholding as in a glass the glory of the Lord, <u>are changed</u> into the **same image from glory to glory,** even as by the Spirit of the Lord."

The word of God says in Matthew 17:1-9, "And after six days Jesus taketh Peter, James, and John his brother, and bringeth them up into a high mountain apart, And was transfigured before them: and his face did shine as the sun, and his raiment was white as the light. And, behold, there appeared unto them Moses and Elijah talking with him. Then answered Peter, and said unto Jesus, Lord, it is good for us to be here: if thou wilt, let us make here three tabernacles; one for thee, and one for Moses, and one for Elijah. While he yet spake, behold, a bright cloud overshadowed them: and behold a voice out of the cloud, which said, This is my beloved Son, in whom I am well pleased; hear ye him. And when the disciples heard it, they fell on their faces, and were sore afraid. And Jesus came and touched them, and said, Arise, and be not afraid. And when they had lifted up their eyes, they saw no man, save Jesus only. And as they came down from the mountain, Jesus charged them, saying, "Tell the vision to no man, until the Son of man be risen again from the dead." Praise The Lord! We see in Matthew 17:1-2 **the glory of God manifested on Jesus' face as it shone as the sun,** and his clothes became white as the light, and yes, Jesus Christ was and is God manifested in the flesh. The word says it was after six days when Jesus was transfigured. In the Old Testament, there were things that pointed to the New Testament. These things were pictures and types that pointed to the anti-type. An example is multitudes of lambs which were slain. This pointed to Jesus as the Lamb of God, who would come centuries later to take away the sins of the world. There were many of these types and shadows in the Old Testament. I believe the transfiguration of Jesus Christ on the mount is a type or a picture that is pointing to what is about to take place, which is the **Rapture**. Praise God! We are at the close of the six thousand years period, or the sixth day period. As Jesus received his glorified immortal body when he was resurrected, I believe that was pointing to what is yet to happen to the Lord's **Victorious! Glorious! Church!** That's what the Church which is the body of Christ should be looking forward to. At that time we are going to be transfigured as well and receive glorified immortal bodies.

In conjunction let's also look at I Corinthians 15:51-57. We know when Jesus returned to the earth after his resurrection, his body was different. As born again believers, we also have that to look forward to. I Corinthians 15:51-57 says, "Behold, I show you a mystery; we shall not all sleep, but we <u>shall all be changed</u>, In a moment, in the twinkling of an eye, at the last trump: for the trumpet shall sound, and the dead shall be raised incorruptible, and we shall be changed. For this corruptible must put on incorruption, and this mortal must put on immortality. So when this corruptible shall have put on incorruption, and this mortal shall have put on immortality, then shall be brought to pass the saying that is written, Death is swallowed up in victory. O death, where is thy sting? O grave, where is thy victory? The sting of death is sin; and the strength of sin is the law. But thanks be to God, which giveth us the victory through our Lord Jesus Christ." We can rejoice in that verse 58 goes on to say: "Therefore, my beloved brethren, be ye steadfast, unmovable, always abounding in the work of the Lord, forasmuch as ye know that your labor is not in vain in the Lord." The day is coming when we who are alive and are part of **Jesus Christ's Victorious! Glorious! Church!** shall be caught up to meet the Lord Jesus Christ in the air. This will be the time when <u>the glory of God</u> is going to be poured upon us in such a way <u>that our mortal bodies will put on immortality</u>, Praise God! **Total Salvation** is a gradual and continual process. At the Rapture, God's will, which are his purposes, will be fulfilled. Praise God, the Lord is taking his people from glory to glory. Amen!

Another supporting scripture is found in I Thessalonians 4:13-18, "But I would not have you to be ignorant, brethren, concerning them which are asleep, that ye sorrow not, even as others which have no hope. For if we believe that Jesus died and rose again, even so them also which sleep in Jesus, will God bring with him." Those who have died and were saved, their spirits are in heaven. Their bodies that died on earth are in the grave, the ocean, and various places; and many have turned back to dust. In the last day when the trumpet sounds, those bodies are going to be resurrected (raised) incorruptible; when Jesus Christ comes in the air with their spirits with him from heaven in the air. Mortals shall put on immortality. Their once dead bodies are going to rejoin their spirits, Praise God! Verse 15 says, "For this we say unto you by the word of the Lord, that we which are alive and remain unto the coming of the Lord shall not prevent them which are asleep." *Them which are asleep is referring to those who have died and their spirits are in the presence of the Lord.* "For the Lord himself shall descend from heaven with a shout, with the voice of the archangel, and with the trump of God: and the dead in Christ shall rise first: **Then we which are *alive* and remain, <u>*shall be caught up*</u> together with them in the clouds to meet the Lord in the air: and so shall we ever be with the Lord**. Wherefore comfort one another with these words."

This is our blessed hope. God is pouring out his glory now as never before. There is going to come a day when everything is going to culminate and that day is fast approaching. Until that day, God has a work for his people to do. There is a purpose for him pouring out his glory, and he has a work for each and every member of his body to do.

Another example of God's glory being poured out is seen in Peter's life. The anointing, the glory and the power of God was on the Apostle Peter in such a mighty, mighty way. Sick people were healed, demons left people from the shadow of Peter. Christians today should pray that God would manifest his glory on each to the point that as sick people pass by, demon spirits will flee, and people will be delivered. *Acts 5:15-16 states: "Insomuch that they brought forth the sick into the streets, and laid them on beds and couches, that at the least the shadow of Peter passing by might overshadow some of them. There came also a multitude out of the cities round about unto Jerusalem, bringing sick folks, and them which were vexed with* unclean spirits: and they were healed every one." It was the presence of God. It was the glory of God showing up in a situation in different peoples' lives, to bring forth various areas of **Total Salvation**, whether it was miracles, healings, deliverances, salvation, or something else, all of this was and is available from God's Total Salvation Package.

Do you want God's glory? That is the question God is asking his people. **Total Salvation** and **Gods glory** is available to all**! God's Glory is a part of Total Salvation** Yes, there are things that believers must do. As God's people, the word of God tells us in **II Corinthians 5:7, we are to walk by faith** and not **by sight.** If you never see the visible outpouring of God's glory, don't worry about that. As God's children we walk by faith. When we go forth, we go forth in the name of the Lord, Jesus Christ. We go forth believing that his glory is being poured out. If God said he's pouring it out, then he's pouring it out by his Spirit. When believers lay hands on the sick they should expect to see results, realizing that we can not do anything in our own strength, or in our own selves. It is God inside of us whose power flows through his people. When we minister to someone, we should always minister in faith. Always expect God to show up. Amen! Remember that we are still walking in God's glory whether we feel it or not. **Do you want God's glory?** God wants his people to realize **that we are <u>now in the day of visitation or the times of refreshing from the presence of the Lord.</u> He's calling his people to repent throughout the world. That's the call to the body of Christ. Repent! Repent! Get your lives right with God. Get sin out of your lives and walk upright and holy before God, who is holy, so that you will be fit for the master's use.**

I Peter 2:11 tells us, "Dearly beloved, I beseech you as strangers and pilgrims, abstain from fleshly lusts, which war against the soul." *There may be temptation, but God does not want us to yield to temptation. We have to make the choice not to. We make the choice not to yield to temptation and sin. It is up to every Christian to choose life and to go God's way. The war is against the soul and we have to bring every thought into captivity to the obedience of Jesus Christ.* V/12, "Having your conversation honest among the Gentiles: that, whereas they speak against you as evildoers, they may by your good works, which they shall behold glorify God in the day of visitation." When they see the good works in Christians' lives, what's going to happen? They are going to give God the glory. When they see God's people ministering to those that are sick, or bound, or blind spiritually and or physically, they will be touched. When the unsaved see their unsaved friend, who has accepted Jesus Christ as their Savior, and their life has been changed by the power of Almighty God; they will begin to ask, what happened to you? You are not the same, and they will tell them about Jesus. When the sinner sees that person living for the Lord; they will begin to give God the glory. When they see a person who is physically blind and God's glory shows up and he receives his sight and begins living for the Lord, they are going to give God the glory. We are in the day of visitation. Hallelujah! We are in the day of refreshing from the presence of the Lord. God is calling his body to get it right. We can't be one way one day and another way another day. We must live holy everyday. Why? Because there are people watching us and God does not want his people to be acting like the world. He desires that his people reflect him. The world wants to see what Jesus looks like. They want to hear what Jesus sounds like. They want to see what Jesus acts like. God is calling his people to be holy people, who will lay down their lives. People who will point others to Jesus Christ, and a people who are ready for the glory of God. When we walk in God's glory, we must glorify him. God is calling us to abstain from fleshly lust and to repent. The book of Acts talks about the times of refreshing from the presence of the Lord. That is where we are in God's prophetic timetable. **Acts 3:19-21 says, "Repent ye therefore, and be converted, that your sins may be blotted out, when the times of refreshing shall come from the presence of the Lord; And he shall send Jesus Christ, which before was preached unto you: Whom the heaven must receive until the times of restitution of all things, which God hath spoken by the mouth of all his holy prophets since the world began**." It is important to continue to go God's way.

God is already pouring out his Spirit and he is going to pour it out in greater measures. He desires that his people be blessed and that the unsaved be blessed by becoming born again. He desires that blinded eyes, spiritually and physically, be opened, and that the dead be raised back to life. Praise God! He does not want people to put any limits on him. Freely, God has given; freely we have received, and freely we are to share with others that which God has given us. We received the new birth, and various parts of **Total Salvation** and God's glory, and it is now time to share with others in need. Remember, as Gods people, we are blessed to be a blessing.

Total Salvation and **God's Glory** is God's will for mankind. Jesus died and shed his blood so that we might enter into the kingdom of God (kingdom of heaven). There is so much in God's kingdom. The kingdom is not just talking about heaven, but it is talking about the kingdom of God here in the earth as well. John the Baptist spoke prophetically in Matthew 3:2 saying, "Repent ye: for the **kingdom of heaven** is at hand." Jesus told his disciples in Luke 12:32, "Fear not little flock; for it is your **Father's good pleasure to give you the kingdom**." Yes, Jesus was talking about eternal life in the kingdom of heaven, but he was also referring to having our daily needs met, be it shelter, food, clothes, health, or whatever his little flock (children) has need of. Amen! (Luke 12:22-32) For too long, much of the body of Christ has fallen short of the purposes; and the provisions of God. Jesus Christ purchased the body of Christ with his precious shed blood and the Lord wants his people to have the best gifts. Each person however must choose to receive their inheritance; and to always remember that <u>the Greatest is the Spiritual</u>. Today is the day of visitation and the times of refreshing from the presence of the Lord. God is pouring out his Spirit as never before. The former and the latter rain have come together. Hallelujah! Yes, his glory was poured out in the Old Testament as well as in the New Testament. People continue to be saved, healed, delivered, and raised from the dead as recorded in the word of God. We who are born again today can rejoice that we are a part of this generation in which God is pouring out the former and the latter rain together. Because we are in the closing moments of time, God wants his people to believe and expect the same manifestations of the former glory, and even greater glory in the latter. He also desires that his people believe and expect what many say is impossible, because Luke 1:37 says, **"For with God nothing shall be impossible."** It's time that the glory of our Daddy, Almighty God, who is the Holy Supernatural God, be seen in his people in this earth. It is time that the body of Christ realizes that we are his supernatural born again sons and daughters; therefore we should demonstrate his power in this earth. It should always be for God's glory. We should demonstrate God's glory by doing even greater signs and wonders than those during the former rain. Jesus said in John 14:12, "Verily, verily, I say unto you, he that believeth on me, the works that I do shall he do also; and greater works shall ye do because I go unto my Father." The Lord desires that every member of the body of Christ yield to him by saying "thy kingdom come, thy will be done" in and through my life, in Jesus' name, Amen!

At the time of the Rapture, we are going to see God's will ultimately fulfilled for his people. His **Victorious! Glorious! Church**! will be Raptured. God's people will be caught up to meet the Lord in the air. Amen! Praise God! Almighty God wants his people to expect that. He wants his people to believe him for his best. Truly, he is worthy of all the honor, all the glory and all the praise.

The word of God tells us that all who live godly will suffer persecution. So persecution for Christ's sake is to be expected. The word of God also tells us in I Peter 4:14, that <u>if the Spirit of glory and of God rests upon you, you will be</u> <u>reproached for his name sake</u>. So, when you are reproached and rejected, praise God because God's glory is resting upon you. God wants Christians to realize that his judgments have already begun. It began first in the house of the Lord. Amen! I Peter 4:13-14 says, "But rejoice, inasmuch as ye are partakers of Christ's suffering; that, when his glory shall be revealed, ye may be glad also with exceeding joy. If ye be reproached for the name of Christ, happy are ye; for the spirit of glory and of God resteth upon you: on their part he is evil spoken of, but on your part he is glorified." God is glorified when we do things his way. He is glorified when we take Total Salvation to others and share the glory of God, and allow his glory to flow through us to others. I Peter 4:17 tells us, "For the time is come that judgment must begin at the house of God: and if it first begin at us, what shall the end be of them that obey not the gospel of God?" It is important to realize that God's judgments have already begun. If we don't want the judgment of God to come upon us, as Christians we must judge ourselves daily. God tells us in his word to judge ourselves so we won't be judged. Get it right now. Repent now! Change now and do it God's way. His way is always best. The word declares that those things that are done in secret will be uncovered. In Matthew 10:26, it states: "Fear them not therefore: for there is nothing covered, that shall not be revealed; and hid that shall not be known." Now is the day of salvation. Now is the day of repentance because we are now in the times of refreshing from the presence of the Lord. We are now in the time of the visitation from Almighty God and he is pouring out his glory as never before. Praise God! We are God's priests; we are a chosen generation. 1 Peter 2:9 declares, "But ye are a chosen generation, a royal priesthood, an holy nation, a peculiar people; that ye should shew forth the praises of him who hath called you out of darkness into his marvelous light." As priests of Almighty God, we are to be sanctified. God's people are called to live holy. Christians must strive always to have pure motives, pure hearts, and pure lives. The word of God tells us in Psalm 24:3-4, "Who shall ascend into the hill of the Lord? or who shall stand in his holy place? He that hath clean hands, and a pure heart; who hath not lifted up his soul unto vanity, nor sworn deceitfully." That's what God is calling for, for the entire body of Christ. Matthew 5:8 tells us, "Blessed are the pure in heart: for they shall see God." Praise God for those that are quick to repent, for those that love God and are sold out to him completely because we will see God in this life as he manifests the blessings in various areas of **Total Salvation** to us, as well as see him in heaven one day. Praise God! As we seek first the kingdom of God and his righteousness, all other things shall be added unto us. Why? Because we are putting God first place and our motives are pure; our hearts are pure before God. In addition to these things as Christians we desire the spiritual to be more like Jesus Christ and to please him more than the things! Amen!

    God is calling for holiness in his people. In Isaiah, the word of God tells us that it is time for God's people to lift up a standard. The standard is holiness. The standard is righteousness. The standard is to be lifted up so that those that are unsaved may see the righteousness and, the glory of God. In Isaiah 62:1-4, it says, "For Zion's sake I will not hold my peace, and for Jerusalem's sake I will not rest, until the righteousness thereof go forth as brightness, and **the salvation** thereof as a lamp that burneth. And the Gentiles shall see thy righteousness, and all kings **thy glory** and thou shalt be called by a new name, which the mouth of the Lord shall name. Thou shalt also be a crown of **glory** in the hand of the Lord, and a royal diadem in the hand of thy God. Thou shalt no more be termed Forsaken; neither shall thy land anymore be termed Desolate: but thou shalt be called Hephzi-bah, (*which in Hebrew means my delight*) and thy land Beulah: (*which means marry*) for the Lord delighteth in thee, and thy land shall be married." **What is the land that God possesses?** It is **his bride. Our body, which houses our spirit, is the temple in which God indwells and we are married to Almighty God**. Amen! Praise God! The Lord is saying lift up a standard. And the Gentiles, those that are unsaved, are going to see God's **glory**. How are they going to see it? They are going to see it in you and me and every member of Christ's body that will totally yield themselves to be used by the Lord for his **glory.** Amen! They are going to see it as God flows through us to do the great and mighty things that he said he would do by his Spirit. Praise God! Verses 10-12 of the same passage says, "Go through, go through the gates*; prepare ye the way of the people*; cast up, cast up the highway; gather out the stones: lift up a standard for the people. Behold, the Lord hath proclaimed unto the ends of the world, Say ye to the daughter of Zion, Behold, thy salvation cometh; behold his reward is with him. **And they shall call them, the holy people**, the redeemed of the Lord: and thou shalt be called, Sought out, A city not forsaken." The word "city" refers to God's people. God's people are going to be sought out even more in these last days. At times, we will be sought out by people who we don't know. Why? Because the glory of the Lord has risen upon us, and his glory will be rising upon his people even more. Why? That the Lord may be glorified and not us. We always must give God the **glory!** The **glory** is his. Isaiah 60:1-5 says, "Arise, shine; for thy light is come, and the glory of the Lord is risen upon thee. For, behold, the darkness shall cover the earth, and gross darkness the people: but the Lord shall arise upon thee, and his glory shall be seen upon thee. And the Gentiles shall come to thy light, and kings to the brightness of thy rising. Lift up thine eyes round about, and see: all they gather themselves together, they come to thee: thy sons shall come from far, and thy daughters shall be nursed at thy side. Then thou shalt see, and flow together, and thine heart shall fear, and be enlarged; because the abundance of the sea shall be converted unto thee, the forces of the Gentiles shall come unto thee." Amen! This scripture is talking about the sea, meaning many people. They are going to come to many, in the body of Christ, which is Jesus Christ's Church. There are going to be multitudes upon multitudes that are going to be converted, that are going to accept Jesus as their Savior! Amen! That should be our hearts' desires. Every believer should have a heart for souls, a heart to be used by God. A heart for **Total Salvation**, whatever the person stands in need of is in God's **Total Salvation Package.** God's people should know that the **glory of the Lord is risen upon many of them,** to bring forth the change that God desires. Whatever areas of **Total Salvation** that any individual may need, God desires to use his people to minister to the areas of need by his Spirit.

We should keep in mind that we are in the times of refreshing from the presence of the Lord, and the times of restitution of all things. God is moving on this earth like never before. Yes, there is gross darkness covering the earth, because time is winding up. There is also a standard that's being lifted up, through God's people who are yielded to him and sanctified. Praise God! Many of his people are saying, "Lord, I am going to live holy before you; I am going to do whatever it takes so that your glory may rest mightily upon me that I may go forth in your name by your Spirit to do that which you would have me to do, to take forth **Total Salvation** to whoever you want me to take it to." Amen! To God Be The Glory! Because Jesus Christ is Lord! Amen!

At the time of the Rapture, God's will for his ultimate glory upon his people will be fulfilled, when we receive the greatest part of **Total Salvation.** At that time Gods people will experience our mortal bodies being changed to immortal, and incorruptible bodies. At the time that our mortal bodies become immortal, they will be like Jesus' glorified body. That's our hope. That is what the **Victorious! Glorious! Church!** should be looking forward to. Before the Rapture occurs, God has a short work that he is doing. He has already started that which he is going to accomplish. He is going to accomplish it in the members of his body that are yielded to him who want to be used by him. The word says in Colossians 1:27, "To whom God would make known what is the riches of the glory of this mystery among the Gentiles; which is Christ in you, the hope of glory." *Hallelujah! That same power that raised Jesus from the dead now flows in you and I who are born again.* Remember, when Jesus Christ was raised from the dead, it was the glory of God that raised him up. It was the same Holy Ghost that raised Jesus from the dead. It is the same power of God that will change our mortal bodies into immortal bodies. It is the same power that will raise the bodies of the saints from the graves to immortality. The spirits of those who have died are already in heaven with Jesus, and will come with Jesus in the air at the Rapture at which time their mortal bodies will rise from the dead to rejoin their spirits in the air as immortal bodies that will be glorified like Jesus Christ' body. Praise God, I Thessalonians 4:17 tells us "then we which are alive and remain shall be caught up together with them in the clouds to meet the Lord in the air: so shall we ever be with the Lord." Therefore, let us say, yes Lord I do want your glory, as well as to be **Raptured,** which is the last part of **Total Salvation and God's glory,** in Jesus' name, Amen! We have that same **glory** in us. This is what Colossians 1:27 is talking about. At that time, God's will for his ultimate **glory** to be poured out upon his people will be fulfilled. To God Be the Glory! **Christ in you the hope of glory!** The Lord is asking, **"Do you want my glory?"** That is the question. We must be willing to pay the price to walk **in God's Glory.** God's glory is intensifying. We must allow **God's Glory** to flow to us and through us to others. Praise God! **Total Salvation and God's Glory**, is for God's **VICTORIOUS! GLORIOUS! CHURCH!** Amen! Amen! and Amen! *I believe your word Lord; I receive it and I thank you for it. I seal it with your blood and I call it done in Jesus' name, Amen! Amen! To God Be The Glory!*

16

Victorious! Glorious! Church!

THE LORD WANTS his people to understand the seasons and the times that we are in now. He wants his people to realize that the members of the body of Christ make up his Church. The Church is made up of those who are born again believers. Which is speaking of everyone who has accepted Jesus Christ as their Savior. Every member of the body of Christ composes the Church. Every blood-washed person that has accepted Jesus as their Savior makes up the Church. Praise God!

The Church was first birthed after Jesus' resurrection, after appearing to Mary and his disciples. The word of God tells us that after Jesus' resurrection, Mary Magdalene was at the tomb. While she was there, Jesus appeared to her. Jesus also commissioned Mary Magdalene to go and tell the disciples the good news of the gospel. The word gospel means good news. The gospel that she was to tell them was that Jesus Christ had risen from the dead. After Jesus was resurrected, he was in his glorified body. The word of God tells us in John 20:19 that the doors were shut when Jesus appeared in the midst of his disciples. The doors being shut was not a problem to Jesus in his resurrected glorified body. When he appeared to his disciples, it was there that he said in verse 21 "Peace be unto you: as my Father hath sent me, even so send I you." Jesus was giving his disciples the commission to do the work that the Father had given him. At that point, the word of God says that Jesus breathed on them and said, "Receive ye the Holy Ghost." I believe it was then that the disciples were born again. I believe it was then that the first members of the Church were birthed. Up to that point, there were no born-again people because Jesus was not yet raised from the dead. It was not until Jesus breathed on them and said, "Receive ye the Holy Ghost" that the Spirit of God entered them. It was then that the Holy Ghost entered into their spirits. Amen!

In Acts 1:4, Jesus told his disciples to wait for the promise of the Father. Jesus said he would send the Holy Ghost upon them. They had already received the Spirit of God in them when the church was first birthed and they were born-again. Jesus told his disciples that they needed additional power. That additional power would be when the Holy Ghost would come upon them so that they could go forth and fulfill the great commission and do the greater works that Jesus had called them to do.

In the word, we see that Jesus was on this earth forty days and forty nights in his resurrected glorified body. He was seen of many in his resurrected glorified body. Before Jesus ascended into heaven, he said in Acts 1:8, for his disciples to tarry and wait in Jerusalem for the promise, for the Spirit of God to come upon them. Then, Jesus ascended into heaven. His disciples saw him ascending back to heaven on a cloud. They were told that Jesus would come back in like manner as stated in Acts 1:11. Ten days later, there were a total of one hundred and twenty persons which were obedient to waiting for the promise that Jesus told them would come. The Holy Spirit came upon those that were obedient disciples. There were both men and women; which were assembled in Jerusalem. They each received the baptism of the Holy Ghost with the evidence of speaking in other tongues.

Shortly after the disciples received the baptism of the Holy Ghost, Peter preached a powerful message, an anointed word of God, and there were about 3,000 souls that came to the Lord, and the body of Christ which is the Church increased (Acts 2:41). The Church has continued to increase throughout the generations. The message that the Apostle Peter preached after having received the baptism of the Holy Ghost and power was so powerful that the word of God states the following as recorded in Acts chapter 2:37-41: "Now when they heard this, they were pricked in their heart, and said unto **Peter and**

to the rest of the apostles, men and brethren, what shall we do? Then Peter said unto them, <u>Repent, and be baptized every one of you in the name of Jesus Christ for the remission of sins, and ye shall receive the gift of the Holy Ghost."</u> **"For the promise is unto you,** and to **your children, and to all that are afar off,** even **as many as the Lord our God shall call.** And with many other words did he testify and exhort, saying, save yourselves from this untoward generation. Then they that gladly received his word were baptized: and the same day there were **added unto them about three thousand souls**." Praise God, the church was continuing to increase in size, and has continued to increase throughout the generations. There has been much persecution of believers throughout the generations. Even with great persecution, the Church of Jesus Christ has continued to grow, and continued to increase with born again believers which comprises the body of Christ, or the Church. Amen!

We are now in the times of refreshing, and the glory of God is intensifying. God wants the body of Christ to come to understand what the times of refreshing are and that we are presently in the times of refreshing. The Lord has much to say about his people that are on the earth now. He wants each to realize that we are the generation that is seeing the things manifest, that were prophesied concerning the rapture of the Church. I believe that we are the generation that will be here at the coming of the Lord Jesus Christ when he comes to catch away his **Victorious! Glorious Church!**

Today, God is calling for each member to walk in the fullness of Jesus Christ as his **Victorious! Glorious! Church**! The glory of God is rising upon God's people that know their God. To know God, you have to spend time with him. At the same time, God's glory is rising upon his **Victorious! Glorious! Church!**, which is the body of Christ, there is darkness in the earth, and the darkness is intensifying in the world. At the same time, God's judgments are already in this earth. The judgments that are in the earth are because of sin and corruption. Unfortunately, many choose to continue to go their own way. I thank God that he is also a loving and a merciful God. Amen! There are apostles and prophets, and other five-fold ministries that have been warning both the saved and the unsaved of the seasons and the times that we are in. It is now the day of **Total Salvation**, and God is calling for all men to come to him, to call on the name of the Lord, to become born again, which is the most important part of **Total Salvation** and the greatest miracle of all! He is calling for all men to repent and to be born again. The day in which we now live is much like the days of Noah. It's a sign to let the body of Christ realize that the Lord is shortly to come. We can see this in the word of God. The disciples asked the Lord, "Lord, how do we know when you will be coming back?" Jesus gave them many signs.

Matthew 24:36-44 tells us, "But of that day and hour knoweth no man, no, not the angels of heaven, but my Father only. But as the days of Noah were, so shall also the coming of the Son of man be. For as in the days before the flood they were eating and drinking, marrying and giving in marriage, until the days that Noah entered into the ark, (Entering the ark symbolizes protection through Jesus Christ, who is our Ark) And knew not until the flood came, and took them all away; so shall also the coming of the Son of man be. Then shall two be in the field; the one shall be taken and the other left. Two women shall be grinding at the mill; the one shall be taken, and the other left. Watch therefore: for ye know not what hour your Lord doth come. But know this, that if the goodman of the house: had known in what watch the thief would come, he would have watched, and would not have suffered his house to be broken up. Therefore be ye also ready: for in such an hour as ye think not the Son of man cometh." God is a God of love. He is a merciful God. He is also the Righteous Judge. Therefore, God does deal with sin. He always gives time for people to repent. He always sends warnings through his apostles and prophets to let people know what hour they are in, to let them know what's coming. It is up to each individual to make the right choice. The same was true in Noah's day, just like today. The alarm is being sounded, just like in the days of Noah. Jesus said it would be like Noah's day. The people did not listen then, and unfortunately many today are not listening.

Noah was a preacher of righteousness. II Peter 2:5-10 talks about the judgment. Verse 5 tells us that Noah was a preacher of righteousness. It also let's us know that Noah was preaching to his generation;

he was warning them, letting them know that God was giving them an opportunity to repent. Verse 5 states, "And spared not the old world, but saved Noah the eighth person, a preacher of righteousness, bringing in the flood upon the world of the ungodly." Today, God's judgments are in the earth. The judgments of God have not yet intensified to the extent that they will. The devil is pulling out every tactic, every maneuver that he can, and using whoever will yield to him. Darkness is increasing; the devil and his demonic plans are escalating. But, I am so glad that God's power is flowing through his people. Hallelujah! The glory of the Lord is risen upon those that know their God. The word of God says in Daniel 11:32, "But the people that do know their God will be strong and do exploits" and that is what is happening with many believers who are totally sold out to Almighty God. Great and mighty exploits are occurring by the power of Almighty God through those who will yield to God, and know their God. Amen! The word of God tells us in Genesis 6:8-9 that Noah found grace in the sight of God. Noah was a just man, and he was perfect in his generations. Praise God! He walked with God. That's what God is looking for today. He is looking for those in his Church, the body of Christ, who will make up their mind to yield to him, to walk with him, to do what he says do. He wants them to spend time with him so they can hear his voice and know what he is saying, much like Noah. Praise God! Noah was a man that loved God, feared God and trusted God. As a result of that, Noah's entire household was saved. The word of God lets us know that everyone else was destroyed, except Noah and his household. God gave everyone the opportunity to repent before the judgment came on the earth, but they chose not to repent. As a result, the rains came and there was a flood on the earth for forty days and forty nights. That was the judgment of God. The word of God says in Genesis 6:13, "And God said unto Noah, The end of all flesh is come before me; for the earth is filled with violence through them; and, behold, I will destroy them with the earth." Noah was instructed by God to prepare an ark. The ark was not only for him and his family, but for seven of every clean animal and two of every unclean animal, so that the earth could be repopulated after the flood. (Genesis 7:1-4) **All nations on the earth came from Noah, who came from Adam,**

who came from God. Noah had three sons, Shem, Ham, and Japheth, from which all people on the earth have come. As recorded in Genesis 11:10-26, Abram, whom God made his covenant with to bless all nations on the earth, descended from Shem. Through Abram's lineage generations later, Jesus Christ was birthed into the earth.

Today there is much corruption in the world. It's not going to get better. It's going to get much, much worse. Even though there is much corruption in the earth, there is a group of God's people that are getting closer to God. They are allowing the glory of God to flow upon them and through them, Hallelujah! God has his righteous seed in the earth. He has his righteous people in the earth that will follow his Spirit. God's revival is now in the earth. Praise God! The word refreshing means revival. We are in the times of refreshing from the presence of the Lord. There is revival throughout the world. In many places, it is intensifying to very high levels. Whenever there is true revival, there are multitudes being birthed into the kingdom of God. This was prophesied of in Joel 2:28-32 and in the book of Acts. In Acts, it says that God would pour out his Spirit and that is exactly what he is doing. God wants his people to be sensitive and to be aware of what is going on. As we see these things happening, it is to wake up the body and to have the members realize that we are the generation that will see the Lord's return. We are seeing the things that were prophesied in Acts 2:16-18, **"But this is that which was spoken by the prophet Joel; And it shall come to pass in the last days, saith God, (I believe that is speaking of today) I will pour out of my Spirit upon all flesh: and your sons and your daughters shall prophesy, your young men shall see visions, and your old men shall dream dreams: And on my servants and on my handmaidens I will pour out in those days of my Spirit; and they shall prophesy."** The Apostle Peter is saying the same thing that the Prophet Joel prophesied hundreds of years earlier. God is pouring out of his Spirit upon all flesh. This is another sign of the close return of the Lord Jesus Christ, Praise God!

We have already seen that there will be much sin, corruption and wickedness in the earth. We are in perilous times and it is getting worse. Jesus said it would be like the days of Noah just before his return. It was so wicked that God had to finally destroy every living thing with the exception of Noah and his family and some animals. Another sign is that our generation is much like the people during Noah's generation. Many are becoming more wicked and sin is becoming more rampant. However, at the same time, there are two rivers in the earth. There is the river of sin, wickedness, and darkness that the enemy, who is the devil, is in charge of. Then there is the river of God, which is clean, pure, and holy, where God is pouring out his anointing, his glory, his Spirit. In order for God to use his people, each must decide to come to the place where they are willing to yield to him. It is important that each person choose to be conformed into his image, and allow the Lord to use them for his glory, and to bring souls to the Lord. Proverbs 11:30 says "The fruit of righteousness is a tree of life; and he that winneth souls is wise." The only thing that really counts is the souls that are going to come to the Lord and how Christians live their lives. All that's going to matter in the end is what we do in the here and now. Hallelujah! We are now in the times of refreshing from the presence of the Lord, Acts 3:19, now is the time to repent and to be converted! Praise the Lord!

Another sign of the coming of the Lord is that in the season in which we are now living, the Lord is pouring out his Spirit, his glory. We are seeing unprecedented healings, miracles, deliverances. Multitudes of people from all races and all walks of life are accepting Jesus Christ as their Savior and being birthed into the body of Christ. The greatest miracle of all is when a soul is saved. As a result of today's technology people are able to hear and see people who have been raised from the dead, and to even view people give their own testimonies. These are examples of what's happening in this revival. This is God pouring out of his Spirit. This is revival. These are the times of refreshing from the presence of the Lord. God said when this season arrived, the times of refreshing from the presence of the Lord, **it would be just before the return of Jesus Christ. (Acts 3:19-21)** We are seeing two things in the earth right now. We are seeing things getting more wicked and more abominable to God. We are seeing men full of themselves, doing what they want to do, doing everything that they can think of that is abominable. Yet, at the same time, there is a group of people, many of the body of Christ, that have made up their minds to do what is right in the sight of Almighty God. They are saying, "Lord I'm selling out to you, Lord I realize that I have been called for a time such as this." As the members of the body of Christ wake up and yield to God, it is then that God pours his anointing upon his people and flows through each to do the greater works that he said we would do. This may be referred to also as the restitution of all things. Restitution may be defined as restore, compensate for loss. **Proverbs 11:31 says, "Behold, the righteous shall be recompensed in the earth: much more the wicked and the sinner**," Amen! Praise God! That's exactly what God is doing. This was prophesied in Acts 3:19, it says "Repent and be converted that your sins may be *blotted out*, (God is giving a warning to this generation), when the times of refreshing shall come from the presence of the Lord." We are now in the times of **revival**. We are in the **times of refreshing from the presence of the Lord**. The Greek word for **refreshing** is **revival.** Praise the Lord! During revivals, there is a mighty outpouring of God's Spirit, his glory. In Acts 3:20-21, it says, "And he shall send Jesus Christ, which before was preached unto you: Whom the heaven must receive until the times of **restitution of all things**, which God hath spoken by the mouth of all his holy prophets since the world began." This day was prophesied by his prophets. Today, his prophets are prophesying the same thing. We are in this time period right now. We are in the times of refreshing from the presence of the Lord. Up until this time, the word says, the heaven has been holding Jesus. Heaven has not released Jesus to come. As soon as this period is over; when mighty revivals that are taking place throughout the world, and restitution is made according to God's plans, Jesus will be released from the heaven. At the same time the times of refreshing are taking place, the enemy is doing his thing. Each one must make up his mind; who is he going to serve? You can't have one foot in the enemy's camp and one foot in God's camp. There must be a decision made because we are in the times of refreshing from the presence of the Lord. The word of the Lord commands his people to repent and be converted! We are in the closing moments of time. Praise God! God's people, who are yielding to him, are coming to know him and are rising to fulfill God's destiny for their lives. The Hebrew word for "know" is "yada." It means to be intimate with God and to spend time with him. They that know their God shall be strong and do exploits, great and mighty exploits. We must have a consistent intimate relationship with Almighty God. How is intimacy developed? Intimacy with God comes from consistent prayer to God, and not only praying, but it is also important to listen to God to hear his voice. Intimacy also comes through praising and worshipping. Praising and worshipping God not only when you go to church, but praising and worshipping him on an ongoing basis, be it in your home, or wherever. It is important to spend time with God through studying God's word, reading God's word, hearing God's word, and doing God's word. It is also important to be planted in a church where the whole word goes forth. These are some of the ways that help to develop intimacy with God. It is not just praying and talking to God, but giving God quiet time to listen to him. We need to listen to his direction, his instruction and then do what the Lord says to do. Amen!

The word of God tells us that we are sanctified by the washing of the water by the word. Ephesians 5:26 states: "That he might sanctify and cleanse it (the Church of Jesus Christ) with the washing of water by the word." As you go to church and sit under the word of God, if it is the whole true unadulterated word of God, you are washed and cleansed. As you get into the word every day, it cleanses you; it washes you, Praise God! That's why it is so important to feed your spirit daily by reading the word of God. As you go to work and travel to various places, God's people are exposed at times to negative things, therefore it is important for God's people to be purified, Christians need to be washed and need to stay in God's word. The word of God tells us in **Ephesians 5:27, "That he might present it to himself a glorious church, not having spot or wrinkle, or any such thing; but that it should be holy and without blemish."** Right now, the church is being prepared. I believe that we are the generation who will be alive to see the coming of the Lord. Amen! All the signs point to it. God's word is showing us that the things that are happening in the world are not by coincidence. It is prophecy being fulfilled. We are a blessed generation. Amen! Yes, we live in perilous times, but we don't have to fear. II Timothy 1:7 says: "For God hath not given us the spirit of fear;

but of power, and of love and of a sound mind." God is sending signs and warnings to wake up his people and make us realize that it is time to do what Jesus Christ has called us to do, which are the greater works. The greater works also includes leading people to the Lord. The Lord wants his people, the body of Christ, to be prepared when he comes. The warning is going out. The alarm is being sounded. It is up to each member of the body of Christ to yield to the call of God. The Lord Jesus Christ is calling for his **Victorious! Glorious! Church!** to do all he said in his word by the power of Almighty God. Jesus said in John 14:12, "Verily, verily, I say unto you. He that believeth on me, the works that I do shall he do also; and greater works then these shall he do: because I go unto my Father."

In I Corinthians 15:51-57, the word of God tells us, "Behold, I show you a mystery: We shall not all sleep, but we shall be changed, In a moment, in the twinkling of an eye, at the last trump: for the trumpet shall sound, and the dead shall be raised incorruptible, and we shall be changed. For this corruptible must put on incorruption and this mortal must put on immortality. So when this corruptible shall have put on incorruption, and this mortal shall have put on immortality, then shall be brought to pass the saying that is written, Death is swallowed up in victory. **O death, where is thy sting? O grave, where is thy victory? The sting of death is sin; and the strength of sin is the law. But thanks be to God, which giveth us the victory through our Lord Jesus Christ.**" We, who choose to walk like <u>the five wise virgins</u> (Matthew 25:1-13), should praise and thank God that Jesus Christ has already given us the victory. Amen! That's why we are called his **Victorious! Glorious! Church!**

I John 5:4-5, it says, "For whatsoever is born of God overcometh the world, and this is the victory that overcometh the world, even our faith. Who is he that overcometh the world, but he that believeth that Jesus is the Son of God." Amen! Praise God! To God Be The Glory for his **Victorious! Glorious! Church! To God Be The Glory Because Jesus Is Lord! Amen!!!**

Blessed Are The Pure In Heart: For They Shall See God. (Matthew 5:8)

I AM THAT I AM

ALMIGHTY GOD

Almighty God		Genesis 17:1
Name Changed		Name Changed
Abram — Abraham	Abrahamic Covenant	Sarai — Sarah

God Almighty	Genesis 28:3	Isaac ---------- Rebecca – wife
God Almighty	Genesis 35:11	Jacob --- name changed – Israel
God Almighty	Genesis 43:14	Twelve Sons – 12 Tribes of Israel
God Almighty	Genesis 48:3	Jacob speaks of God's Promise

Tribe of Judah – Jesus came from
Genesis 49:10 – Promise of Messiah

Boaz ------------------------Ruth

1948- Israel recognized as a nation by man

King David

Psalm 122:6 – Pray for the peace of Jerusalem

Mary overshadowed by Holy Spirit
Luke 1:35   Luke 1:38

Matthew 24:34 – Verily I say unto you, This generation shall not pass til all these things be fulfilled.

Book of Generations of Jesus Christ
Matthew 1:1-17

Jesus manifested in the flesh
Luke 10:11 (To God be the Glory!)
Amen!

Psalm 22:30-31

Matthew 24:44 – Therefore be ye ready; for in such an hour as ye think not the Son of man cometh.

What Is Total Salvation?

Total Salvation encompasses everything that is good and perfect based on God's word. The word of God says in James 1:17, "Every good gift and every perfect gift is from above, and cometh down from the Father of lights with whom is no variableness, neither shadow of turning." Total Salvation was paid for through the shedding of Jesus Christ's precious blood when he was crucified, died and arose to redeem mankind. Jesus Christ demonstrated his great love for man in paying the redemption price for mankind. God's love is so extensive that Christians will be learning about the depths of God's love for his people throughout the endless ages of eternity. AMEN!

THE FOLLOWING ARE SOME THINGS THAT ARE INCLUDED IN TOTAL SALVATION

Total Salvation includes being Born Again, which is the most Important part of total salvation, this occurs when a person accepts Jesus Christ as their Savior. The Greatest gift and Miracle of all is the new birth, which occurs when a person accepts the Lord as their Savior. This is also referred to as being saved, receiving salvation, the new birth, and the second birth. Total Salvation also includes the Baptism of the Holy Spirit with the evidence of speaking in other tongues, the Fruit of the Spirit, Holiness, the Gifts of the Spirit, Deliverance, Transformation, Restoration, Reconciliation, Restitution, Justice, Healings, Miracles, Translations, Resurrected Glorified bodies and More.

The Total Salvation package also encompasses: Prosperity: Spiritually, Emotionally, Physically, Socially, and Financially, Prosperity in every area. God's desire is that his people prosper.

III John 1:2 says: "Beloved I wish above all things that thou mayest prosper and be in <u>health</u>, even as thy <u>soul</u> prospereth."

Psalm 35:27 says: "Let them shout for joy, and be glad, that favor my righteous cause: yea, let them say continually, Let the Lord be magnified, which hath pleasure in the prosperity of his servant."

The SPIRITUAL Is Most Important!

Each Christian should have or desire to have a servant's heart and a heart that is pure like Jesus Christ which comes from renewing the mind through the word of God; then obeying God's word consistently. Jesus Christ said in Matthew 5:8, "Blessed are the pure in heart: for they shall see God." The Greatest desire of Christians should be for the SPIRITUAL, and to Focus and Trust in Almighty God. Each should seek first the Spiritual and to be more and more like Jesus Christ each day. Jesus Christ also said in Matthew 6:33, "But seek ye first the kingdom of God, and his righteousness; and all these things shall be added unto you."

The Hebrew and Greek Definitions of Salvation

Salvation in the Hebrew is defined as deliverance, aid, victory, prosperity, health, helping, welfare, save, saving, salvation. Salvation in the Greek is defined as: to rescue, safety, deliver, health, save, saving, salvation.

Total Salvation also includes Christians receiving immortal bodies. This includes those whose spiritual bodies are now in heaven that Jesus Christ will bring in the air at the Rapture as well as the Christians on the earth who are like the five wise virgins, who shall be CAUGHT UP, RAPTURED to meet Jesus Christ in the air. In Matthew 25:10, Jesus said: "And while they went to buy, the Bridegroom came: and they that were ready went in with him to the marriage: and the door was shut."

The word of God states in I Corinthians 15: 50-57, "Now this I say, brethren, that flesh and blood cannot inherit the kingdom of God; neither doth corruption inherit incorruption. V51: Behold, I shew you a mystery; we shall not all sleep, but we shall all be changed, V52: In a moment, in the twinkling of an eye, at the last trump: for the trumpet shall sound, and the dead shall be raised incorruptible, and we shall be changed. V53: For this corruptible must put on incorruption, and this mortal must put on immortality. V54: So when this corruptible shall have put on incorruption, and this mortal shall have put on immortality, then shall be brought to pass the saying that is written, Death is swallowed up in victory. V55: O death, where is thy sting? O grave, where is thy victory? V56: The sting of death is sin; and the strength of sin is the law. V57: But thanks be to God, which giveth us the victory through our Lord Jesus Christ."

PRAISE GOD, TOTAL SALVATION INCLUDES THE THINGS THAT HAVE BEEN LISTED AND MORE, THROUGH THE SHEDDING OF THE PRECIOUS BLOOD OF JESUS CHRIST. THANK YOU JESUS FOR PAYING THE PRICE FOR MANKIND.

PSALMS 122:6 says: Pray for the peace of Jerusalem they shall prosper that love thee. AMEN!!!

TOTAL SALVATION! AMEN.

Love In Jesus Christ,

Apostle Crystal Moore Naylor

God's Plan For Man - Total Salvation

John 3:16 - For God so loved the world that He gave His only begotten Son, that whosoever believeth in Him should not perish, but have everlasting life.

John 10:10 - The thief cometh not, but for to steal, and to kill, and to destroy: I am come that they might have life, and that they might have it more abundantly.

Man's Fall, Sin - Alienation from God

Romans 5:8 - But God commendeth His love to us, in that, while we were yet sinners, Christ died for us.

Romans 3:23-24 - For all have sinned, and come short of the glory of God, v/24 Being justified freely by His grace through the redemption that is in Christ Jesus.

Romans 6:23 - For the wages of sin is death; but the gift of God is eternal life through Jesus Christ our Lord.

Colossians 1:21 - And you, that were sometime alienated and enemies in your mind by wicked works, yet now hath He reconciled.

God's Provision To Man, Reconciliation - God's Gift To Man, Jesus Christ

John 14:6 - Jesus saith unto him, I am the way, the truth and the life: no man cometh unto the father, but by me.

Ephesians 2:8-9 - For by grace are **ye saved** through **faith**; and that not of yourselves: it is the **gift** of God: v/9 Not of **works** lest any man should boast.

II Corinthians 5:21 - For He hath made Him to be sin for us, who knew no sin; that we might be made the righteousness of God in Him

Man's Choice - To Choose Jesus Christ, Life

Romans - 10:9-10 - That if thou shalt confess with thy mouth the Lord Jesus, and shalt believe in thine heart that God hath raised Him from the dead, thou shalt be saved. v/10 For with the heart man believeth unto righteousness; and with the mouth confession is made unto salvation.

I John 1:9 - If we confess our sins, he is faithful and just to forgive us our sins, and to cleanse us from all unrighteousness.

John 1:12 - But as many as received Him, to them gave He power to become the sons of God, even to them that believe on His name.

We Believe

We believe that Jesus Christ is the Son of God.
(John 3:16), (Mark 1:11)

We believe that Jesus Christ is God, the second person of the trinity, and he is now, after his earthly birth, both God and man.
(1 John 4:2), (Matthew 1:20-23)

We believe that Jesus Christ was born of a virgin who was overshadowed by the Holy Spirit.
(Luke 1:26-38), (Isaiah 7:14)

We believe that one must accept Jesus Christ as their Savior to become saved, or born again.
(John 3:3-7), (Romans 10:9-13)

We believe that Jesus Christ never sinned, and that he was crucified for sinners and that he arose from the dead and paid the price of redemption.
(2 Corinthians 5:21), (Roman 3:23-26), (Galatians 4:4-5)

We believe that there is forgiveness of believers' sins if they truly repent of their sins, because of the holy, precious, and sinless blood of Jesus Christ which was shed for sins.
(1 John 1:9) (Romans 3:25)

We believe that Jesus Christ is now in heaven with Father God and that he will very, very, very, very soon return to catch away his church.
(1 Thessalonians 4:13-18), (1 Corinthians 15:49-57)

We believe the bible is the inspired word of God, both the Old and New Testaments.
(2 Timothy 3:16), (Proverbs 4:20-22)

We believe that there is a real heaven and a real hell.
Hell - (Isaiah 14:15-17), (Revelation 1:18), (Revelation 20:13-14) –
Heaven - (John 14:1-3), (Revelation 4:1-4), (Revelation 19:11)

We believe in the Fruit of the Holy Spirit (**Galatians 5:22-23),** the Gifts of the Holy Spirit **(1 Corinthians 12:4-12),** and the Baptism of the Holy Spirit with the evidence of speaking in tongues **(Acts 1:5-8), (Acts 2:1-4), (Acts 10:44-46)**

We believe in water baptism by immersion.
(Matthew 3: 13-17), (Luke 3:21-22)

We believe that salvation is a gift of God and that it can never be earned. **(Ephesians 2:8-9), (Romans 5:15), (Romans 6:23)**

WHERE WILL YOU SPEND ETERNITY HEAVEN OR HELL?

For **God** so loved the **world**, that he gave his only begotten **Son**, **that whosoever believeth in him** should not perish but have **everlasting life** (John 3:16).

Are you saved? To be saved means that you have accepted Jesus as your Savior by asking Him to come into your heart. Jesus loves you and he shed His holy blood on Calvary's cross, died, and arose from the dead so that you could become a child of God which entitles you to eternal life in heaven.

The word of God tells us that if thou shalt **confess** with thy **mouth** the **Lord Jesus**, and shalt **believe** in thine **heart** that **God** hath raised him from the dead, thou shalt be **saved (Romans 10:9).**

If you desire to be saved and become a child of God, pray this prayer: Heavenly Father, I believe that Jesus died for me, and that He arose from the dead and is now in heaven. I want to be your child. Please help me to live a life that is pleasing to you, in Jesus name. Amen.

Thank you for saving me!

Sign:_____Date:_____

You are now a born again child of God. You are saved because you have accepted Jesus as your Savior. Don't go by your feelings but by God's words. Now ask God to help you find a church that he wants you to attend.

Write and let me know of your decision to choose Jesus Christ as your Savior along with any prayer request. You may go to my e-mail address to share your testimony.

My e-mail address is: **OSCK777@verizon.net**

To hear and view my messages, go to www.iccmtv.com, go to the page with my picture and name, Crystal Naylor.

VICTORIOUS! GLORIOUS! CHURCH! ▪ 203

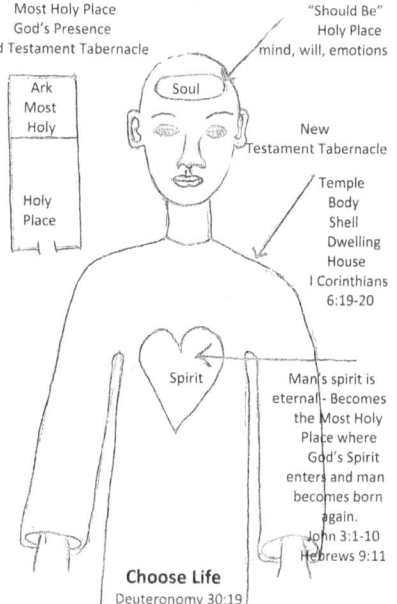

What Is Going Into Your Soul?

Death
Eph 5:4 - jesting
Eph 5:11-12 - pornography
Prov 24:9 - foolishness
Prov 19:1 - perversion

OR

Life
John 8:32 - The word of God is truth
John 6:63 - God's words are Spirit and Life
Prov 30:5 - God's word is pure
Prov 4:22 - God's word is health to the flesh

Proverbs 18:21

Death and life are in the power of the tongue; and they that love it shall eat the fruit thereof.

God's Temple!
Born Again Man

Most Holy Place
God's Presence
Old Testament Tabernacle

"Should Be"
Holy Place
mind, will, emotions

Ark Most Holy

Soul

New Testament Tabernacle

Holy Place

Temple
Body
Shell
Dwelling
House
I Corinthians
6:19-20

Spirit

Man's spirit is eternal - Becomes the Most Holy Place where God's Spirit enters and man becomes born again.
John 3:1-10
Hebrews 9:11

Choose Life
Deuteronomy 30:19

© By Apostle Crystal Naylor

TO GOD BE THE GLORY!

THE RAPTURE

I give God Honor, and the Praise, all the Glory, for he alone is worthy. In 1995 the Lord gave me a double vision of the Rapture. The first vision was in the morning praise and worship service. The second vision was in the evening praise and worship on the same day Sunday, at the church that I was a member. Prior to that time, years before the Lord had given me a pencil sketch, and a cut and paste of the Rapture, that was to be the cover for my book, the Lord wanted me to do. After the double vision of the Rapture, I did a quick color sketch of the vision that I had seen during the praise and worship. I also did a poem titled The Rapture on April 15, 1996. I gave copies to my husband and family, the pastor of the church, and several friends. Shortly after this I asked a lady of the church who was on the praise and worship team and a graphic artist if she would do my drawing of the Rapture. After giving her a copy of my color sketch she said yes, however, the Lord dealt with me to do the picture myself, and I obeyed him. What you see is a result of my obedience to God.

The lady that was a graphic artist of our church later showed me a pencil sketch of the rapture that was very similar to mine. One of the youth leaders and his wife had done a similar drawing to mine unknowing and wanted the graphic artist to do their's for a bulletin for a Wednesday night youth service. Their's would show youth in a cartoon style being raptured from the earth to Jesus, while mine showed born again people being raptured from the earth to Jesus in a realistic style.

I was asked what to do. I told all I did not want to get in the way of what God was doing, and to pray. The youth leader and his wife decided to do something different for the youth service. I shared all this with the pastor. I realized that the reason I had the double vision, as well as someone else being given a similar vision by God was to confirm that God will shortly bring it to pass, and that what I had shared about the visions were of God and not of me. Amen! (Read Genesis 41:32 and I Thessalonians 4:13-18) To God Be The Glory! Praise God, Amen!

Love in Jesus Christ,
Rev. Crystal M. Naylor

© (1997)

OUR SOON COMING KING, INC.
P.O. BOX 799
CROWNSVILLE, MD 21032 0799
U.S.A.

ITEMS FOR SALE

BY

APOSTLE CRYSTAL MOORE NAYLOR

Picture - The Rapture – Vision II
Vision I Is Also Available

Vision Explained – Heart

Book – What Total Salvation Gives Through Jesus Christ The Son

Book - Why Three Baptisms?

Ordering Materials

If You Desire To Purchase Additional Copies Of This Book:
"VICTORIOUS! GLORIOUS! CHURCH!"
For more information, go to:
www.outskirtspress.com/cmnvictoriousgloriouschurchbook

THERE ARE A VARIETY OF OTHER PRODUCTS THAT ARE AVAILABLE THAT CAN BE ORDERED. IF YOU ARE INTERESTED IN PURCHASING OTHER PRODUCTS, PLEASE GO TO THE WEBSITE ADDRESS, SEE BELOW:

www.osck.org

TO CONTACT APOSTLE CRYSTAL M. NAYLOR, PLEASE SEND CORRESPONDENCE BY E-MAIL. SEE E-MAIL ADDRESS BELOW:
Email: osck777@verizon.net

LOVE IN JESUS CHRIST,
APOSTLE CRYSTAL MOORE NAYLOR

www.ingramcontent.com/pod-product-compliance
Lightning Source LLC
Chambersburg PA
CBHW061253110426
42742CB00012BA/1899